C-1131   CAREER EXAMINATION SERIES

This is your
PASSBOOK for...

Automotive Mechanic (USPS)

Test Preparation Study Guide
Questions & Answers

COPYRIGHT NOTICE

This book is SOLELY intended for, is sold ONLY to, and its use is RESTRICTED to individual, bona fide applicants or candidates who qualify by virtue of having seriously filed applications for appropriate license, certificate, professional and/or promotional advancement, higher school matriculation, scholarship, or other legitimate requirements of education and/or governmental authorities.

This book is NOT intended for use, class instruction, tutoring, training, duplication, copying, reprinting, excerption, or adaptation, etc., by:

1) Other publishers
2) Proprietors and/or Instructors of "Coaching" and/or Preparatory Courses
3) Personnel and/or Training Divisions of commercial, industrial, and governmental organizations
4) Schools, colleges, or universities and/or their departments and staffs, including teachers and other personnel
5) Testing Agencies or Bureaus
6) Study groups which seek by the purchase of a single volume to copy and/or duplicate and/or adapt this material for use by the group as a whole without having purchased individual volumes for each of the members of the group
7) Et al.

Such persons would be in violation of appropriate Federal and State statutes.

PROVISION OF LICENSING AGREEMENTS – Recognized educational, commercial, industrial, and governmental institutions and organizations, and others legitimately engaged in educational pursuits, including training, testing, and measurement activities, may address request for a licensing agreement to the copyright owners, who will determine whether, and under what conditions, including fees and charges, the materials in this book may be used them. In other words, a licensing facility exists for the legitimate use of the material in this book on other than an individual basis. However, it is asseverated and affirmed here that the material in this book CANNOT be used without the receipt of the express permission of such a licensing agreement from the Publishers. Inquiries re licensing should be addressed to the company, attention rights and permissions department.

All rights reserved, including the right of reproduction in whole or in part, in any form or by any means, electronic or mechanical, including photocopying, recording, or by any information storage and retrieval system, without permission in writing from the Publisher.

Copyright © 2024 by
National Learning Corporation

212 Michael Drive, Syosset, NY 11791
(516) 921-8888 • www.passbooks.com
E-mail: info@passbooks.com

PUBLISHED IN THE UNITED STATES OF AMERICA

PASSBOOK® SERIES

THE *PASSBOOK® SERIES* has been created to prepare applicants and candidates for the ultimate academic battlefield – the examination room.

At some time in our lives, each and every one of us may be required to take an examination – for validation, matriculation, admission, qualification, registration, certification, or licensure.

Based on the assumption that every applicant or candidate has met the basic formal educational standards, has taken the required number of courses, and read the necessary texts, the *PASSBOOK® SERIES* furnishes the one special preparation which may assure passing with confidence, instead of failing with insecurity. Examination questions – together with answers – are furnished as the basic vehicle for study so that the mysteries of the examination and its compounding difficulties may be eliminated or diminished by a sure method.

This book is meant to help you pass your examination provided that you qualify and are serious in your objective.

The entire field is reviewed through the huge store of content information which is succinctly presented through a provocative and challenging approach – the question-and-answer method.

A climate of success is established by furnishing the correct answers at the end of each test.

You soon learn to recognize types of questions, forms of questions, and patterns of questioning. You may even begin to anticipate expected outcomes.

You perceive that many questions are repeated or adapted so that you can gain acute insights, which may enable you to score many sure points.

You learn how to confront new questions, or types of questions, and to attack them confidently and work out the correct answers.

You note objectives and emphases, and recognize pitfalls and dangers, so that you may make positive educational adjustments.

Moreover, you are kept fully informed in relation to new concepts, methods, practices, and directions in the field.

You discover that you are actually taking the examination all the time: you are preparing for the examination by "taking" an examination, not by reading extraneous and/or supererogatory textbooks.

In short, this PASSBOOK®, used directedly, should be an important factor in helping you to pass your test.

AUTOMOTIVE MECHANIC (USPS)

DUTIES

Under supervision, overhauls, repairs and maintains engines and component assembles used in automotive, construction and special equipment powered by internal combustion engines; diagnoses mechanical and operating difficulties of vehicles, repairs defects, replaces work or broken parts; adjusts and tunes up engines, and makes other necessary adjustments to maintain proper operating condition for trucks that are in service; repairs or replaces automotive electrical equipment such as generators, starters, ignition systems, distributors and wiring; installs and sets new spark plugs. Duties also include conducting road tests of vehicles after repairs, noting performance of engine, clutch, transmission, brakes, and other parts; operating standard types of modern garage testing equipment. In addition, may perform any one of the following duties:

1. Removes, disassembles, reassembles, and installs entire engines;
2. Overhauls transmissions, rear-end assemblies, and braking systems;
3. Straightens frames and axles;
4. Makes road calls to make emergency repairs; and
5. Makes required truck inspection.

SCOPE OF THE EXAMINATION

The written test will be of the multiple-choice type and may include questions on the operating principles of internal combustion automotive components such as engines, transmissions, clutches, electronic ignition, front end, steering and suspension systems, cooling and electrical systems, brakes, wheels, tires; trouble shooting and repair of motor vehicle components, accessories and systems; tools, safety, basic mathematics, reading comprehension, materials and electricity; shop equipment and shop techniques commonly used in effecting overhaul and reconstruction of automotive components; training, reports, records, and other related areas.

HOW TO TAKE A TEST

I. YOU MUST PASS AN EXAMINATION

A. WHAT EVERY CANDIDATE SHOULD KNOW

Examination applicants often ask us for help in preparing for the written test. What can I study in advance? What kinds of questions will be asked? How will the test be given? How will the papers be graded?

As an applicant for a civil service examination, you may be wondering about some of these things. Our purpose here is to suggest effective methods of advance study and to describe civil service examinations.

Your chances for success on this examination can be increased if you know how to prepare. Those "pre-examination jitters" can be reduced if you know what to expect. You can even experience an adventure in good citizenship if you know why civil service exams are given.

B. WHY ARE CIVIL SERVICE EXAMINATIONS GIVEN?

Civil service examinations are important to you in two ways. As a citizen, you want public jobs filled by employees who know how to do their work. As a job seeker, you want a fair chance to compete for that job on an equal footing with other candidates. The best-known means of accomplishing this two-fold goal is the competitive examination.

Exams are widely publicized throughout the nation. They may be administered for jobs in federal, state, city, municipal, town or village governments or agencies.

Any citizen may apply, with some limitations, such as the age or residence of applicants. Your experience and education may be reviewed to see whether you meet the requirements for the particular examination. When these requirements exist, they are reasonable and applied consistently to all applicants. Thus, a competitive examination may cause you some uneasiness now, but it is your privilege and safeguard.

C. HOW ARE CIVIL SERVICE EXAMS DEVELOPED?

Examinations are carefully written by trained technicians who are specialists in the field known as "psychological measurement," in consultation with recognized authorities in the field of work that the test will cover. These experts recommend the subject matter areas or skills to be tested; only those knowledges or skills important to your success on the job are included. The most reliable books and source materials available are used as references. Together, the experts and technicians judge the difficulty level of the questions.

Test technicians know how to phrase questions so that the problem is clearly stated. Their ethics do not permit "trick" or "catch" questions. Questions may have been tried out on sample groups, or subjected to statistical analysis, to determine their usefulness.

Written tests are often used in combination with performance tests, ratings of training and experience, and oral interviews. All of these measures combine to form the best-known means of finding the right person for the right job.

II. HOW TO PASS THE WRITTEN TEST

A. NATURE OF THE EXAMINATION

To prepare intelligently for civil service examinations, you should know how they differ from school examinations you have taken. In school you were assigned certain definite pages to read or subjects to cover. The examination questions were quite detailed and usually emphasized memory. Civil service exams, on the other hand, try to discover your present ability to perform the duties of a position, plus your potentiality to learn these duties. In other words, a civil service exam attempts to predict how successful you will be. Questions cover such a broad area that they cannot be as minute and detailed as school exam questions.

In the public service similar kinds of work, or positions, are grouped together in one "class." This process is known as *position-classification*. All the positions in a class are paid according to the salary range for that class. One class title covers all of these positions, and they are all tested by the same examination.

B. FOUR BASIC STEPS

1) Study the announcement

How, then, can you know what subjects to study? Our best answer is: "Learn as much as possible about the class of positions for which you've applied." The exam will test the knowledge, skills and abilities needed to do the work.

Your most valuable source of information about the position you want is the official exam announcement. This announcement lists the training and experience qualifications. Check these standards and apply only if you come reasonably close to meeting them.

The brief description of the position in the examination announcement offers some clues to the subjects which will be tested. Think about the job itself. Review the duties in your mind. Can you perform them, or are there some in which you are rusty? Fill in the blank spots in your preparation.

Many jurisdictions preview the written test in the exam announcement by including a section called "Knowledge and Abilities Required," "Scope of the Examination," or some similar heading. Here you will find out specifically what fields will be tested.

2) Review your own background

Once you learn in general what the position is all about, and what you need to know to do the work, ask yourself which subjects you already know fairly well and which need improvement. You may wonder whether to concentrate on improving your strong areas or on building some background in your fields of weakness. When the announcement has specified "some knowledge" or "considerable knowledge," or has used adjectives like "beginning principles of…" or "advanced … methods," you can get a clue as to the number and difficulty of questions to be asked in any given field. More questions, and hence broader coverage, would be included for those subjects which are more important in the work. Now weigh your strengths and weaknesses against the job requirements and prepare accordingly.

3) Determine the level of the position

Another way to tell how intensively you should prepare is to understand the level of the job for which you are applying. Is it the entering level? In other words, is this the position in which beginners in a field of work are hired? Or is it an intermediate or advanced level? Sometimes this is indicated by such words as "Junior" or "Senior" in the class title. Other jurisdictions use Roman numerals to designate the level – Clerk I, Clerk II, for example. The word "Supervisor" sometimes appears in the title. If the level is not indicated by the title, check the description of duties. Will you be working under very close supervision, or will you have responsibility for independent decisions in this work?

4) Choose appropriate study materials

Now that you know the subjects to be examined and the relative amount of each subject to be covered, you can choose suitable study materials. For beginning level jobs, or even advanced ones, if you have a pronounced weakness in some aspect of your training, read a modern, standard textbook in that field. Be sure it is up to date and has general coverage. Such books are normally available at your library, and the librarian will be glad to help you locate one. For entry-level positions, questions of appropriate difficulty are chosen – neither highly advanced questions, nor those too simple. Such questions require careful thought but not advanced training.

If the position for which you are applying is technical or advanced, you will read more advanced, specialized material. If you are already familiar with the basic principles of your field, elementary textbooks would waste your time. Concentrate on advanced textbooks and technical periodicals. Think through the concepts and review difficult problems in your field.

These are all general sources. You can get more ideas on your own initiative, following these leads. For example, training manuals and publications of the government agency which employs workers in your field can be useful, particularly for technical and professional positions. A letter or visit to the government department involved may result in more specific study suggestions, and certainly will provide you with a more definite idea of the exact nature of the position you are seeking.

III. KINDS OF TESTS

Tests are used for purposes other than measuring knowledge and ability to perform specified duties. For some positions, it is equally important to test ability to make adjustments to new situations or to profit from training. In others, basic mental abilities not dependent on information are essential. Questions which test these things may not appear as pertinent to the duties of the position as those which test for knowledge and information. Yet they are often highly important parts of a fair examination. For very general questions, it is almost impossible to help you direct your study efforts. What we can do is to point out some of the more common of these general abilities needed in public service positions and describe some typical questions.

1) General information

Broad, general information has been found useful for predicting job success in some kinds of work. This is tested in a variety of ways, from vocabulary lists to questions about current events. Basic background in some field of work, such as sociology or economics, may be sampled in a group of questions. Often these are principles which have become familiar to most persons through exposure rather than through formal training. It is difficult to advise you how to study for these questions; being alert to the world around you is our best suggestion.

2) Verbal ability

An example of an ability needed in many positions is verbal or language ability. Verbal ability is, in brief, the ability to use and understand words. Vocabulary and grammar tests are typical measures of this ability. Reading comprehension or paragraph interpretation questions are common in many kinds of civil service tests. You are given a paragraph of written material and asked to find its central meaning.

3) **Numerical ability**

Number skills can be tested by the familiar arithmetic problem, by checking paired lists of numbers to see which are alike and which are different, or by interpreting charts and graphs. In the latter test, a graph may be printed in the test booklet which you are asked to use as the basis for answering questions.

4) **Observation**

A popular test for law-enforcement positions is the observation test. A picture is shown to you for several minutes, then taken away. Questions about the picture test your ability to observe both details and larger elements.

5) **Following directions**

In many positions in the public service, the employee must be able to carry out written instructions dependably and accurately. You may be given a chart with several columns, each column listing a variety of information. The questions require you to carry out directions involving the information given in the chart.

6) **Skills and aptitudes**

Performance tests effectively measure some manual skills and aptitudes. When the skill is one in which you are trained, such as typing or shorthand, you can practice. These tests are often very much like those given in business school or high school courses. For many of the other skills and aptitudes, however, no short-time preparation can be made. Skills and abilities natural to you or that you have developed throughout your lifetime are being tested.

Many of the general questions just described provide all the data needed to answer the questions and ask you to use your reasoning ability to find the answers. Your best preparation for these tests, as well as for tests of facts and ideas, is to be at your physical and mental best. You, no doubt, have your own methods of getting into an exam-taking mood and keeping "in shape." The next section lists some ideas on this subject.

IV. KINDS OF QUESTIONS

Only rarely is the "essay" question, which you answer in narrative form, used in civil service tests. Civil service tests are usually of the short-answer type. Full instructions for answering these questions will be given to you at the examination. But in case this is your first experience with short-answer questions and separate answer sheets, here is what you need to know:

1) Multiple-choice Questions

Most popular of the short-answer questions is the "multiple choice" or "best answer" question. It can be used, for example, to test for factual knowledge, ability to solve problems or judgment in meeting situations found at work.

A multiple-choice question is normally one of three types—

- It can begin with an incomplete statement followed by several possible endings. You are to find the one ending which *best* completes the statement, although some of the others may not be entirely wrong.
- It can also be a complete statement in the form of a question which is answered by choosing one of the statements listed.

- It can be in the form of a problem – again you select the best answer.

Here is an example of a multiple-choice question with a discussion which should give you some clues as to the method for choosing the right answer:

When an employee has a complaint about his assignment, the action which will *best* help him overcome his difficulty is to
- A. discuss his difficulty with his coworkers
- B. take the problem to the head of the organization
- C. take the problem to the person who gave him the assignment
- D. say nothing to anyone about his complaint

In answering this question, you should study each of the choices to find which is best. Consider choice "A" – Certainly an employee may discuss his complaint with fellow employees, but no change or improvement can result, and the complaint remains unresolved. Choice "B" is a poor choice since the head of the organization probably does not know what assignment you have been given, and taking your problem to him is known as "going over the head" of the supervisor. The supervisor, or person who made the assignment, is the person who can clarify it or correct any injustice. Choice "C" is, therefore, correct. To say nothing, as in choice "D," is unwise. Supervisors have and interest in knowing the problems employees are facing, and the employee is seeking a solution to his problem.

2) True/False Questions

The "true/false" or "right/wrong" form of question is sometimes used. Here a complete statement is given. Your job is to decide whether the statement is right or wrong.

SAMPLE: A roaming cell-phone call to a nearby city costs less than a non-roaming call to a distant city.

This statement is wrong, or false, since roaming calls are more expensive.

This is not a complete list of all possible question forms, although most of the others are variations of these common types. You will always get complete directions for answering questions. Be sure you understand *how* to mark your answers – ask questions until you do.

V. RECORDING YOUR ANSWERS

Computer terminals are used more and more today for many different kinds of exams.

For an examination with very few applicants, you may be told to record your answers in the test booklet itself. Separate answer sheets are much more common. If this separate answer sheet is to be scored by machine – and this is often the case – it is highly important that you mark your answers correctly in order to get credit.

An electronic scoring machine is often used in civil service offices because of the speed with which papers can be scored. Machine-scored answer sheets must be marked with a pencil, which will be given to you. This pencil has a high graphite content which responds to the electronic scoring machine. As a matter of fact, stray dots may register as answers, so do not let your pencil rest on the answer sheet while you are pondering the correct answer. Also, if your pencil lead breaks or is otherwise defective, ask for another.

Since the answer sheet will be dropped in a slot in the scoring machine, be careful not to bend the corners or get the paper crumpled.

The answer sheet normally has five vertical columns of numbers, with 30 numbers to a column. These numbers correspond to the question numbers in your test booklet. After each number, going across the page are four or five pairs of dotted lines. These short dotted lines have small letters or numbers above them. The first two pairs may also have a "T" or "F" above the letters. This indicates that the first two pairs only are to be used if the questions are of the true-false type. If the questions are multiple choice, disregard the "T" and "F" and pay attention only to the small letters or numbers.

Answer your questions in the manner of the sample that follows:

32. The largest city in the United States is
    A. Washington, D.C.
    B. New York City
    C. Chicago
    D. Detroit
    E. San Francisco

1) Choose the answer you think is best. (New York City is the largest, so "B" is correct.)
2) Find the row of dotted lines numbered the same as the question you are answering. (Find row number 32)
3) Find the pair of dotted lines corresponding to the answer. (Find the pair of lines under the mark "B.")
4) Make a solid black mark between the dotted lines.

VI. BEFORE THE TEST

Common sense will help you find procedures to follow to get ready for an examination. Too many of us, however, overlook these sensible measures. Indeed, nervousness and fatigue have been found to be the most serious reasons why applicants fail to do their best on civil service tests. Here is a list of reminders:

- Begin your preparation early – Don't wait until the last minute to go scurrying around for books and materials or to find out what the position is all about.
- Prepare continuously – An hour a night for a week is better than an all-night cram session. This has been definitely established. What is more, a night a week for a month will return better dividends than crowding your study into a shorter period of time.
- Locate the place of the exam – You have been sent a notice telling you when and where to report for the examination. If the location is in a different town or otherwise unfamiliar to you, it would be well to inquire the best route and learn something about the building.
- Relax the night before the test – Allow your mind to rest. Do not study at all that night. Plan some mild recreation or diversion; then go to bed early and get a good night's sleep.
- Get up early enough to make a leisurely trip to the place for the test – This way unforeseen events, traffic snarls, unfamiliar buildings, etc. will not upset you.
- Dress comfortably – A written test is not a fashion show. You will be known by number and not by name, so wear something comfortable.

- Leave excess paraphernalia at home – Shopping bags and odd bundles will get in your way. You need bring only the items mentioned in the official notice you received; usually everything you need is provided. Do not bring reference books to the exam. They will only confuse those last minutes and be taken away from you when in the test room.
- Arrive somewhat ahead of time – If because of transportation schedules you must get there very early, bring a newspaper or magazine to take your mind off yourself while waiting.
- Locate the examination room – When you have found the proper room, you will be directed to the seat or part of the room where you will sit. Sometimes you are given a sheet of instructions to read while you are waiting. Do not fill out any forms until you are told to do so; just read them and be prepared.
- Relax and prepare to listen to the instructions
- If you have any physical problem that may keep you from doing your best, be sure to tell the test administrator. If you are sick or in poor health, you really cannot do your best on the exam. You can come back and take the test some other time.

VII. AT THE TEST

The day of the test is here and you have the test booklet in your hand. The temptation to get going is very strong. Caution! There is more to success than knowing the right answers. You must know how to identify your papers and understand variations in the type of short-answer question used in this particular examination. Follow these suggestions for maximum results from your efforts:

1) Cooperate with the monitor

The test administrator has a duty to create a situation in which you can be as much at ease as possible. He will give instructions, tell you when to begin, check to see that you are marking your answer sheet correctly, and so on. He is not there to guard you, although he will see that your competitors do not take unfair advantage. He wants to help you do your best.

2) Listen to all instructions

Don't jump the gun! Wait until you understand all directions. In most civil service tests you get more time than you need to answer the questions. So don't be in a hurry. Read each word of instructions until you clearly understand the meaning. Study the examples, listen to all announcements and follow directions. Ask questions if you do not understand what to do.

3) Identify your papers

Civil service exams are usually identified by number only. You will be assigned a number; you must not put your name on your test papers. Be sure to copy your number correctly. Since more than one exam may be given, copy your exact examination title.

4) Plan your time

Unless you are told that a test is a "speed" or "rate of work" test, speed itself is usually not important. Time enough to answer all the questions will be provided, but this does not mean that you have all day. An overall time limit has been set. Divide the total time (in minutes) by the number of questions to determine the approximate time you have for each question.

5) Do not linger over difficult questions

If you come across a difficult question, mark it with a paper clip (useful to have along) and come back to it when you have been through the booklet. One caution if you do this – be sure to skip a number on your answer sheet as well. Check often to be sure that you have not lost your place and that you are marking in the row numbered the same as the question you are answering.

6) Read the questions

Be sure you know what the question asks! Many capable people are unsuccessful because they failed to *read* the questions correctly.

7) Answer all questions

Unless you have been instructed that a penalty will be deducted for incorrect answers, it is better to guess than to omit a question.

8) Speed tests

It is often better NOT to guess on speed tests. It has been found that on timed tests people are tempted to spend the last few seconds before time is called in marking answers at random – without even reading them – in the hope of picking up a few extra points. To discourage this practice, the instructions may warn you that your score will be "corrected" for guessing. That is, a penalty will be applied. The incorrect answers will be deducted from the correct ones, or some other penalty formula will be used.

9) Review your answers

If you finish before time is called, go back to the questions you guessed or omitted to give them further thought. Review other answers if you have time.

10) Return your test materials

If you are ready to leave before others have finished or time is called, take ALL your materials to the monitor and leave quietly. Never take any test material with you. The monitor can discover whose papers are not complete, and taking a test booklet may be grounds for disqualification.

VIII. EXAMINATION TECHNIQUES

1) Read the general instructions carefully. These are usually printed on the first page of the exam booklet. As a rule, these instructions refer to the timing of the examination; the fact that you should not start work until the signal and must stop work at a signal, etc. If there are any *special* instructions, such as a choice of questions to be answered, make sure that you note this instruction carefully.

2) When you are ready to start work on the examination, that is as soon as the signal has been given, read the instructions to each question booklet, underline any key words or phrases, such as *least, best, outline, describe* and the like. In this way you will tend to answer as requested rather than discover on reviewing your paper that you *listed without describing*, that you selected the *worst* choice rather than the *best* choice, etc.

3) If the examination is of the objective or multiple-choice type – that is, each question will also give a series of possible answers: A, B, C or D, and you are called upon to select the best answer and write the letter next to that answer on your answer paper – it is advisable to start answering each question in turn. There may be anywhere from 50 to 100 such questions in the three or four hours allotted and you can see how much time would be taken if you read through all the questions before beginning to answer any. Furthermore, if you come across a question or group of questions which you know would be difficult to answer, it would undoubtedly affect your handling of all the other questions.

4) If the examination is of the essay type and contains but a few questions, it is a moot point as to whether you should read all the questions before starting to answer any one. Of course, if you are given a choice – say five out of seven and the like – then it is essential to read all the questions so you can eliminate the two that are most difficult. If, however, you are asked to answer all the questions, there may be danger in trying to answer the easiest one first because you may find that you will spend too much time on it. The best technique is to answer the first question, then proceed to the second, etc.

5) Time your answers. Before the exam begins, write down the time it started, then add the time allowed for the examination and write down the time it must be completed, then divide the time available somewhat as follows:
    - If 3-1/2 hours are allowed, that would be 210 minutes. If you have 80 objective-type questions, that would be an average of 2-1/2 minutes per question. Allow yourself no more than 2 minutes per question, or a total of 160 minutes, which will permit about 50 minutes to review.
    - If for the time allotment of 210 minutes there are 7 essay questions to answer, that would average about 30 minutes a question. Give yourself only 25 minutes per question so that you have about 35 minutes to review.

6) The most important instruction is to *read each question* and make sure you know what is wanted. The second most important instruction is to *time yourself properly* so that you answer every question. The third most important instruction is to *answer every question*. Guess if you have to but include something for each question. Remember that you will receive no credit for a blank and will probably receive some credit if you write something in answer to an essay question. If you guess a letter – say "B" for a multiple-choice question – you may have guessed right. If you leave a blank as an answer to a multiple-choice question, the examiners may respect your feelings but it will not add a point to your score. Some exams may penalize you for wrong answers, so in such cases *only*, you may not want to guess unless you have some basis for your answer.

7) Suggestions
    a. Objective-type questions
        1. Examine the question booklet for proper sequence of pages and questions
        2. Read all instructions carefully
        3. Skip any question which seems too difficult; return to it after all other questions have been answered
        4. Apportion your time properly; do not spend too much time on any single question or group of questions

5. Note and underline key words – *all, most, fewest, least, best, worst, same, opposite,* etc.
6. Pay particular attention to negatives
7. Note unusual option, e.g., unduly long, short, complex, different or similar in content to the body of the question
8. Observe the use of "hedging" words – *probably, may, most likely,* etc.
9. Make sure that your answer is put next to the same number as the question
10. Do not second-guess unless you have good reason to believe the second answer is definitely more correct
11. Cross out original answer if you decide another answer is more accurate; do not erase until you are ready to hand your paper in
12. Answer all questions; guess unless instructed otherwise
13. Leave time for review

    b. Essay questions
      1. Read each question carefully
      2. Determine exactly what is wanted. Underline key words or phrases.
      3. Decide on outline or paragraph answer
      4. Include many different points and elements unless asked to develop any one or two points or elements
      5. Show impartiality by giving pros and cons unless directed to select one side only
      6. Make and write down any assumptions you find necessary to answer the questions
      7. Watch your English, grammar, punctuation and choice of words
      8. Time your answers; don't crowd material

8) Answering the essay question

Most essay questions can be answered by framing the specific response around several key words or ideas. Here are a few such key words or ideas:

M's: manpower, materials, methods, money, management
P's: purpose, program, policy, plan, procedure, practice, problems, pitfalls, personnel, public relations

    a. Six basic steps in handling problems:
      1. Preliminary plan and background development
      2. Collect information, data and facts
      3. Analyze and interpret information, data and facts
      4. Analyze and develop solutions as well as make recommendations
      5. Prepare report and sell recommendations
      6. Install recommendations and follow up effectiveness

    b. Pitfalls to avoid
      1. *Taking things for granted* – A statement of the situation does not necessarily imply that each of the elements is necessarily true; for example, a complaint may be invalid and biased so that all that can be taken for granted is that a complaint has been registered

2. *Considering only one side of a situation* – Wherever possible, indicate several alternatives and then point out the reasons you selected the best one
3. *Failing to indicate follow up* – Whenever your answer indicates action on your part, make certain that you will take proper follow-up action to see how successful your recommendations, procedures or actions turn out to be
4. *Taking too long in answering any single question* – Remember to time your answers properly

IX. AFTER THE TEST

Scoring procedures differ in detail among civil service jurisdictions although the general principles are the same. Whether the papers are hand-scored or graded by machine we have described, they are nearly always graded by number. That is, the person who marks the paper knows only the number – never the name – of the applicant. Not until all the papers have been graded will they be matched with names. If other tests, such as training and experience or oral interview ratings have been given, scores will be combined. Different parts of the examination usually have different weights. For example, the written test might count 60 percent of the final grade, and a rating of training and experience 40 percent. In many jurisdictions, veterans will have a certain number of points added to their grades.

After the final grade has been determined, the names are placed in grade order and an eligible list is established. There are various methods for resolving ties between those who get the same final grade – probably the most common is to place first the name of the person whose application was received first. Job offers are made from the eligible list in the order the names appear on it. You will be notified of your grade and your rank as soon as all these computations have been made. This will be done as rapidly as possible.

People who are found to meet the requirements in the announcement are called "eligibles." Their names are put on a list of eligible candidates. An eligible's chances of getting a job depend on how high he stands on this list and how fast agencies are filling jobs from the list.

When a job is to be filled from a list of eligibles, the agency asks for the names of people on the list of eligibles for that job. When the civil service commission receives this request, it sends to the agency the names of the three people highest on this list. Or, if the job to be filled has specialized requirements, the office sends the agency the names of the top three persons who meet these requirements from the general list.

The appointing officer makes a choice from among the three people whose names were sent to him. If the selected person accepts the appointment, the names of the others are put back on the list to be considered for future openings.

That is the rule in hiring from all kinds of eligible lists, whether they are for typist, carpenter, chemist, or something else. For every vacancy, the appointing officer has his choice of any one of the top three eligibles on the list. This explains why the person whose name is on top of the list sometimes does not get an appointment when some of the persons lower on the list do. If the appointing officer chooses the second or third eligible, the No. 1 eligible does not get a job at once, but stays on the list until he is appointed or the list is terminated.

X. HOW TO PASS THE INTERVIEW TEST

The examination for which you applied requires an oral interview test. You have already taken the written test and you are now being called for the interview test – the final part of the formal examination.

You may think that it is not possible to prepare for an interview test and that there are no procedures to follow during an interview. Our purpose is to point out some things you can do in advance that will help you and some good rules to follow and pitfalls to avoid while you are being interviewed.

What is an interview supposed to test?

The written examination is designed to test the technical knowledge and competence of the candidate; the oral is designed to evaluate intangible qualities, not readily measured otherwise, and to establish a list showing the relative fitness of each candidate – as measured against his competitors – for the position sought. Scoring is not on the basis of "right" and "wrong," but on a sliding scale of values ranging from "not passable" to "outstanding." As a matter of fact, it is possible to achieve a relatively low score without a single "incorrect" answer because of evident weakness in the qualities being measured.

Occasionally, an examination may consist entirely of an oral test – either an individual or a group oral. In such cases, information is sought concerning the technical knowledges and abilities of the candidate, since there has been no written examination for this purpose. More commonly, however, an oral test is used to supplement a written examination.

Who conducts interviews?

The composition of oral boards varies among different jurisdictions. In nearly all, a representative of the personnel department serves as chairman. One of the members of the board may be a representative of the department in which the candidate would work. In some cases, "outside experts" are used, and, frequently, a businessman or some other representative of the general public is asked to serve. Labor and management or other special groups may be represented. The aim is to secure the services of experts in the appropriate field.

However the board is composed, it is a good idea (and not at all improper or unethical) to ascertain in advance of the interview who the members are and what groups they represent. When you are introduced to them, you will have some idea of their backgrounds and interests, and at least you will not stutter and stammer over their names.

What should be done before the interview?

While knowledge about the board members is useful and takes some of the surprise element out of the interview, there is other preparation which is more substantive. It *is* possible to prepare for an oral interview – in several ways:

1) Keep a copy of your application and review it carefully before the interview

This may be the only document before the oral board, and the starting point of the interview. Know what education and experience you have listed there, and the sequence and dates of all of it. Sometimes the board will ask you to review the highlights of your experience for them; you should not have to hem and haw doing it.

2) Study the class specification and the examination announcement

Usually, the oral board has one or both of these to guide them. The qualities, characteristics or knowledges required by the position sought are stated in these documents. They offer valuable clues as to the nature of the oral interview. For example, if the job involves supervisory responsibilities, the announcement will usually indicate that knowledge of modern supervisory methods and the qualifications of the candidate as a supervisor will be tested. If so, you can expect such questions, frequently in the form of a hypothetical situation which you are expected to solve. NEVER go into an oral without knowledge of the duties and responsibilities of the job you seek.

3) Think through each qualification required

Try to visualize the kind of questions you would ask if you were a board member. How well could you answer them? Try especially to appraise your own knowledge and background in each area, *measured against the job sought*, and identify any areas in which you are weak. Be critical and realistic – do not flatter yourself.

4) Do some general reading in areas in which you feel you may be weak

For example, if the job involves supervision and your past experience has NOT, some general reading in supervisory methods and practices, particularly in the field of human relations, might be useful. Do NOT study agency procedures or detailed manuals. The oral board will be testing your understanding and capacity, not your memory.

5) Get a good night's sleep and watch your general health and mental attitude

You will want a clear head at the interview. Take care of a cold or any other minor ailment, and of course, no hangovers.

What should be done on the day of the interview?

Now comes the day of the interview itself. Give yourself plenty of time to get there. Plan to arrive somewhat ahead of the scheduled time, particularly if your appointment is in the fore part of the day. If a previous candidate fails to appear, the board might be ready for you a bit early. By early afternoon an oral board is almost invariably behind schedule if there are many candidates, and you may have to wait. Take along a book or magazine to read, or your application to review, but leave any extraneous material in the waiting room when you go in for your interview. In any event, relax and compose yourself.

The matter of dress is important. The board is forming impressions about you – from your experience, your manners, your attitude, and your appearance. Give your personal appearance careful attention. Dress your best, but not your flashiest. Choose conservative, appropriate clothing, and be sure it is immaculate. This is a business interview, and your appearance should indicate that you regard it as such. Besides, being well groomed and properly dressed will help boost your confidence.

Sooner or later, someone will call your name and escort you into the interview room. *This is it*. From here on you are on your own. It is too late for any more preparation. But remember, you asked for this opportunity to prove your fitness, and you are here because your request was granted.

What happens when you go in?

The usual sequence of events will be as follows: The clerk (who is often the board stenographer) will introduce you to the chairman of the oral board, who will introduce you to the other members of the board. Acknowledge the introductions before you sit down. Do not be surprised if you find a microphone facing you or a stenotypist sitting by. Oral interviews are usually recorded in the event of an appeal or other review.

Usually the chairman of the board will open the interview by reviewing the highlights of your education and work experience from your application – primarily for the benefit of the other members of the board, as well as to get the material into the record. Do not interrupt or comment unless there is an error or significant misinterpretation; if that is the case, do not hesitate. But do not quibble about insignificant matters. Also, he will usually ask you some question about your education, experience or your present job – partly to get you to start talking and to establish the interviewing "rapport." He may start the actual questioning, or turn it over to one of the other members. Frequently, each member undertakes the questioning on a particular area, one in which he is perhaps most competent, so you can expect each member to participate in the examination. Because time is limited, you may also expect some rather abrupt switches in the direction the questioning takes, so do not be upset by it. Normally, a board member will not pursue a single line of questioning unless he discovers a particular strength or weakness.

After each member has participated, the chairman will usually ask whether any member has any further questions, then will ask you if you have anything you wish to add. Unless you are expecting this question, it may floor you. Worse, it may start you off on an extended, extemporaneous speech. The board is not usually seeking more information. The question is principally to offer you a last opportunity to present further qualifications or to indicate that you have nothing to add. So, if you feel that a significant qualification or characteristic has been overlooked, it is proper to point it out in a sentence or so. Do not compliment the board on the thoroughness of their examination – they have been sketchy, and you know it. If you wish, merely say, "No thank you, I have nothing further to add." This is a point where you can "talk yourself out" of a good impression or fail to present an important bit of information. Remember, *you close the interview yourself*.

The chairman will then say, "That is all, Mr. _____, thank you." Do not be startled; the interview is over, and quicker than you think. Thank him, gather your belongings and take your leave. Save your sigh of relief for the other side of the door.

How to put your best foot forward

Throughout this entire process, you may feel that the board individually and collectively is trying to pierce your defenses, seek out your hidden weaknesses and embarrass and confuse you. Actually, this is not true. They are obliged to make an appraisal of your qualifications for the job you are seeking, and they want to see you in your best light. Remember, they must interview all candidates and a non-cooperative candidate may become a failure in spite of their best efforts to bring out his qualifications. Here are 15 suggestions that will help you:

1) Be natural – Keep your attitude confident, not cocky

If you are not confident that you can do the job, do not expect the board to be. Do not apologize for your weaknesses, try to bring out your strong points. The board is interested in a positive, not negative, presentation. Cockiness will antagonize any board member and make him wonder if you are covering up a weakness by a false show of strength.

2) Get comfortable, but don't lounge or sprawl

Sit erectly but not stiffly. A careless posture may lead the board to conclude that you are careless in other things, or at least that you are not impressed by the importance of the occasion. Either conclusion is natural, even if incorrect. Do not fuss with your clothing, a pencil or an ashtray. Your hands may occasionally be useful to emphasize a point; do not let them become a point of distraction.

3) Do not wisecrack or make small talk

This is a serious situation, and your attitude should show that you consider it as such. Further, the time of the board is limited – they do not want to waste it, and neither should you.

4) Do not exaggerate your experience or abilities

In the first place, from information in the application or other interviews and sources, the board may know more about you than you think. Secondly, you probably will not get away with it. An experienced board is rather adept at spotting such a situation, so do not take the chance.

5) If you know a board member, do not make a point of it, yet do not hide it

Certainly you are not fooling him, and probably not the other members of the board. Do not try to take advantage of your acquaintanceship – it will probably do you little good.

6) Do not dominate the interview

Let the board do that. They will give you the clues – do not assume that you have to do all the talking. Realize that the board has a number of questions to ask you, and do not try to take up all the interview time by showing off your extensive knowledge of the answer to the first one.

7) Be attentive

You only have 20 minutes or so, and you should keep your attention at its sharpest throughout. When a member is addressing a problem or question to you, give him your undivided attention. Address your reply principally to him, but do not exclude the other board members.

8) Do not interrupt

A board member may be stating a problem for you to analyze. He will ask you a question when the time comes. Let him state the problem, and wait for the question.

9) Make sure you understand the question

Do not try to answer until you are sure what the question is. If it is not clear, restate it in your own words or ask the board member to clarify it for you. However, do not haggle about minor elements.

10) Reply promptly but not hastily

A common entry on oral board rating sheets is "candidate responded readily," or "candidate hesitated in replies." Respond as promptly and quickly as you can, but do not jump to a hasty, ill-considered answer.

11) Do not be peremptory in your answers

A brief answer is proper – but do not fire your answer back. That is a losing game from your point of view. The board member can probably ask questions much faster than you can answer them.

12) Do not try to create the answer you think the board member wants

He is interested in what kind of mind you have and how it works – not in playing games. Furthermore, he can usually spot this practice and will actually grade you down on it.

13) Do not switch sides in your reply merely to agree with a board member

Frequently, a member will take a contrary position merely to draw you out and to see if you are willing and able to defend your point of view. Do not start a debate, yet do not surrender a good position. If a position is worth taking, it is worth defending.

14) Do not be afraid to admit an error in judgment if you are shown to be wrong

The board knows that you are forced to reply without any opportunity for careful consideration. Your answer may be demonstrably wrong. If so, admit it and get on with the interview.

15) Do not dwell at length on your present job

The opening question may relate to your present assignment. Answer the question but do not go into an extended discussion. You are being examined for a *new* job, not your present one. As a matter of fact, try to phrase ALL your answers in terms of the job for which you are being examined.

Basis of Rating

Probably you will forget most of these "do's" and "don'ts" when you walk into the oral interview room. Even remembering them all will not ensure you a passing grade. Perhaps you did not have the qualifications in the first place. But remembering them will help you to put your best foot forward, without treading on the toes of the board members.

Rumor and popular opinion to the contrary notwithstanding, an oral board wants you to make the best appearance possible. They know you are under pressure – but they also want to see how you respond to it as a guide to what your reaction would be under the pressures of the job you seek. They will be influenced by the degree of poise you display, the personal traits you show and the manner in which you respond.

ABOUT THIS BOOK

This book contains tests divided into Examination Sections. Go through each test, answering every question in the margin. We have also attached a sample answer sheet at the back of the book that can be removed and used. At the end of each test look at the answer key and check your answers. On the ones you got wrong, look at the right answer choice and learn. Do not fill in the answers first. Do not memorize the questions and answers, but understand the answer and principles involved. On your test, the questions will likely be different from the samples. Questions are changed and new ones added. If you understand these past questions you should have success with any changes that arise. Tests may consist of several types of questions. We have additional books on each subject should more study be advisable or necessary for you. Finally, the more you study, the better prepared you will be. This book is intended to be the last thing you study before you walk into the examination room. Prior study of relevant texts is also recommended. NLC publishes some of these in our Fundamental Series. Knowledge and good sense are important factors in passing your exam. Good luck also helps. So now study this Passbook, absorb the material contained within and take that knowledge into the examination. Then do your best to pass that exam.

EXAMINATION SECTION

EXAMINATION SECTION
TEST 1

DIRECTIONS: Each question or incomplete statement is followed by several suggested answers or completions. Select the one that BEST answers the question or completes the statement. *PRINT THE LETTER OF THE CORRECT ANSWER IN THE SPACE AT THE RIGHT.*

1. All of the following are probable causes of an engine's failure to start EXCEPT   1.____
   A. cylinders not wired in proper order
   B. poor coolant circulation
   C. resistance unit burned out
   D. defective condenser

2. In an *expert* system for offboard computer diagnosis, which stage of knowledge acquisition in developing problem-solving rules occurs FIRST?   2.____
   A. Implementation   B. Identification
   C. Formalization   D. Conceptualization

3. Some suspension units consist of tandem axles joined by a single cross support that also acts as a vertical pivot for the entire unit.   3.____
   These units are known as
   A. axials   B. field frames   C. bogies   D. helicals

4. In automotive electronics, the fractional duration that ignition points are closed is known as   4.____
   A. slip   B. gain   C. dwell   D. delay

5. A brake system's warning lights may be tested by   5.____
   A. testing the bulbs with an ohmmeter
   B. depressing the brake pedal and opening a wheel cylinder bleeder screw
   C. jumping the wires at the brake distributor switch assembly
   D. testing the system with an ammeter

6. Of the following procedures performed prior to grinding a valve seat, which should be performed FIRST?   6.____
   A. Reaming   B. Adjusting   C. Cleaning   D. Replacement

7. What type of clutch is responsible for controlling a car's air conditioning compressor?   7.____
   A. Centrifugal   B. Free-wheeling
   C. Magnetic   D. Mechanical

8. Which of the following is a DISADVANTAGE associated with onboard computer diagnostic systems?   8.____
    A. Inability to incorporate self-diagnosis
    B. Limited number of systems available for diagnosis
    C. Cannot be manually activated
    D. Inability to detect intermittent failures

9. Which parts in a motor or generator contact the rotating armature commutator or rings?   9.____
    A. Cams   B. Brushes   C. Rod caps   D. Bushings

10. What is the MAIN advantage associated with the use of offboard computer diagnostic systems?   10.____
    A. Decreased task load
    B. Continuous testing intervals
    C. Can be manually activated by the driver
    D. Capable of simultaneous multiple diagnoses

11. An EGO sensor used in a microprocessor-based control/diagnostic system   11.____
    A. is perfectly linear
    B. is unaffected by temperature
    C. has two different output levels, depending on the fuel mixture
    D. is unaffected by engine exhaust levels

12. To what drive train component is the ring gear in the differential bolted?   12.____
    A. Drive pinion   B. Axle shaft
    C. Differential case   D. Carrier

13. What is transmitted by the slip rings on an automotive alternator?   13.____
    A. Alternating current to the field coils
    B. Alternating current from the stator windings
    C. Direct current from the field coils
    D. Direct current to the alternator output terminals

14. Which of the following is a PROBABLE cause of an engine's missing at low speed?   14.____
    A. Poor compression   B. Leaky head gasket
    C. Carbon deposits in cylinders   D. Loose flywheel

15. In order for an onboard computer diagnostic system to detect a failure in the cars electronic system, the failure must be   15.____
    A. associated with engine performance
    B. intermittent
    C. symptomatic
    D. nonreversible

16. What is the term for the part of a shaft which rotates in a bearing?   16.____
    A. Lunette   B. Journal   C. Jackshaft   D. Kingpin

17. What is the USUAL steering gear reduction for passenger vehicles? _____-to-1.
    A. 2 B. 4 C. 8 D. 12

18. What is indicated by a low reading from 5 to 10 on an engine vacuum test?
    A. Broken piston ring
    B. Weak cylinders
    C. Late valve timing
    D. Valve sticking

19. Which of the following is NOT a component of the automotive power train?
    A. Steering gear
    B. Clutch
    C. Transmission
    D. Differential

20. Which instrument is NORMALLY used to check the condition of a resistance spark plug?
    A. Voltmeter B. Ohmmeter C. Ammeter D. Potentiometer

21. Which device is used to measure the resistance of a circuit or electrical machine?
    A. Ohmmeter B. Voltmeter C. Resistor D. Ammeter

22. What reading will appear on an infrared meter which indicates a failure of the catalytic converter? _____ HC/ _____ CO
    A. Low; high B. Low; low C. High; low D. High; high

23. In automatic transmissions, the servo
    A. operates the shifter valves
    B. applies the clutch
    C. applies the bands
    D. controls the output from the variable vane pump

24. If an onboard diagnostic system's fault code indicates that the O_2 sensor is not ready, all of the following are possible causes EXCEPT
    A. O_2 sensor is not functioning correctly
    B. defective connections or leads
    C. lack of O_2 contacting sensor
    D. control unit is not processing O_2 signal

25. The mechanical compressor in a car's air conditioning system is driven by
    A. an electric motor
    B. the axles
    C. the propeller shaft
    D. the crankshaft

KEY (CORRECT ANSWERS)

1.	B	11.	C
2.	B	12.	C
3.	C	13.	C
4.	C	14.	A
5.	B	15.	D
6.	C	16.	B
7.	C	17.	B
8.	D	18.	C
9.	B	19.	A
10.	A	20.	B

21.	A
22.	C
23.	C
24.	C
25.	D

TEST 2

DIRECTIONS: Each question or incomplete statement is followed by several suggested answers or completions. Select the one that BEST answers the question or completes the statement. *PRINT THE LETTER OF THE CORRECT ANSWER IN THE SPACE AT THE RIGHT.*

1. When installing disc brake linings, a hammer should be used to 1.____
    A. tighten the shoe retainer
    B. seat the pads in the calipers
    C. shape the pads
    D. remove the linings

2. What engine component is lubricated by the oil squirt hole in the connecting rod? 2.____
    A. Connecting rod bearing
    B. Crankshaft
    C. Cylinder wall
    D. Piston pin

3. Which of the following is a PROBABLE cause of backfiring through a carburetor? 3.____
    A. Short circuit in switch
    B. Water in gasoline
    C. Overheating
    D. Sticky thermostat

4. What is the GREATEST danger associated with hydraulic braking systems? 4.____
    A. Uneven braking
    B. Defective metering valve
    C. Loss of brake fluid
    D. Dirty or clogged wheel cylinder

5. Under what conditions must an engine be operated during a cylinder balance test? 5.____
    A. With the spark plugs firing, one at a time, at 1500 rpm
    B. With all plugs shorted but two which fire at non-simultaneous equal intervals
    C. At idle speed, with all plugs shorted but two which fire at non-simultaneous equal intervals
    D. At idle speed, with the spark plugs shorted, one at a time

6. Which of the following is a requisite property of brake fluid? 6.____
    A. Has detergents for keeping hoses unobstructed
    B. High wetting characteristics
    C. High viscosity
    D. High boiling point and low freezing point

7. What is measured by the mass airflow sensor in a microprocessor-based control/diagnostic system? The 7.____
    A. rate at which air is flowing into an engine
    B. composition of a given mass of air
    C. rate at which exhaust is flowing out of an engine
    D. density of atmospheric air

8. What is placed at the joint of a steel frame in order to strengthen the joint? 8.____
    A. Wobble plate
    B. Gusset plate
    C. Jackshaft
    D. Lint pin

9. What is indicated if a combustion meter reading is 10% higher with the air cleaner in place than when the air cleaner has been removed?
   A. Clogged injectors
   B. Dirty air cleaner
   C. Clogged vent
   D. Normal operation

10. Which of the following is a PROBABLE cause of an engine failing to stop?
    A. Lack of pressure on gasoline tank
    B. Disconnected magneto ground
    C. High altitude
    D. Spark plug gaps too wide

11. Automotive sensors used in computer-operated diagnostic or control systems typically see changes in each of the following EXCEPT
    A. electrical signals
    B. temperature
    C. position
    D. pressure

12. What type of feeler gauge should be used to set the gap on a new set of spark plugs?
    A. Flat   B. Ramp-type   C. Wire   D. Round

13. Intake and exhaust manifolds are built with their walls contacting each other in order to
    A. reduce atomization
    B. pre-heat the fuel mixture
    C. facilitate valve action
    D. conserve space

14. Fuel tank vapors stored in the charcoal canister
    A. are released to the atmosphere through a bleed valve
    B. are released to the atmosphere through a port in the canister
    C. are cycled back into the fuel tank
    D. become part of the fuel mixture when the engine is started

15. The information handled by a computerized engine control system flows from
    A. computer to sensor to display
    B. actuator to display to computer
    C. sensor to computer to actuator
    D. sensor to display to computer

16. In a car with manual transmission, spring pressure clamps the friction disc between the pressure plate and the _____ when the clutch is engaged.
    A. sun gear
    B. reaction plate
    C. flywheel
    D. differential

17. If the insulation material used with a crimp connector on electric wiring is coded red, what range of gauges is considered typical?
    A. 10-12   B. 12-18   C. 14-16   D. 18-22

18. An air conditioning system's expansion valve controls the
    A. pressure of refrigerant in the compressor
    B. temperature of refrigerant in the condenser
    C. amount of refrigerant in the evaporator
    D. temperature of air in the car's interior

19. Each of the following is a probable cause of engine overheating EXCEPT 19.____
    A. slipping fan belt
    B. frozen radiator
    C. improper valve timing
    D. short circuit in distributor rotor

20. When using a short finder to trace a short circuit, which of the following steps 20.____
    should be performed LAST?
    A. Turn on all switches in a series with the circuit being tested
    B. Move the short finder meter along circuit wiring
    C. Remove the blown fuse while leaving the battery connected
    D. Connect the pulse unit of short finder across the fuse terminals

21. If a light load test is performed on a battery and the battery shows less than 21.____
    1.95 volts in all cells, then the battery
    A. is overly discharged
    B. should be replaced
    C. needs charging
    D. is in good condition

22. A *thermistor* is a 22.____
    A. newly-developed type of transistor
    B. device for regulating engine temperature
    C. temperature control system operated by a car passenger
    D. semiconductor temperature sensor

23. An *expert* system for offboard computer diagnosis differs from other 23.____
    computerized diagnostic systems because it is capable of
    A. carrying out several diagnostic operations at once
    B. recommending repair procedures
    C. determining the causes of problems without manual assistance
    D. sensing faults in a circuitry that is not related to engine performance

24. In which type of engine are all valve contained in the cylinder block? 24.____
    A. V-type   B. Two-stroke   C. F-head   D. L-head

25. The function of a MAP sensor in a microprocessor-based control/diagnostic 25.____
    system is to
    A. sense anomalous changes in a vehicle's traveling direction
    B. measure changes in mean atmospheric pressure
    C. measure manifold absolute pressure
    D. measure fluctuations in manifold air flow

KEY (CORRECT ANSWERS)

1.	C	11.	A
2.	C	12.	C
3.	D	13.	B
4.	C	14.	D
5.	B	15.	C
6.	D	16.	C
7.	A	17.	D
8.	B	18.	C
9.	B	19.	C
10.	B	20.	B

21. A
22. D
23. B
24. D
25. C

TEST 3

DIRECTIONS: Each question or incomplete statement is followed by several suggested answers or completions. Select the one that BEST answers the question or completes the statement. *PRINT THE LETTER OF THE CORRECT ANSWER IN THE SPACE AT THE RIGHT.*

1. What is indicated by a sudden periodic drop of 1 or 2 points during a vacuum test on a car's engine? 1.____
    A. Spark plug failure
    B. Damaged distributor cap
    C. Coil failure
    D. Low oil pressure

2. A stud axle is articulated to an axle-beam or steering head by means of a 2.____
    A. journal   B. kingpin   C. gusset plate   D. poppet

3. Which of the following should be checked FIRST when examining a front suspension? 3.____
    A. Kingpins
    B. Steering connections
    C. Bumper and frame level
    D. Suspension arm pivots

4. Which of the following procedures involving a combustion efficiency tester will detect manifold leaks? 4.____
    A. Accelerating the engine to fast speed and checking for meter deflection
    B. Pumping the accelerator and checking for instant response in the combustion meter
    C. Applying a kerosene/oil mixture to the flange and manifold gaskets and checking for meter deflection
    D. Placing the engine on full choke and checking for meter deflection

5. If a car's battery is always fully charged, which of the following should be checked? 5.____
    A. Short circuiting in alternator
    B. Output amperage of the alternator
    C. volt regulator output
    D. Volt regulator points

6. Which of the following are companion cylinders in a car's V-8 engine? 6.____
    A. 1 and 8   B. 2 and 8   C. 3 and 4   D. 2 and 7

7. Which of the following is a PROBABLE cause of firing in a car's muffler? 7.____
    A. Too rich a fuel mixture
    B. Carbon deposits in cylinder
    C. Improperly adjusted valve tappets
    D. Water in gasoline

8. What is the MAJOR benefit associated with the use of *expert* offboard computer diagnostic systems? 8.____
    A. High task load capability
    B. Continuous testing intervals
    C. Consistent application of problem-solving strategies
    D. Simultaneous multiple-system capability

9

9. Which type of valve is used to sense how fast a vehicle is traveling? 9.____
   A. Throttle   B. Governor   C. Manual   D. Modulator

10. A two-unit alternator is composed of a 10.____
    A. voltage limiter and current limiter
    B. current limiter and reverse current relay
    C. voltage limiter and field relay
    D. current limiter and field relay

11. Which type of gears are used for the forward speeds of fully synchronized standard transmissions? 11.____
    A. Helical   B. Double helical
    C. Hypoid   D. Spur

12. When checking a circuit for voltage drop, which of the following steps should be performed FIRST? 12.____
    A. Select the voltmeter range just above the battery circuit
    B. Connect the positive lead of the voltmeter to the end of the wire closest to the battery
    C. Connect the negative lead of the voltmeter to the end of the wire farthest from the battery
    D. Switch on the circuit

13. Each of the following is a probable cause of engine knocking EXCEPT 13.____
    A. compression too low   B. loose piston
    C. spark too far advanced   D. engine overheated

14. In what portion of an *expert* system for offboard computer diagnosis are logical operation performed? 14.____
    A. Domain   B. Inference engine
    C. Knowledge base   D. Interface

15. In the propeller shaft of an automotive transmission, a universal joint allows variation in the 15.____
    A. speed of rotation   B. angle of drive
    C. length of the shaft   D. direction of rotation

16. Which of the following is a POSSIBLE use for an engine analyzer? 16.____
    A. Setting the choke   B. Measuring intake fuel flow rate
    C. Setting ignition points D. Measuring fuel mixture

17. What is the term for the smaller of two mating or meshing gears? 17.____
    A. Linch   B. Master   C. Pinion   D. Pilot

18. Conditioned air in an automotive air conditioning system is cooled as it passes through the 18.____
    A. condenser   B. evaporator   C. compressor   D. receiver

19. In order to determine the correct valve timing of an engine, the opening and closing of the valves should be measured in reference to the
    A. cylinder compression ratio
    B. fuel mixing jets
    C. distributor setting
    D. piston position

19._____

20. In modern engines using computer-based control systems, diagnosis is performed
    A. with an engine analyzer
    B. with a timing light only
    C. with a timing light and voltmeter
    D. in the digital control system

20._____

21. What is the MOST probable cause of a car drifting from side to side on a level road?
    A. Bent steering arm
    B. Tight shock absorber
    C. Loose steering connections
    D. Bent axle

21._____

22. Which device, as part of a special type of pump, drives plunger back and forth as it rotates, producing the pumping action?
    A. Trunnion
    B. Torus
    C. Camber link
    D. Wobble plate

22._____

23. In a microprocessor-based control/diagnostic system, a typical engine crankshaft angular position sensor is MOST effectively located on the
    A. camshaft
    B. crankshaft
    C. compressor pulley
    D. flywheel

23._____

24. Which type of gauge will allow a mechanic to MOST accurately set the proper electrode gap on a spark plug?
    A. Flat feeler
    B. Round wire feeler
    C. Square wire feeler
    D. Dial

24._____

25. What type of logical rule bases are programmed into MOST expert diagnostic systems?
    A. Either/or
    B. Set/subset
    C. If/then
    D. Inductive

25._____

KEY (CORRECT ANSWERS)

1.	A	11.	A
2.	B	12.	B
3.	C	13.	A
4.	C	14.	B
5.	C	15.	B
6.	B	16.	C
7.	A	17.	C
8.	C	18.	B
9.	B	19.	D
10.	C	20.	D

21. C
22. D
23. B
24. B
25. C

EXAMINATION SECTION
TEST 1

DIRECTIONS: Each question or incomplete statement is followed by several suggested answers or completions. Select the one that BEST answers the question or completes the statement. *PRINT THE LETTER OF THE CORRECT ANSWER IN THE SPACE AT THE RIGHT.*

1. A mechanic who discovers that the friction-disc facing of a dry clutch is saturated with oil should
   A. use a heavier oil
   B. wash the facing in solvent
   C. replace the facing
   D. increase clutch spring pressure

   1.____

2. Which of the following steps, performed prior to the removal of a transmission oil cooler, should occur FIRST?
   A. Removal of transmission case
   B. Removal of valve body assembly
   C. Checking transmission fluid level
   D. Draining radiator

   2.____

3. An alternator voltage regulator controls alternator output by
   A. grounding the negative diodes
   B. grounding the stator windings
   C. controlling the voltage output at the B terminal
   D. controlling the current feed to the rotor

   3.____

4. Which clutch part is located between the engine flywheel and the pressure plate?
   A. Release lever
   B. Fork
   C. Friction disc
   D. Adjusting screw

   4.____

5. In a digital microcomputer used for the control or diagnosis of automotive engine, some device is needed to convert the computer's output data into a form readable by people.
   The component which serve this function are known as
   A. data buses
   B. microprocessors
   C. peripherals
   D. accumulators

   5.____

6. What is being adjusted when a mechanic pulls the entire control arm toward the frame?
   A. Caster
   B. Camber
   C. Tracking
   D. Kingpin inclination

   6.____

7. Which of the following is a characteristic that could NOT typically be identified by a onboard computer diagnostic system?
   A. Faulty EGR circuits
   B. The cause of a short circuit
   C. Low ECT input
   D. Lean fuel mixture

   7.____

8. In an automatic transmission, the oil filter is USUALLY secured by means of   8._____
   A. screws or a clip	B. the oil pan
   C. a bracket assembly	D. a spring

9. In a microprocessor-based control/diagnostic system, which type of actuator   9._____
   recirculates exhaust gas to the intake charge?
   A. Fuel metering B. Ignition	C. EGR	D. EGO

10. Which of the following is a PROBABLE cause of an engine's missing at high   10._____
    speed?
    A. Carbon deposits in cylinder	B. Scored cylinder
    C. Short circuit in distributor rotor	D. Weak valve spring

11. Which of the following operations is performed by a sensor in a microprocessor-   11._____
    based control/diagnostic system?
    A. Sending signals to the driver
    B. Selecting the transmission gear ratio
    C. Measuring variables in physical qualities
    D. Serving as an output device

12. When a hydraulic brake pedal is released quickly, the initial makeup fluid is   12._____
    supplied to the master cylinder's pressure chamber through the
    A. piston bleeder holes	B. compensating port
    C. check valve	D. port holes

13. Which part of a transaxle drives the output shafts?   13._____
    A. Ring gear assembly	B. Pinion gears
    C. Side gears	D. Chain

14. Which of the following problems would be MOST difficult to solve with an   14._____
    onboard computer diagnostic system?
    A. Air pump switching valve failure
    B. Imbalanced injectors
    C. Fuel pump circuit fault
    D. Defective electronic spark timing circuit

15. What is the MOST likely cause of a buzzing noise in the automatic transmission?   15._____
    A. Vacuum leakage	B. Malfunctioning front pump
    C. Bent pilot shaft	D. Worn clutch plates

16. What is the function of an actuator in a microprocessor-based control/diagnostic   16._____
    system?
    A. Indicates results of a measurement
    B. Creates a response to an electrical signal
    C. Serves as an input device
    D. Provides a mathematical model for an engine

17. The constant flow method of fuel injection places its burden on each of the following components EXCEPT
    A. an engine-driven injection pump equipped with plungers
    B. injector nozzles
    C. metering valve
    D. bypass unit

17.____

18. Which device is used specifically to regulate current by means of variable resistance?
    A. Capacitor   B. Rheostat   C. Ohmmeter   D. Volute

18.____

19. Which type of spring is used in a spring-loaded disc clutch?
    A. Cantilever   B. Volute   C. Helical   D. Diaphragm

19.____

20. When the engine is running, power steering fluid travels from
    A. control valve to reservoir to pump
    B. pump to control valve to reservoir
    C. reservoir to pump to control valve
    D. reservoir to control valve to pump

20.____

21. Piezoresistivity is
    A. a resistance property of insulators
    B. a property of certain semiconductors in which resistivity varies with strain
    C. the ratio of resistivity in a semiconductor to the property being measured by a sensor
    D. a type of metal bonding pad

21.____

22. Which of the following would be a PROBABLE cause of engine stoppage?
    A. Fuel pump breakdown   B. Disconnected magneto ground
    C. High altitude   D. Blown cylinder-head gasket

22.____

23. If the insulation material used with a crimp connector on electric wiring is coded yellow, what range of gauges is considered typical?
    A. 10-12   B. 12-18   C. 14-16   D. 18-22

23.____

24. What is the MOST common firing order of an in-line 6-cylinder engine?
    A. 1-6-2-5-3-4   B. 1-3-6-4-2-5   C. 1-2-5-6-3-4   D. 1-5-3-6-2-4

24.____

25. The pressure sensor of most fuel injection systems is located
    A. in the injection chamber
    B. at the nozzle port
    C. within the pump housing
    D. beneath the floor, at the side of the engine compartment

25.____

KEY (CORRECT ANSWERS)

1.	C	11.	C
2.	D	12.	D
3.	C	13.	C
4.	C	14.	A
5.	C	15.	B
6.	B	16.	B
7.	B	17.	A
8.	A	18.	B
9.	C	19.	A
10.	D	20.	B

21. C
22. A
23. A
24. D
25. D

TEST 2

DIRECTIONS: Each question or incomplete statement is followed by several suggested answers or completions. Select the one that BEST answers the question or completes the statement. *PRINT THE LETTER OF THE CORRECT ANSWER IN THE SPACE AT THE RIGHT.*

1. What is the term for a spring-loaded ball that engages a notch? 1.____
   A. Roller bearing   B. Poppet   C. Venturi   D. Lunette

2. What changes alternating current to direct current in the alternator? 2.____
   A. Field relay
   B. Stator windings
   C. Rotor slip rings
   D. Diodes

3. If a mechanic is using an expert diagnostic system and encounters no rules in the conflict set, what should be done? 3.____
   A. Use highest-priority rules for predicted condition
   B. Stop the procedure
   C. Use the rule that most commonly appears under similar conditions
   D. Switch to a different database

4. With which drive train component does a transmission's reverse idler gear ALWAYS mesh? 4.____
   A. Clutch plate
   B. Second gear
   C. Countershaft reverse gear
   D. Main shaft reverse gear

5. Which of the following is the MOST probable cause for a noise that is present in the rear end only when a car goes around curves? 5.____
   A. Loose universal joint
   B. Trouble in the differential case assembly
   C. Trouble in the drive-pinion assembly
   D. Dry wheel bearing

6. In a microprocessor-based control/diagnostic system, which type of sensor is basically a resistor with a movable contact? 6.____
   A. Crankshaft position
   B. Throttle angle
   C. EGO
   D. Knock

7. What is being indicated by bubbles in an air conditioning sight gauge if the unit has been running for several minutes? 7.____
   A. Low refrigerant
   B. Low compressor pressure
   C. System leakage
   D. Normal operation

8. When checking connecting rods for alignment, the angle the rod aligner mandrel makes with the face plate should be _____ degrees, depending on the type of jig used. 8.____
   A. 10 or 20   B. 45 or 90   C. 90 or 180   D. 180 or 320

17

9. Which type of fuel injection system typically sprays fuel into each intake port on the manifold side of the intake valve?
    A. Direct
    B. Port
    C. Sequential
    D. Single-point

10. The purpose of a suction throttling valve used in an automotive air conditioning system is to
    A. prevent freezing in the evaporator
    B. control compressor cycles
    C. control the metering of the expansion valve
    D. maintain low condenser pressure

11. In a microprocessor-based control/diagnostic system, which type of actuator consists of a spray nozzle and a solenoid-operated plunger?
    A. Thermostat
    B. Ignition
    C. EGO
    D. Fuel injector

12. Which component of a band and servo assembly is DIRECTLY affected by hydraulic pressure?
    A. Anchor
    B. Band
    C. Servo piston
    D. Stem

13. If an ammeter shows a small fluctuating reading and a spark test reveals no spark, what is the MOST likely source of the trouble?
    A. Primary circuit
    B. Secondary circuit
    C. Battery
    D. Ignition switch

14. All of the following are characteristics of a top-feed fuel injector, as opposed to a bottom-feed EXCEPT
    A. uses incoming air for cooling purposes
    B. higher cost
    C. greater pressure requirements
    D. heavier mass

15. All of the following are probable causes of an engine's lacking power EXCEPT
    A. too rich a fuel mixture
    B. lack of coolant
    C. high altitude
    D. leaky manifold gaskets

16. Which device should be used to check for runout or wobble on a disc brake that has been lathe-mounted?
    A. Timing light
    B. Electric meter
    C. Dial indicator
    D. Torque wrench

17. A(n) _____ is the term for a wire or wires that form a common path to and from the various components a microcomputer uses for the diagnosis or control of an automotive engine.
    A. analog
    B. runner
    C. bus
    D. port

18. The notch on the head of a piston should be facing the _____ during the installation of a piston assembly.
    A. minor thrust side
    B. major thrust side
    C. rear of the engine
    D. front of the engine

18.____

19. The requisite knowledge and expertise used in an expert diagnostic system's programming is acquired from a person known as the
    A. domain expert
    B. user
    C. inference engine
    D. knowledge engineer

19.____

20. All of the following are probable causes of an engine's missing at all speeds EXCEPT
    A. valve tappets adjusted too closely
    B. dirty plug
    C. loose piston
    D. leak in intake manifold

20.____

21. The function of a MAP sensor in a microprocessor-based control/diagnostic system is to measure
    A. anomalous changes in a vehicle's traveling direction
    B. changes in mean atmospheric pressure
    C. manifold absolute pressure
    D. fluctuations in manifold air flow

21.____

22. What procedure is recommended upon discovering that brake fluid is contaminated?
    A. Bleed the hydraulic system
    B. Flush the system with alcohol, and then adding clean fluid
    C. Add a detergent oil to the system
    D. Replace the fluid, along with all hydraulic rubber cups and seals

22.____

23. Which of the following could be indicated by a vibrating reading on a vacuum gauge that appears only at high engine speeds?
    A. Pitted distributor points
    B. Incorrect ignition timing
    C. Blow-by
    D. Weak valve springs

23.____

24. In a microprocessor-based control/diagnostic system, which type of sensor uses magnetostrictive techniques?
    A. Knock
    B. Throttle angle
    C. EGO
    D. MAP

24.____

25. The amount that the steering knuckle pivots are angled away from a true vertical is known as
    A. camber
    B. phase
    C. tilt
    D. caster

25.____

KEY (CORRECT ANSWERS)

1.	B	11.	D
2.	D	12.	C
3.	B	13.	B
4.	C	14.	A
5.	C	15.	D
6.	B	16.	C
7.	A	17.	C
8.	C	18.	D
9.	B	19.	D
10.	A	20.	C

21. C
22. D
23. D
24. A
25. D

TEST 3

DIRECTIONS: Each question or incomplete statement is followed by several suggested answers or completions. Select the one that BEST answers the question or completes the statement. *PRINT THE LETTER OF THE CORRECT ANSWER IN THE SPACE AT THE RIGHT.*

1. All of the following are components of a positive crankcase ventilating system EXCEPT the 1._____
    A. manifold suction tube
    B. metering valve
    C. road draft tube
    D. intake breather

2. The MAXIMUM voltage for sensor and actuator circuits used in onboard diagnostic systems is 2._____
    A. 3
    B. 5
    C. 10
    D. 15

3. Which of the following is a PROBABLE result of adjusting valves with too little clearance? 3._____
    A. Delayed timing
    B. Burning oil
    C. Lower fuel economy
    D. Overheated valves

4. In a fuel metering actuator that is used in a microprocessor-based control/diagnostic system, *duty cycle* refers too the ratio of fuel 4._____
    A. *off* time to fuel *on* time
    B. *on* time to fuel *off* time
    C. *on* time to fuel *on* time plus fuel *off* time
    D. *off* time to fuel *off* time pus fuel *on* time

5. In a synchromesh transmission, gears are engaged by a _____ in order to prevent gear clashing. 5._____
    A. slip joint or spline
    B. friction and dog clutch
    C. planetary unit
    D. dog clutch

6. An EGO sensor is a 6._____
    A. device for measuring the oxygen concentration in automotive engine exhaust
    B. spark plug advance mechanism
    C. device for measuring crankshaft acceleration
    D. device for measuring the concentrations of various exhaust gases

7. What type of expander must be used under an oil ring? 7._____
    A. Step joint
    B. Diagonal joint
    C. Rigid
    D. Vented

8. Which of the following procedures is included in the performance of a compression test on a car engine? 8._____
    A. Perform entire test while engine is cold
    B. Test one cylinder at a time, with the corresponding plug temporarily removed

21

C. Crank for no more than two compression strokes
D. Block open throttle and choke

9. Air enters most Bosch electronic fuel injection systems through the
   A. oil bath cleaner
   B. injector choke
   C. compressor line
   D. injector manifold

10. The idler arm is attached to the _____ in a typical steering mechanism
    A. center link
    B. tie rod
    C. pitman arm
    D. spindle

11. In a microprocessor-based control/diagnostic system, which type of crankshaft position sensor uses a disk having several holes?
    A. Optical
    B. Ignition timing
    C. Hall-effect
    D. Magnetic reluctance

12. In a mechanical fuel pump, pressure is maintained by means of
    A. a spring under the diaphragm
    B. a motor
    C. a needle valve
    D. rotating vanes

13. If a third pump is used in a fuel injection system, it is mounted
    A. on the fuel tank pump pickup tube
    B. in the line between the pickup tube and the pressure pump
    C. in the line between the pressure pump and fuel metering assembly
    D. at the fuel metering assembly

14. Which part of a cooling system thermostat opens and closes system valves?
    A. Pressure valve
    B. Vacuum valve
    C. Bellows
    D. Seater

15. What is the term for the front portion of a vehicle body or cab which partially encloses the dash panel and forms the windshield frame?
    A. Cowl
    B. Hull
    C. Head
    D. Mask

16. How many digits make up a fault code used in a typical onboard computer diagnostic system?
    A. 1
    B. 2
    C. 3
    D. 4

17. Which of the following should be checked FIRST when all brakes are dragging?
    A. Brake fluid level
    B. Master cylinder compensating port
    C. Wheel cylinders
    D. Brake pedal free travel

18. Which type of sensor measure is NOT capable of measuring the amount of air flowing through a fuel injection system?
    A. Speed-density
    B. Plate
    C. Differential
    D. Mass airflow

19. Which type of engine contains valves both in the head and the cylinder block?
    A. V-type
    B. Two-stroke
    C. F-head
    D. L-head

20. Toe-in adjustments made by turning the adjusting sleeves on the tie rods in equal amounts in opposite directions are done to
    A. keep the wheels in balance
    B. keep the steering wheel centered
    C. avoid over-adjustment
    D. prevent excessive steering wheel play

21. Which of the following is NOT a possible cause of an overly lean fuel mixture that appears during a no-load carburetor mixture test?
    A. Plugged metering jets
    B. Stuck float
    C. Bad metering rod adjustment
    D. Manifold air leak

22. Which of the following is NOT a component of a pressure regulator used in fuel injection systems?
    A. Spring
    B. Manifold
    C. Diaphragm
    D. Valve

23. During installation of the transmission, _____ can be used to turn the drive plate in order to connect it with the converter.
    A. the transmission unit
    B. the cranking motor
    C. the output shaft
    D. a wrench

24. Which type of bearing is NOT used on automotive drive axles?
    A. Sleeve
    B. Roller
    C. Taper
    D. Ball

25. What is the term for the action or process of producing voltage by the relative motion of a magnetic field and a conductor?
    A. Induction
    B. Resistance
    C. Condensation
    D. Conduction

KEY (CORRECT ANSWERS)

1. C
2. B
3. D
4. C
5. B

6. A
7. B
8. D
9. A
10. A

11. A
12. A
13. D
14. C
15. A

16. B
17. D
18. C
19. C
20. B

21. C
22. B
23. B
24. A
25. A

EXAMINATION SECTION
TEST 1

DIRECTIONS: Each question or incomplete statement is followed by several suggested answers or completions. Select the one that BEST answers the question or completes the statement. *PRINT THE LETTER OF THE CORRECT ANSWER IN THE SPACE AT THE RIGHT.*

1. All of the following are probable sources of drivability problems EXCEPT the 1.____
   A. battery system
   B. engine condition
   C. ignition system
   D. fuel delivery system

2. Bending the _____ is the BEST way to adjust the ignition point contact. 2.____
   A. movable point arm
   B. breaker plate
   C. stationary point bracket
   D. pivot post

3. If an ignition system's breaker points are pitted, what should a mechanic check FIRST? 3.____
   A. Distributor condenser
   B. Distributor cap
   C. Circuit breaker
   D. Coil

4. Which cooling system component should be checked if a car's air conditioning blower operates properly but system output is still inadequate? 4.____
   A. Receiver-drier
   B. Evaporator core
   C. Temperature control
   D. Condenser

5. Excessive wear of brake linings will MOST likely cause 5.____
   A. stiff pedal
   B. drum scoring
   C. sticky wheel
   D. drag on brakes

6. The PCV valve is connected between the 6.____
   A. transmission and clutch
   B. injector and fuel pump
   C. exhaust pipe and intake manifold
   D. crankcase and intake manifold

7. What device is MOST effective for checking fuel pump performance? 7.____
   A. Vacuum switch
   B. Micrometer
   C. Voltmeter
   D. Stethoscope prod

8. For what purpose are the points of a conventional ignition system adjusted to increase the point gap? To 8.____
   A. advance the ignition timing
   B. increase the dwell angle
   C. decrease the dwell angle with no change in timing
   D. slow the ignition timing

9. Which of the following is NOT a type of temperature sensor used in microprocessor-based control/diagnostic systems?
   A. Wire-wound resistor
   B. Potentiometer
   C. Semiconductor resistor
   D. Thermistor

10. The various relationships and fundamental data associated with the use of an expert diagnostic system are known as the
    A. domain
    B. inference engine
    C. knowledge base
    D. interface

11. Which type of electric starting motor is often used because of its high starting torque?
    A. Compound-wound
    B. Shunt-wound
    C. Series-wound
    D. Capacitor

12. The auto system that is LEAST likely to cause engine operating problems is the _____ system.
    A. starting
    B. charging
    C. ignition
    D. fuel injection

13. Which device is capable of measuring volts, ohms, and amperes in solid-state electronic equipment?
    A. Digital multimeter
    B. Analog multimeter
    C. Jumper wires
    D. Continuity tester

14. Which of the following is a PROBABLE cause of backfiring in an intake manifold?
    A. Broken connecting rod
    B. Incorrect valve timing
    C. Sticky choke valve
    D. A lean cold-engine fuel mixture

15. An EGO sensor that is used in a microprocessor-based control/diagnostic system should NOT be used for control at a temperature less than _____ °C.
    A. 0
    B. 100
    C. 200
    D. 300

16. What is the PROBABLE result of setting a spark plug gap more closely than normal?
    A. Smoother idling
    B. Hard starting
    C. Easier starting
    D. Rougher idling

17. Adjusting the _____ will help the steering of a car return to a straight position after cornering.
    A. toe-in
    B. toe-out
    C. caster
    D. camber

18. What is the basic work register in microcomputers that is used for automotive engine control an diagnostics?
    A. Status register
    B. Condition code register
    C. Brancher
    D. Accumulator

19. A car lacks power and a popping sound can be heard. 19.____
What is the MOST likely cause?
   A. Shorted spark plug
   B. Uneven fuel supply
   C. Pitted breaker points
   D. Bad distributor timing

20. What is the term for the reinforcing ridge around a tire opening where it fits 20.____
the wheel rim?
   A. Piping   B. Binder   C. Ram   D. Bead

21. When checking a circuit for voltage drop, which of the following steps 21.____
should be performed LAST?
   A. Select the voltmeter range just above the battery circuit
   B. Connect the positive lead of the voltmeter to the end of the wire closest to the battery
   C. Connect the negative lead of the voltmeter to the end of the wire farthest from the battery
   D. Switch on the circuit

22. If a battery frequently needs recharging, all of the following are probable 22.____
causes EXCEPT
   A. poorly sized alternator drive pulley
   B. cell leakage
   C. poorly grounded voltage regulator
   D. sulfated battery

23. The diagnosis of intermittent failures in computer-based engine control systems 23.____
is
   A. readily found using standard service bay equipment
   B. accomplished by displaying fault codes to the driver at the time of the failure
   C. sometimes accomplished by means of warning lamps on the dash display
   D. routinely accomplished with the onboard diagnostic capability of the control system

24. Before disassembling an air-release parking brake, it is necessary to FIRST 24.____
   A. remove the diaphragm clamp
   B. remove the quick release valve
   C. compress the apply spring
   D. fill the air reservoir

25. What is the MOST probable result of incorrect camber on car wheels? 25.____
   A. Abnormal tire wear along one side of the tread
   B. Damaged shocks
   C. Front-end shimmy
   D. Pulling to the side while braking

KEY (CORRECT ANSWERS)

1.	A		11.	C
2.	C		12.	D
3.	A		13.	A
4.	C		14.	D
5.	B		15.	D
6.	D		16.	D
7.	D		17.	B
8.	A		18.	D
9.	B		19.	B
10.	C		20.	D

21. D
22. B
23. C
24. C
25. A

TEST 2

DIRECTIONS: Each question or incomplete statement is followed by several suggested answers or completions. Select the one that BEST answers the question or completes the statement. *PRINT THE LETTER OF THE CORRECT ANSWER IN THE SPACE AT THE RIGHT.*

1. The fuel pump in MOST fuel injection systems operates when the engine has oil pressure, and when the cranking speed is above _____ rpm. 1.____
   A. 50-75   B. 150-200   C. 500-1000   D. 1000-2000

2. What is indicated by an occasional 3-4 inch drop in a vacuum gauge test? 2.____
   A. Slowed timing
   B. Carburetor failure
   C. Valve sticking
   D. Incorrectly gapped plugs

3. All of the following are types of compressors used in automotive air conditioning systems EXCEPT 3.____
   A. 90-degree V
   B. 2-cylinder in-line
   C. axial
   D. hermetically sealed

4. How much free action does a mechanic typically allow in the brake pedal? 4.____
   A. None   B. 1/8 inch   C. 1/4 inch   D. 1/2 inch

5. Tire wear that is concentrated on both sides of the tread is USUALLY the result of 5.____
   A. toe-out
   B. improper balance
   C. over-inflation
   D. under-inflation

6. Temperature sensors that are a part of microprocessor-based electronic control/diagnostic systems use a type of semiconductor to measure temperature. 6.____
   The resistance of this semiconductor
   A. is always 100,000 ohms
   B. varies in direct proportion to temperature
   C. varies in inverse proportion to temperature
   D. varies in direct proportion to engine speed

7. Using a test lamp across the breaker points, and with the ignition switch on, a mechanic will rotate the _____ to obtain the correct timing. 7.____
   A. distributor housing until the light goes out
   B. distributor housing until the light goes on
   C. engine until the light goes out
   D. engine until the light goes on

8. In constant-flow fuel injection systems, pressure and circulation are provided by a(n) 8.____
   A. injection pump
   B. hydraulic line
   C. engine-driven rotary pump
   D. bellows

29

9. Which of the following could NOT be determined by using an armature growler to test a starting motor armature?
   A. Insulation condition
   B. Location of short circuits
   C. Amount of resistance
   D. Commutator condition

10. What is measured by the crankcase angular position sensor in a microprocessor-based control/diagnostic system? The
    A. oil pressure angle
    B. angle between a line drawn through a crankshaft axis, a mark on the flywheel, and a reference line
    C. angle between the connecting rods and the crankshaft
    D. pitch angle of the crankshaft

11. If the insulation material used with a crimp conector on electric wiring is coded blue, what range of gauges is considered typical?
    A. 10-12   B. 12-18   C. 14-16   D. 18-22

12. Which type of pump is used ONLY as a supply pump in some fuel injection systems?
    A. Rotary   B. Diaphragm   C. Turbine   D. Roller

13. In what part of a car's air conditioning system does the refrigerant lose heat?
    A. Receiver   B. Compressor   C. Condenser   D. Evaporator

14. When disc brake pads are retracted so as not to make contact with the rotor surface, the amount of retraction
    A. is limited by the metering valve
    B. must be a minimum of 1/16 inch
    C. is affected by the piston return springs
    D. is affected by the piston seals

15. What is the term for the high curved portion of a cam that produce maximum valve lift?
    A. Peak
    B. Nose circle
    C. Flank circle
    D. Radial circle

16. The current from a battery generally flows to the alternator _____ when a vehicle is started?
    A. rectifier
    B. rotor winding
    C. stator windings
    D. commutator

17. If the cam dwell angle of a distributor is less than the specified minimum, it is LIKELY that the
    A. rubbing block will wear down
    B. distributor contact points will become pitted
    C. ignition coil output will increase at high engine speeds
    D. ignition timing will be off

18. The ignition quality of diesel fuel is measured against an index known as the
    A. lean parameter	B. cetane rating
    C. atomization ratio	D. vortex flow chart

    18.____

19. During timing operations on a six-cylinder engine, a timing light should be connected to spark plug number
    A. 6	B. 4	C. 2	D. 1

    19.____

20. In a microprocessor-based control/diagnostic system, which type of actuator serves to lower NO emissions?
    A. Ignition	B. Fuel metering
    C. EGR	D. EGO

    20.____

21. What is indicated by a faintly vibrating needle during an engine vacuum test?
    A. Weak cylinders
    B. Leaking valves
    C. Obstruction in the exhaust system
    D. A broken piston ring

    21.____

22. Which of the following components is NOT carried by a car's wheel knuckle assembly?
    A. Disc brake caliper mounting	B. Rotor
    C. Steering arm	D. Drum backing plate

    22.____

23. If a mechanic hears a squealing noise during operation after the installation of an automatic transmission, what is the MOST likely source of the trouble?
    A. Rear bearing
    B. Regulator body mating surfaces
    C. Speedometer pinion
    D. Front pump drive sleeve or pump pinion

    23.____

24. How should a mechanic decrease ignition point dwell?
    A. Rotate distributor body in the direction opposite the distributor shaft rotation
    B. Install weaker springs in the advance unit
    C. Increase the point gap
    D. Decrease the point gap

    24.____

25. Before charging a battery, the battery ground cable should be disconnected at the battery.
    This is done in order to protect the
    A. alternator regulator	B. alternator diodes
    C. ignition coil	D. ignition module

    25.____

KEY (CORRECT ANSWERS)

1.	B	11.	C
2.	C	12.	C
3.	D	13.	C
4.	C	14.	D
5.	D	15.	B
6.	C	16.	B
7.	B	17.	D
8.	C	18.	B
9.	C	19.	D
10.	B	20.	C

21.	A
22.	B
23.	D
24.	A
25.	B

TEST 3

DIRECTIONS: Each question or incomplete statement is followed by several suggested answers or completions. Select the one that BEST answers the question or completes the statement. *PRINT THE LETTER OF THE CORRECT ANSWER IN THE SPACE AT THE RIGHT.*

1. Against what part of a bearing do rollers or balls move? 1.____
    A. Sleeve B. Spread C. Knuckle D. Race

2. All of the following are desirable characteristics of an EGO sensor used in a microprocessor-based electronic control/diagnostic system EXCEPT 2.____
    A. variable voltages with respect to exhaust temperature
    B. rapid switching of output voltage in response to exhaust gas oxygen changes
    C. abrupt change in voltage at the optimal combustion ratio
    D. large difference in sensor output voltage between rich and lean mixture conditions

3. A _____ joint is used to allow changes in the length of a propeller shaft. 3.____
    A. slip B. shaft C. universal D. idler

4. Which of the following should be adjusted LAST in performing a tune-up on a car with a carburetor? 4.____
    A. Drive belts
    B. Manifold heat control valve
    C. Carburetor
    D. EGR valve

5. What device operates the plungers in a fuel injection pump? 5.____
    A. Pump camshaft
    B. Belt
    C. Engine camshaft
    D. Drive chain

6. Ignition of the combustion charge before the spark has formed across the plug electrodes is known as 6.____
    A. cold firing
    B. knocking
    C. backfiring
    D. preignition

7. Gear-train end play can be adjusted by 7.____
    A. changing the snap ring
    B. removing the clutch plates and installing retainer ring
    C. changing the selective thrust washer
    D. installing different pinion carriers

8. Unlike a conventional spark plug, a resistor plug will 8.____
    A. require higher voltage to function
    B. lengthen the capacitive part of the spark
    C. shrink the inductive part of the spark
    D. have an auxiliary air gap

9. Which measuring device is used MAINLY to check for voltage in a circuit while power is connected to the circuit?
   A. Digital multimeter
   B. Jumper wires
   C. Test lights
   D. Short finder

10. The flexible link that allows a suspension spring's length to change as it flexes is the
    A. shackle
    B. strut
    C. flange
    D. trailing arm

11. What type of electrical connectors are generally used with component that are occasionally disconnected?
    A. Crimp
    B. Bullet
    C. Butt
    D. Snap-splice

12. Which of the following device is NOT appropriate for checking the distributor automatic advance operations?
    A. Tachometer
    B. Voltmeter
    C. Vacuum pump
    D. Timing light

13. Engine bearings are commonly made from each of the following materials EXCEPT
    A. babbit
    B. case-hardened steel
    C. aluminum
    D. copper-lead mix

14. What should be used with bolts or screws on bearing surface designed to retain end thrust?
    A. Toggles
    B. Plain washers
    C. Thrust washers
    D. Lock washers

15. An automotive technician's basic measurement tool is the
    A. dial gauge
    B. feeler gauge
    C. telescopic gauge
    D. micrometer

16. What is used to attach a thrust plate to an engine block?
    A. Sheet metal screws
    B. Cap screws
    C. Wire spring clips
    D. Stamped metal clips

17. In an *expert* system for offboard computer diagnosis, which stage of knowledge acquisition in developing problem-solving rules occurs LAST?
    A. Implementation
    B. Identification
    C. Formalization
    D. Conceptualization

18. All of the following are possible causes of incorrect steering axis inclination and toe-out figures EXCEPT
    A. worn tires
    B. bent suspension
    C. worn ball joint
    D. worn steering parts

19. In a magnetic circuit, reluctance is a quality that is analogous to the _____ of an electrical circuit.
    A. capacitance
    B. voltage
    C. amperage
    D. resistance

19.____

20. Which device is used MAINLY to check for both open and short circuits?
    A. Short finder
    B. Jumper wires
    C. Test light
    D. Continuity tester

20.____

21. Which type of spring is MOST commonly used in automotive suspension systems?
    A. Torsion bar
    B. Coil spring
    C. Multiple-leaf spring
    D. Monoleaf spring

21.____

22. At the most basic level, the special type of language used to form microcomputer instructions, such as the ones used in automotive controls and diagnostics, is known as
    A. digital coding
    B. assembly language
    C. branch language
    D. fault coding

22.____

23. Most automotive camshafts are made from
    A. hardened alloy cast-iron
    B. steel'
    C. sintered iron
    D. tempered aluminum alloy

23.____

24. What progressively increasing quality should be indicated by a combustion tester as an engine accelerates from idle to cruising speeds?
    A. Higher rate of combustion
    B. Higher fuel-air ratio
    C. Lower thermal efficiency
    D. Leaner fuel mixture

24.____

25. What sizing process conforms metal to size by applying pressure?
    A. Stamping
    C. Burnishing
    C. Canting
    D. Beading

25.____

KEY (CORRECT ANSWERS)

1. D
2. A
3. A
4. C
5. A

6. D
7. C
8. C
9. C
10. A

11. B
12. B
13. B
14. C
15. D

16. B
17. A
18. A
19. D
20. D

21. B
22. B
23. A
24. D
25. B

EXAMINATION SECTION
TEST 1

DIRECTIONS: Each question or incomplete statement is followed by several suggested answers or completions. Select the one that BEST answers the question or completes the statement. *PRINT THE LETTER OF THE CORRECT ANSWER IN THE SPACE AT THE RIGHT.*

1. Of the following, the SMALLEST taper which would require the reboring of a common automotive engine cylinder, which is otherwise in good condition, is

   A. .001"   B. .003"   C. .007"   D. .013"

2. In order to prevent oil pumping, the maximum permissible clearance between the top piston ring and the land should be MOST NEARLY _____ inches.

   A. .0015   B. .002   C. .006   D. .010

3. Of the following, the SMALLEST out-of-roundness which would require reboring of a common automotive engine cylinder, which is otherwise in good condition, is

   A. .010"   B. .006"   C. .002"   D. .001"

Questions 4-5.

DIRECTIONS: Questions 4 and 5 are to be answered in accordance with Fig. 1 below.

Figure 1 represents an automobile engine cylinder in which measurements K and L were made at the top and measurements and N were made at the bottom. These measurements are, in inches:
K = 3.886
L = 3.879
M = 3.875
N = 3.874

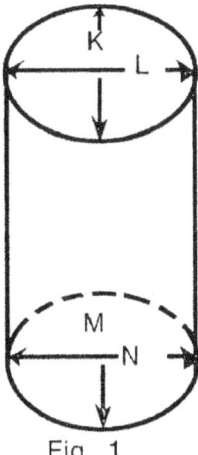
Fig. 1

4. The MAXIMUM out-of-roundness in the cylinder shown in Fig. 1 is MOST NEARLY _____ inches.

   A. .003   B. .005   C. .007   D. .009

5. The MAXIMUM taper in the cylinder shown in Fig. 1 is MOST NEARLY _____ inches.

   A. .002   B. .007   C. .011   D. .01

6. The most nearly CORRECT of the following statements regarding piston *scraper* rings is that they

   A. usually have grooved faces
   B. are usually installed in the lowest ring groove
   C. must be installed with the steel segment above the cast iron section
   D. are similar in construction to oil control rings

7. After a precision type bearing insert has been installed in a main bearing cap, it is determined that the ends of the bearing are both .010 inches below the surface of the cap that contacts the block.
   The statement that BEST indicates the action to be taken is that the bearing

   A. should be returned to the supplier because it is defective
   B. should be exchanged for one of the correct standard OD oversize
   C. should be left in place as it is within specifications as to allowance for expansion
   D. cap should be machined flush with the ends of the insert and a shim installed to allow for future adjustment

8. The most nearly CORRECT of the following statements concerning an *engineered* set of piston rings is that they

   A. will give superior sealing and improved gas mileage in a rebored engine
   B. have weaker expander rings than a factory set in order to reduce drag for high performance operation
   C. should be used in cylinders with less than .005 inch wear
   D. should be used in cylinders with more than .008 inch wear

9. Camshaft lobes are normally ground tapered in order to

   A. cause the tappet lifter to rotate
   B. insure that motion is transmitted through the hardened edge of the cam
   C. eliminate thrust loading on the tappet
   D. place the highest point under the centerline of the tappet bore

10. When inspecting engine crankshaft main bearings and camshaft bearings, one would NORMALLY expect that the

    A. crankshaft and camshaft bearings would show equal wear
    B. crankshaft bearings would be more worn than the camshaft bearings
    C. camshaft bearings would be more worn than the crankshaft bearings
    D. crankshaft bearings may or may not be more worn than the camshaft bearings

11. An automobile mechanic usually uses a wire gage for checking

    A. spark plug gaps
    B. the resistance of secondary circuit wires
    C. the diameter of secondary circuit wires
    D. the wall thickness of tubing

12. The terms *Reed and Prince* or *Clutch,* in connection with hand tools, USUALLY refer to

    A. box wrenches   B. pliers
    C. screwdrivers   D. vise grips

13. When a dial indicator is being used to measure the end play of a shaft, it is MOST important that the   13._____

    A. actuating rod of the indicator be perpendicular to the movement of the shaft
    B. face of the dial indicator be in the horizontal plane
    C. face of the dial indicator be in the vertical plane
    D. actuating rod of the indicator be parallel to the movement of the shaft

14. In automotive work, stud wrenches are MOST generally used when   14._____

    A. installing studs   B. driving 12 point bolts
    C. removing flare nuts   D. working in tight places

15. When a hydrometer is used to check a fully charged lead-acid battery, the reading should be MOST NEARLY   15._____

    A. 1.370   B. 1.270   C. 1.240   D. 1.120

16. Of the following statements about the use of a positive crankcase vent (PCV) valve on an automotive engine, the one that is CORRECT is that the valve   16._____

    A. controls the flow of gases from the crankcase into the air filter
    B. controls the flow of gases from the crankcase into the exhaust manifold
    C. is solenoid operated
    D. will cause rough idling if it does not seat properly

17. Of the following, the one that the use of a pressure cap on the radiator tank of an automotive cooling system does NOT permit is   17._____

    A. relief of excess pressure when required
    B. admission of air to the system when the system is cooling
    C. the rise of water temperature to a temperature above 212° F
    D. increased cavitation in the pump

18. In adjusting roller bearing type wheel bearings, it is PROPER to   18._____

    A. tighten the nut to 25 ft. lbs. before locking
    B. have .001 to .003 in. end play after locking
    C. have no end play with a slight preload after locking
    D. tighten the nut to 10 ft. lbs. and back off three flats of the nut

19. The MOST likely cause of a continuous noise coming from a rear axle when pulling straight ahead is   19._____

    A. worn differential pinions
    B. excessive axle end play
    C. loose pinion shaft bearings
    D. excessive side gear backlash

20. When cleaning hydraulic brake cylinder parts, the BEST solvent to use is   20._____

    A. gasoline   B. kerosene   C. alcohol   D. acetone

21. A force of 50 pounds is applied to the push rod of the one-inch bore master cylinder in a properly connected and properly operating hydraulic brake system. The master cylinder is connected to a 1 1/2 inch bore wheel cylinder. The fluid pressure developed in the wheel cylinder is

   A. less than the pressure in the master cylinder
   B. approximately 64 pounds per sq. in.
   C. greater than the pressure in the master cylinder
   D. approximately 113 pounds

22. With regard to a paper carburetor air cleaner element, the BEST procedure to follow is to

   A. clean it by soaking it in solvent for half hour and blowing it dry with compressed air
   B. clean it by blowing it out with compressed air in the direction opposite the direction of flow when it is in use
   C. clean it by tapping on the edge of the element, rotating it frequently to cover the whole element
   D. replace it since it is a sealed unit and is impossible to clean

23. In order to decrease the ignition point dwell, it is necessary to

   A. rotate the distributor body in the direction opposite that of the rotation of the distributor shaft
   B. install weaker springs in the advance unit
   C. increase the point gap
   D. decrease the point gap

24. Of the following, the range of torques which require the use of a torque wrench, in an automotive shop, or garage, is MOST NEARLY from

   A. -50 inch pounds to 50 inch pounds
   B. 0 to 150 foot pounds
   C. 0 to 200 inch pounds
   D. -50 foot pounds to 50 foot pounds

Questions 25-26.

DIRECTIONS: Questions 25 and 26 are to be answered in accordance with Fig. 2 below.

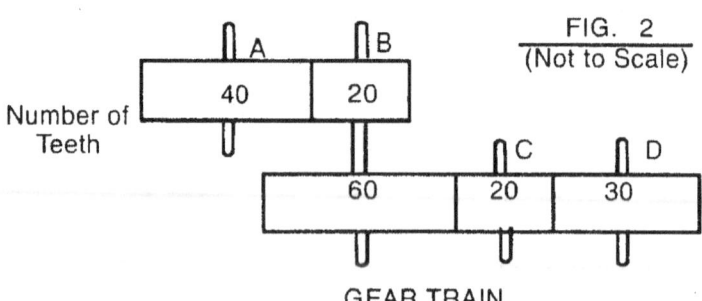

25. Fig. 2 shows the number of teeth on each gear of the gear train.
    If the 40-tooth gear makes 100 rpm, then the 30-tooth gear will make MOST NEARLY _____ rpm.

   A. 200   B. 400   C. 600   D. 800

26. If Gear A in Fig. 2 is rotating counterclockwise, the rotation of Gears B, C, and D will be: 26.____
    A. B counterclockwise, C counterclockwise, D clockwise
    B. B clockwise, C clockwise, D counterclockwise
    C. B clockwise, C clockwise, D clockwise
    D. B clockwise, C counterclockwise, D clockwise

27. An alternator is driven by a belt connected to a pulley on the engine crankshaft. The crankshaft pulley is 8 inches in diameter and the alternator pulley is 3 inches in diameter. If the engine is operating at 1000 rpm, the alternator is rotating at MOST NEARLY _____ rpm. 27.____
    A. 2700   B. 2500   C. 2000   D. 1500

28. The one of the following statements about diesel engines that is CORRECT is that they are exclusively _____ engines. 28.____
    A. 2 stroke cycle   B. 4 stroke cycle
    C. high compression   D. truck

29. Automotive engines are frequently classified by valve location.
    The engine in which both the intake and the exhaust valves are located in the cylinder head is the _____-Head. 29.____
    A. H   B. L   C. F   D. I

30. The fuel in the cylinder of an automotive diesel engine running under full load is ignited by 30.____
    A. a hot wire   B. hot air
    C. a glowing plug   D. a Ricardo Lead

31. The gears used for the forward speeds of MOST standard transmissions of the fully synchronized type are _____ gears. 31.____
    A. helical   B. hypoid
    C. spur   D. double helical

32. A snap ring with eyelets is BEST removed with the aid of 32.____
    A. snap ring pliers
    B. two screwdrivers
    C. chain nose pliers
    D. a screwdriver and slip joint pliers

33. Air brake compressor governors are MOST usually adjusted so that the compressor 33.____
    A. will maintain an unvarying pressure of 100 Psi in the system
    B. will cut in at a pressure of 50 Psi and cut out at a pressure of 100 Psi
    C. will cut in at a pressure of 100 Psi and cut out at a pressure of 115 Psi
    D. pressure will never exceed 100 Psi

34. The instrument USUALLY used to check the condition of a resistance-type spark plug is a(n) 34.____
    A. voltmeter   B. ammeter   C. ohmmeter   D. potentiometer

35. One of the machinists in your shop enjoys the reputation of being a great equivocator. This means MOST NEARLY that he

    A. takes pride and is happy in his work
    B. generally hedges and often gives misleading answers
    C. is a strong union man with great interest in his fellow workers' welfare
    D. is good at resolving disputes

36. When a machinist has the reputation of persistently making foolish or silly remarks, it may be said that he is

    A. inane
    B. meticulous
    C. a procrastinator
    D. a prevaricator

37. When two mechanics, called A and B, make measurements of the same workpiece and find significant discrepancies in their measurements, it is MOST NEARLY CORRECT to state that

    A. mechanic B made an erroneous reading
    B. mechanic A was careless in making his measurements
    C. both mechanics made their measurements correctly
    D. there was considerable difference in the two sets of measurements

38. The taper and out-of-roundness of an automotive engine cylinder can be determined accurately and MOST rapidly by use of a(n)

    A. inside micrometer
    B. telescoping gage
    C. micrometer depth gage
    D. cylinder dial gage

39. Among the ordinary taps that are used in general garage work, the tap that has the LONGEST chamfer in usually the _____ tap.

    A. machine screw
    B. tape
    C. bottoming
    D. plug

40. In cutting very thick work with a hand hacksaw, it is MOST desirable to use a hacksaw blade with _____ teeth per inch.

    A. 14
    B. 18
    C. 24
    D. 32

KEY (CORRECT ANSWERS)

1.	D	11.	A	21.	B	31.	A
2.	C	12.	C	22.	B	32.	A
3.	B	13.	D	23.	C	33.	C
4.	C	14.	A	24.	B	34.	C
5.	C	15.	B	25.	B	35.	B
6.	A	16.	D	26.	D	36.	A
7.	A	17.	D	27.	A	37.	D
8.	D	18.	B	28.	C	38.	D
9.	A	19.	C	29.	D	39.	B
10.	B	20.	C	30.	B	40.	A

TEST 2

DIRECTIONS: Each question or incomplete statement is followed by several suggested answers or completions. Select the one that BEST answers the question or completes the statement. *PRINT THE LETTER OF THE CORRECT ANSWER IN THE SPACE AT THE RIGHT.*

1. When the head of an OHV gasoline engine is removed, it is noted that all the exhaust valves are dark colored and that the combustion chambers are dry.
These conditions MOST probably indicate that

   A. the engine is in good condition
   B. the spark plugs are too hot
   C. compression is low because of bad rings
   D. compression is low because of leaking valves

   1.____

2. A slot-shaped opening in the air horn of a carburetor, just above the throttle valve when it is in the closed position, would MOST probably be

   A. a part of the low-speed circuit
   B. the accelerating pump inlet
   C. the high-speed bleeder
   D. the full power bypass jet discharge

   2.____

3. In a carburetor, the full power bypass jet NORMALLY supplies additional fuel when the

   A. venturi vacuum increases
   B. venturi vacuum decreases
   C. manifold vacuum increases
   D. manifold vacuum decreases

   3.____

4. A DC generator of the type in which the field winding is externally grounded is USUALLY polarized by using a jumper and flashing between the

   A. generator and battery terminals on the regulator
   B. armature and field terminals on the generator
   C. generator and the field terminals on the regulator
   D. battery and the field terminals on the regulator

   4.____

5. The slip rings on an automotive alternator transmit

   A. alternating current from the stator windings
   B. direct current to the field coils
   C. alternating current to the field coils
   D. direct current to the alternator output terminals

   5.____

6. You have been instructed to set up a 24 volt source of DC and have been supplied two six-cell and four three-cell lead-acid batteries.
In order to produce the required voltage, and to insure maximum current capacity, the batteries should be connected

   A. with one set of two six-cell batteries connected in series and one set of four three-cell batteries connected in series, with the outer terminals of both sets then connected in parallel
   B. with two sets of one six-cell and two three-cell batteries connected in series, with both sets then connected in series

   6.____

C. in series, making certain that each positive terminal is connected to the negative terminal of another battery
D. in parallel, with all positive terminals connected together and all negative terminals connected together

7. A two-unit alternator regulator consists of a

   A. field relay and a voltage limiter
   B. reverse current relay and a current limiter
   C. voltage limiter and a current limiter
   D. field relay and current limiter

8. The number of diodes NORMALLY found on an automotive alternator is

   A. 3 B. 4 C. 6 D. 7

9. In attempting to operate the starting motor of an automotive engine with the headlamps burning brightly, it is noticed that the lamps go out as the starter solenoid is energized. This MOST probably indicates that

   A. the primary windings of the solenoid are short-circuited
   B. there is a poor connection at one of the battery terminals
   C. the battery requires charging
   D. the solenoid switch is not completing the circuit

10. The MAXIMUM permissible drop in voltage at the battery terminals during a cranking voltage test on a starter motor is MOST NEARLY

    A. 10% B. 20% C. 30% D. 40%

11. An ignition system test is made by taking the end of the high tension wire from the coil and holding it near the engine block. At the same time, the movable ignition point arm is shorted to the breaker plate with the points open and the ignition on. No spark is obtained at the end of the high tension wire.
    This indicates MOST likely that there is a defect in the

    A. rotor   B. ignition points
    C. coil   D. distributor cap

12. If the result of the test described in the preceding question was a good spark between the coil wire and the block, and if no spark is obtained at any of the spark plugs when cranking the engine with the ignition on, the MOST likely cause of the trouble is the

    A. coil   B. ignition points
    C. condenser   D. spark plug wires

13. When performing a compression test on an automotive engine, the PROPER procedure includes

    A. removing only one spark plug at a time and reinstalling it after completing the test on that cylinder
    B. having the throttle and choke blocked open
    C. cranking the engine for a maximum of two compression strokes
    D. performing the test when the engine is cold

14. A cylinder balance test is NORMALLY performed by operating the engine 14._____

    A. with the spark plugs shorted, one at a time, at idle speed
    B. with the spark plugs firing, one at a time, at 1500 rpm
    C. at idle speed, shorting all plugs but two, with those firing at equal intervals (but not simultaneously)
    D. at 1500 rpm, shorting all plugs but two, with those firing at equal intervals (but not simultaneously)

15. In order to properly adjust a recirculating ball worm and nut steering gear, it is necessary to 15._____

    A. make the pitman shaft gear over-center adjustment prior to making the worm bearing preload adjustment
    B. have the gear in the center position when making the worm bearing preload adjustment
    C. have the gear in the center position when making the pitman shaft gear over-center adjustment
    D. eliminate all play between the sector and ball nut teeth in the extreme right and left positions

16. In a typical steering mechanism linkage, the idler arm is NORMALLY attached to the 16._____

    A. tie rod B. spindle C. center link D. pitman arm

17. The no-flow discharge pressure of an automotive diaphragm type fuel pump is controlled by the _____ spring. 17._____

    A. rocker arm   B. diaphragm
    C. outlet valve   D. inlet valve

18. In air brake systems, a push-pull control valve with automatic pressure release is USUALLY used in conjunction with the 18._____

    A. tractor protection valve   B. limiting quick release valve
    C. compressor unloader   D. brake relay valve

19. A vapor discharge valve would MOST likely be found on a 19._____

    A. fuel pump   B. gas tank
    C. carburetor   D. vacuum booster unit

20. In automatic transmissions, a servo is USUALLY used to 20._____

    A. control the output from the variable volume vane pump
    B. apply the clutches
    C. apply the bands
    D. operate the shifter valve

21. In connection with the control of pollution from automotive engines, an air pump is NORMALLY an important component in the _____ system. 21._____

    A. ECS   B. Thermactor   C. TCS   D. CCS

22. The one of the following statements about primary brake shoes in single anchor duo-servo systems which is CORRECT is that they

    A. face front on the right side brakes and face the rear on the left side brakes
    B. face front on all brakes
    C. face the rear on all brakes
    D. are identical to the secondary shoes

23. The statement pertaining to the use of proportioning and metering valves in hydraulic brake systems that is CORRECT is that a

    A. proportioning valve is installed in the line to the front brakes of a 4-drum brake system to balance the pressures on the front and rear brake shoes
    B. metering valve is installed directly after the master cylinder to prevent brake lock-up during panic stops
    C. proportioning valve is placed in the line to the rear drum brakes when disk brakes are used in the front
    D. metering valve is placed in the line to the rear drum brakes when disk brakes are used in the front

24. When the brake pedal operating an hydraulic brake system is released quickly, the initial make-up fluid is supplied to the pressure chamber of the master cylinder through the

    A. compensating port
    B. check valve
    C. breather port
    D. bleeder holes in the piston

25. In order to check ball joint wear on a vehicle that has the coil spring between the body and the lower suspension arm, it is USUALLY necessary to

    A. place a support wedge between the upper arm and the frame and jack up the lower arm
    B. place a support wedge between the upper arm and the frame and jack up the frame
    C. jack up the lower suspension arm
    D. jack up the frame

26. When adjusting the alignment on the left front wheel of a vehicle in which the upper suspension arm is attached to the vehicle by means of an arm inner shaft and two bolts, a mechanic adjusts the shims to move only the front of the inner shaft closer to the centerline of the vehicle.
    This adjustment would move the caster in the _____ direction and the camber in the _____ direction.

    A. negative; negative
    B. negative; positive
    C. positive; negative
    D. positive; positive

27. In a three-speed standard transmission, synchronized in all forward speeds and with two shifting yokes, the synchronizer closest to the input shaft must be engaged when the transmission is in _____ gears.

    A. second and high
    B. first and reverse
    C. first and high
    D. second and reverse

28. The gears on a certain car, equipped with a standard transmission, clash when the clutch pedal is depressed and the transmission is shifted into reverse.
The LEAST likely cause of this difficulty would be

   A. excessive free travel of the clutch pedal
   B. broken springs in the clutch hub
   C. a high spot on the clutch facing
   D. a sticking release bearing sleeve

29. A feathered edge on a tire thread is USUALLY an indication of improper

   A. camber
   B. caster
   C. toe-in or toe-out
   D. inflation

30. It is necessary to torque a nut to 120 foot pounds. If the wrench handle is 18 inches long, the tangential force that would have to be applied to the end of the wrench handle would be MOST NEARLY _____ pounds.

   A. 180   B. 120   C. 80   D. 40

31. In connection with measurements made on worm crankshaft journals, it is MOST NEARLY CORRECT to state that

   A. the up-and-down diameter is usually greater than the sideways diameter
   B. grinding is not indicated unless the journal is out of round by more than .008"
   C. bearings must be ordered for the smallest diameter of the journal
   D. measurements taken sideways on the journal usually determine the true wear

32. A semi-floating piston pin is secured in position by

   A. tightening a set screw in the piston
   B. fixing snap rings at each end of the piston
   C. being press fitted in the piston
   D. being clamped to the connecting rod

33. A heat-sink support is USUALLY used in connection with the repair of

   A. alternators
   B. automatic chokes
   C. cooling systems
   D. automatic transmissions

34. The manufacturer's specifications for a particular engine indicate a bore of 4.00" and a stroke of 3.50" for a four-stroke cycle 8-cylinder engine with a 10.0 compression ratio and an output of 325 hp at 5600 rpm.
The piston displacement of this engine, in cubic inches, is MOST NEARLY

   A. 225   B. 325   C. 350   D. 400

35. Two properly mating spur gears have the following specifications: One has 22 teeth with a pitch diameter of 5.50" and an outside diameter of 6"; the other gear has 43 teeth with a pitch diameter of 10.75" and an outside diameter of 11.25". Each gear has an addendum of .250".
The distance from the outside tooth tip of the smaller gear to the outside tooth tip of the larger gear, measured along the sides of the two gears and through their centers, is _____ inches.

   A. 16.0   B. 16.25   C. 16.5   D. 16.75

36. In a four-stroke cycle gasoline engine, the distributor rotor rotates at   36._____

    A. the same speed as the crankshaft
    B. the same speed as the camshaft
    C. twice the speed of the camshaft
    D. half the speed of the camshaft

37. Of the following conditions, the one that could cause an engine to overheat in service is that the   37._____

    A. fan belt is too tight
    B. thermostat is stuck open
    C. ignition timing is late
    D. engine oil level is too high

38. A certain engine fires with the ignition key in the start position but stops when returned to the on position.   38._____
    The MOST likely cause for the engine stopping is a(n)

    A. defective safety switch
    B. open resistor
    C. shorted condenser
    D. shorted secondary winding in the coil

39. The one of the following problems which is NOT caused by improper caster angles is   39._____

    A. hard steering   B. pulling to one side
    C. high speed instability D. rapid tire wear

40. In an automotive air conditioning system, the conditioned air is cooled as it passes through the   40._____

    A. evaporator   B. condenser   C. receiver   D. compressor

---

KEY (CORRECT ANSWERS)

1. D	11. C	21. B	31. D
2. A	12. B	22. B	32. D
3. D	13. B	23. C	33. A
4. A	14. D	24. D	34. C
5. B	15. C	25. C	35. D
6. A	16. C	26. A	36. B
7. A	17. B	27. A	37. C
8. C	18. A	28. D	38. B
9. B	19. A	29. C	39. D
10. B	20. C	30. C	40. A

EXAMINATION SECTION
TEST 1

DIRECTIONS: Each question or incomplete statement is followed by several suggested answers or completions. Select the one that BEST answers the question or completes the statement. *PRINT THE LETTER OF THE CORRECT ANSWER IN THE SPACE AT THE RIGHT.*

1. If a carburetor drips continually, the MOST likely cause is a 1.____
   A. loose Venturi tube
   B. needle valve not seating
   C. loose idle set screw
   D. float set too low

2. The part used to control the ratio of air and gasoline in a truck engine is the 2.____
   A. bogie   B. filter   C. carburetor   D. pump

3. During cranking, all electrical energy is supplied by the 3.____
   A. alternator   B. battery   C. generator   D. engine

4. A device for storing electric charges is known as a(n) 4.____
   A. commutator   B. condenser   C. capacitance   D. exciter

5. Hydraulic brake fluid is a mixture of _____ and _____. 5.____
   A. kerosene; engine oil
   B. mineral oil; denatured alcohol
   C. castor oil; denatured alcohol
   D. ethelene glycol; mineral oil

6. When you are servicing the air brake chambers located at each wheel, the bolts and nuts holding the diaphragm plates should be tightened 6.____
   A. more tightly on the pressure plate than on the non-pressure plate
   B. more tightly on the non-pressure plate than on the pressure plate
   C. with only sufficient pressure to insure an air-tight seal
   D. with as much pressure as possible

7. The temperature gauge indicates the temperature of the 7.____
   A. air surrounding the engine
   B. water surrounding the cylinders
   C. oil in the crankcase
   D. pistons

8. Air drawn into the cooling system through the pump or hoses causes 8.____
   A. better cooling of the water
   B. the water to stop circulating
   C. a boost in the circulation
   D. rusting of the cylinder block

9. Diesel fuel filter elements on an International Harvester or Allis-Chalmers tractor are USUALLY serviced when too dirt for continued use by 9.____
   A. washing in kerosene
   B. steam cleaning
   C. washing in carbon tetrachloride
   D. oiling

10. To find out if a cylinder of a diesel engine is firing, it is necessary to
    A. remove the fuel pump
    B. disconnect the vent valve
    C. remove the vent valve
    D. prime the injection pump

11. In diesel engines, piston rings are held against the side of the cylinder PRIMARILY by
    A. gas pressure behind the ring
    B. thermal expansion of the ring
    C. an oil wedge behind the ring
    D. spring forces within the ring itself

12. In addition to lighter weight, the PRINCIPAL advantage of aluminum alloy pistons in diesel engines is that
    A. piston rings have less tendency to collect sludge and stick
    B. they have a much higher heat transfer rate than cast iron pistons
    C. they expand less under heat and thus reduce liner wear
    D. area for area, they are stronger than cast iron

13. All the refrigerant now used for automotive air conditioners is R
    A. 10   B. 12   C. 18   D. 22

14. When the right front wheel is turned 20° to the left, the left front wheel should turn APPROXIMATELY _____ degrees.
    A. 16   B. 18   C. 20   D. 24

15. In placing a new tire and a well-worn tire on dual wheels, it is BEST to place
    A. the new tire on the inside
    B. the worn tire on the inside
    C. either tire on the inside; it makes no difference
    D. the tires separately

16. The color of iron at welding heat is USUALLY a
    A. creamy white   B. dull yellow   C. light yellow   D. light red

17. The _____ raring method measures the amount of current a battery can supply steadily for 20 hours, with no cell falling below 1.75 volts.
    A. cold-cranking
    B. reserve-capacity
    C. watts
    D. ampere-hour

18. In an automotive gasoline engine, the camshaft is used PRIMARILY to
    A. drive the transmission
    B. operate the valve lifters
    C. change the reciprocating motion of the pistons to rotary motion
    D. operate the choke mechanism

19. The PRIMARY function of the thermostat in the cooling system of an automobile engine is to
    A. control the operating temperature of the engine
    B. keep the operating temperature of the engine as low as possible
    C. provide the proper amount of heat for the heater
    D. retain engine heat when the engine gets hot

3 (#1)

20. The PRIMARY purpose of the condenser in the ignition circuit of a gasoline engine is to
    A. boost the ignition voltage
    B. rectify the ignition voltage
    C. adjust the coil voltage
    D reducing arcing of the distributor breaker points

    20.____

21. The PRIMARY purpose of the differential in the rear drive train of an automotive vehicle is to allow each of the rear wheels to
    A. rotate at different speeds
    B. go in reverse
    C. rotate with maximum torque
    D. absorb road shocks

    21.____

22. Of the following, the BEST tool to use for securely tightening a one-inch standard hexagonal nut is a(n)
    A. monkey wrench
    B. open-end wrench
    C. Stillson wrench
    D. pair of heavy duty pliers

    22.____

23. The purpose of the ignition coil in a gasoline engine is PRIMARILY to
    A. smooth the voltage
    B. raise the voltage
    C. raise the current
    D. smooth the current

    23.____

24. Vapor lock in a vehicle with a gasoline engine is caused by excessive heat. To prevent vapor lock, it may be necessary to relocate
    A. the ignition system
    B. the cooling system
    C. the starter motor
    D. a part of the fuel line

    24.____

25. It is important to use safety shoes PRIMARILY to guard the feet against
    A. tripping hazards
    B. heavy falling objects
    C. shock hazards
    D. mud and dirt

    25.____

KEY (CORRECT ANSWERS)

1.	B		11.	D
2.	C		12.	C
3.	B		13.	B
4.	B		14.	D
5.	C		15.	D
6.	C		16.	A
7.	B		17.	B
8.	D		18.	B
9.	A		19.	A
10.	B		20.	D

21.	A
22.	B
23.	B
24.	D
25.	B

TEST 2

DIRECTIONS: Each question or incomplete statement is followed by several suggested answers or completions. Select the one that BEST answers the question or completes the statement. *PRINT THE LETTER OF THE CORRECT ANSWER IN THE SPACE AT THE RIGHT.*

1. Which of the following is a PROBABLE result of a malfunctioning PCV valve? 1.____
   A. High fuel tank pressure
   B. Improper idling
   C. Noisy engine valves
   D. High fuel consumption

2. When a car goes into overdrive, the _____ gear is held stationary. 2.____
   A. pinion   B. ring   C. sun   D. planetary

3. A puller is NOT commonly used to remove or install 3.____
   A. valves   B. gears   C. pulleys   D. bearings

4. An engine turbocharger draws its energy from 4.____
   A. ignition spark
   B. engine fan airflow
   C. cylinder combustion
   D. hot exhaust gases

5. A four-gas automotive emissions analyzer will NOT measure the presence of 5.____
   A. HC   B. CO   C. CO_2 D. NO

6. An automotive cylinder head is attached to the 6.____
   A. bearing saddle
   B. pan rail
   C. boss
   D. block deck

7. Which of the following is a DISADVANTAGE associated with a magnetic reluctance crankshaft position sensor that is used in a microprocessor-based control/diagnostic system? 7.____
   A. Inability to directly measure crankshaft position
   B. Inability to exploit flywheel rotation
   C. Requires additional installation of a harmonic damper
   D. Inability to set engine timing statically

8. Which valve train component CANNOT be used on overhead cam engines? 8.____
   A. Finger follower
   B. Bucket follower
   C. Tappet
   D. Rocker arm

9. Which of the following would likely be indicated by uneven firing voltages that are displayed on an oscilloscope? 9.____
   A. Worn plug electrodes
   B. Condenser failure
   C. Arcing contact points
   D. Point contact failure

10. Power steering systems typically use each of the following types of pumps EXCEPT 10.____
    A. vane   B. diaphragm   C. roller   D. slipper

11. Most exhaust gas analyzers used in emission control maintenance indicate the percentage of _____ in the exhaust.
    A. HC   B. CO   C. NO   D. CO_2

12. What is the term for the portion of a cam that has a constant diameter, and does not produce lift as it rotates?
    A. Offset   B. Nose circle   C. Flank circle   D. Radial circle

13. In a microprocessor-based control/diagnostic system, which type of sensor uses the compound zirconia oxide?
    A. MAP
    B. Throttle angle
    C. EGO
    D. Knock

14. Which measuring device is MAINLY used to find open circuits and excessive resistance by imposing a bypass on a portion of the existing circuit?
    A. Digital multimeter
    B. Jumper wires
    C. Test light
    D. Continuity tester

15. If a car engine is operating at 1500 rpm, at what speed (rpm) is the distributor running?
    A. 750   B. 1500   C. 3000   D. 4500

16. Throttle body fuel injection refers to
    A. the insertion of fuel below the throttle plate
    B. unregulated fuel flow
    C. a continuous flow fuel injection
    D. a form of fuel metering actuator used in microprocessor-based control/diagnostic systems

17. Which of the following conditions in the valve train is NOT consistent with the *open valve* position in engine operation?
    A. Upward oil flow
    B. Plunger extended
    C. Slight leakage between plunger and body
    D. Ball check valve closed

18. What is the term for projections on a plate or disc that interlock in hub or drum slots?
    A. Drive lugs
    B. Toe cams
    C. Axial teeth
    D. Plate threads

19. Which of the following conditions is a POSSIBLE result of evaporation control system failure?
    A. Collapsed fuel tank
    B. High fuel tank pressure
    C. Improper idle
    D. Vapor low from air cleaner

20. Each of the following is a problem commonly associated with improper casting angles EXCEPT
    A. pulling to one side
    B. hard steering
    C. high speed instability
    D. rapid tire wear

21. In a microprocessor-based control/diagnostic system, which type of crankshaft position sensor is located in the distributor?
    A. Optical
    B. Ignition timing
    C. Hall-effect
    D. Magnetic reluctance

22. When using a short finder to trace a short circuit, which of the following steps should be performed FIRST?
    A. Turn on all switches in a series with the circuit being tested
    B. Move the short finder meter along circuit wiring
    C. Remove the blown fuse while leaving the battery connected
    D. Connect the pulse unit of short finder across the fuse terminals

23. In a fuel injection system, which type of pump is used PRIMARILY as a transfer pump?
    A. Rotary
    B. Diaphragm
    C. Turbine
    D. Roller

24. What type of electrical connectors are used to permanently join two stripped wire ends?
    A. Crimp
    B. Flat blade
    C. Butt
    D. Snap-splice

25. Discharges from the _____ appear as high voltage surges on an oscilloscope tester.
    A. distributor
    B. contact points
    C. coil high-tension terminal
    D. battery

KEY (CORRECT ANSWERS)

1.	B	11.	B
2.	C	12.	C
3.	A	13.	C
4.	D	14.	B
5.	D	15.	A
6.	D	16.	D
7.	D	17.	B
8.	C	18.	A
9.	A	19.	D
10.	B	20.	D

21.	C
22.	C
23.	B
24.	C
25.	C

EXAMINATION SECTION
TEST 1

DIRECTIONS: Each question or incomplete statement is followed by several suggested answers or completions. Select the one that BEST answers the question or completes the statement. *PRINT THE LETTER OF THE CORRECT ANSWER IN THE SPACE AT THE RIGHT.*

1. The gage that is generally used in the United States for sizing non-ferrous wires and non-ferrous sheets is the   1.____

   A. Birmingham Wire Gage
   B. Brown & Sharpe Wire Gage
   C. United States Standard (Revised)
   D. Stubs Wire Gage

2. The number of threads per inch for a screw with a pitch of .3125" is MOST NEARLY   2.____

   A. 3 1/4   B. 4 1/4   C. 2 1/4   D. 5 1/4

3. A center gage is used to check   3.____

   A. cylinder bore diameters
   B. tapers
   C. 60° threading tools
   D. lines on rough work

4. The portion of a gear tooth between the pitch circle and the root circle is called the   4.____

   A. clearance
   B. dedendum
   C. addendum
   D. pressure angle

5. Which one of the following is NOT used as an abrasive for lapping?   5.____

   A. Emery
   B. Alundum
   C. Diamond dust
   D. Quartz

6. If the air gap between the pole pieces and armature of a generator increases due to worn bearings, the result would be   6.____

   A. a decrease in generator output
   B. an increase in magnetic lines of force
   C. an increase in generator output
   D. no change in the number of magnetic lines of force

7. When the generator is not operating on a passenger car, the cutout relay USUALLY   7.____

   A. closes the circuit between the generator and battery
   B. sends residual current through the circuit to supply the electrical equipment
   C. prevents any damaging current to flow from the battery to the electrical devices
   D. prevents the battery from discharging back through the generator

8. In looking over an alteration job on car bodies, you find that 96 pieces of 1" x 1" x 1'6" long square steel stock are needed to do this job. Steel weighs 480 lbs. per cu.ft. and costs $0.12 per lb.
   The total cost of this material is MOST NEARLY   8.____

   A. $40.00   B. $60.00   C. $80.00   D. $100.00

57

9. The Shore's Scleroscope is an instrument which measures the hardness of materials by means of a

   A. steel ball
   B. diamond penetrator
   C. diamond-tipped hammer
   D. square-based diamond pyramid

10. A process of annealing white cast iron in which the carbon is wholly or in part transformed to graphitic or free carbon, and, in some cases, part of the carbon is removed completely, is called

   A. spheroidizing B. carburizing
   C. malleablizing D. nitriding

11. Relative to driving axles, which one of the following statements is MOST NEARLY correct?

   A. The types of live axles are distinguished by the way in which the axle shafts are connected and the stresses they must carry.
   B. For plain live axles, all stresses caused by turning corners, skidding, or wobbling wheels are not taken by the axle shafts.
   C. In the semifloating axle, the differential case is carried on the inner ends of the axle shafts.
   D. In a fullfloating rear axle, the axle shafts are rigidly connected to the wheels.

12. A passenger car is equipped with a fluid coupling and an automatic transmission. When the engine is idling and the vehicle is stationary, the percentage *slip* is MOST NEARLY

   A. 100   B. 80   C. 10   D. 2

13. In front wheel alignment work, the term *axle caster* is defined as the

   A. amount the wheels incline at the top from a vertical position
   B. outward inclination of wheels at top
   C. backward inclination between the steering knuckle kingpin and the vertical plane
   D. run out of the front wheels with respect to the steering knuckle kingpin

14. Which one of the following statements concerning milling machine operations is MOST NEARLY true?

   A. Climb-milling means that the feeding movement of the work and the cutting movement are in opposite directions.
   B. Conventional-milling means that the feeding movement of the work and the cutting movement are in the same direction.
   C. Cutters used in the conventional-milling manner tend to seat the work firmly in the holding device.
   D. The cutters used in climb-milling tend to seat the work firmly in the holding devices.

15. Crankshafts are USUALLY manufactured of

   A. steel and nickel   B. iron and vanadium
   C. steel and cobalt   D. steel and tungsten

16. In brazing, the filler metal GENERALLY

    A. is a ferrous metal or alloy
    B. is heated only to a red heat
    C. has a melting point lower than 1000° F
    D. has a melting point lower than that of the base metals to be joined

17. In welding certain alloy steels with electric arc welding, the effect of a coating on the electrode is to

    A. reduce arc stability
    B. increase attractive force between molten metal and the end of the electrode
    C. protect the molten weld metal from the ambient atmosphere while cooling
    D. provide ingredients which, when melted, prevent formation of slag over molten metal

18. In the operation of a 6-cylinder, 4-cycle diesel engine, you observe that the engine is missing erratically or intermittently on all cylinders.
    The trouble in this case is MOST likely NOT due to

    A. sticking nozzle valve
    B. plugged air cleaner
    C. improper fuel
    D. badly worn piston pins or bushings

19. In a *common rail* system of fuel injection as used in many high-speed diesel engines, the pressure, in lbs. per sq. in., maintained by the master pump is MOST NEARLY

    A. 6,000   B. 15,000   C. 500   D. 150

20. The SMALLEST diameter of a circular steel plate from which a 7/8" square can be cut is MOST NEARLY

    A. 0.951"   B. 1.279"   C. 1.217"   D. 1.237"

21. A large majority of industrial applications require that motor speeds remain approximately constant under all conditions of loading. Lathes and milling machines are examples.
    The D.C. motor which meets the above conditions is MOST NEARLY a _____ motor.

    A. series   B. shunt
    C. induction   D. wound-rotor

22. In timing the fuel injection of a 4-cycle diesel engine, when the end of compression is reached,

    A. both intake and exhaust valves are open
    B. the intake valve only is closed
    C. the exhaust valve only is closed
    D. both intake and exhaust valves are closed

23. The ease with which gasoline and other liquids vaporize or pass from the liquid to a vapor state is known as its

    A. kinematic viscosity   B. viscous friction
    C. volatility   D. surface viscosity

24. Suppose a piece of work on a milling machine requires 69 divisions, and this is to be done by means of compound indexing.
Which one of the following indexing movements would you suggest your machinist to use to do this job?

   A. 9/21 + 3/33
   B. 21/23 - 11/33
   C. 23/29 - 11/33
   D. 3/31 + 11/33

25. A gear with 80 teeth is driven by a pinion having 30 teeth.
If the pinion gear revolves at 600 RPM, the speed of the gear, in revolutions per minute, is MOST NEARLY

   A. 225
   B. 1600
   C. 200
   D. 1500

26. In cam grinding pistons, you observe that the grinding wheel becomes glazed frequently. In order to remedy this condition, you should substitute another wheel which has a

   A. harder bond
   B. softer bond
   C. larger diameter
   D. smaller diameter

27. A replacement part for a truck engine is to be made from S.A.E. 4140 steel. This type of steel is MOST likely a _____ steel.

   A. molybdenum
   B. nickel
   C. chrome-nickel
   D. chrome vanadium

28. The mechanical efficiency of a gasoline engine is obtained by dividing the brake horsepower by the

   A. S.A.E. horsepower
   B. indicated horsepower
   C. volumetric horsepower
   D. thermal efficiency

29. An empty truck weighs 4,000 lbs., and its center of gravity is 100 inches in front of the rear axle. The truck carries a load of 3,000 lbs., and the center of gravity of this load is 50 inches in front of the rear axle.
If the wheel base is 150 inches, then the total weight on the rear wheels is MOST NEARLY _____ lbs.

   A. 3525
   B. 3625
   C. 3425
   D. 3325

30. A hydraulic hoisting cylinder on a truck operates with a pressure of 800 lbs. per sq.in. The piston has a diameter of 3.25 inches.
The maximum load, in tons, that can be raised is MOST NEARLY

   A. 5
   B. 4
   C. 3
   D. 6

31. Relative to an Auto-Lite vacuum advance mechanism of the type which is mounted on the side of the distributor, the basic principle of operation is that the

   A. spring retards the spark and the vacuum advances it
   B. spring retards and advances the spark
   C. vacuum retards the spark and the spring advances it
   D. vacuum retards and advances the spark

32. The condenser that is used in the distributor circuit of an auto ignition system is

    A. usually an electrolytic type condenser
    B. below the required capacity if the breaker lever contact develops a pitted cavity
    C. under normal operating conditions, usually about .250 microfarads
    D. usually about 0.5 microfarad

33. During discharge, the internal resistance of a storage battery

    A. decreases
    B. remains the same
    C. is negative
    D. increases

34. In low speed, a passenger car has a 2.39 to 1 transmission ratio.
    If, at the rear, the drive pinion has 10 teeth and the bevel gear has 39 teeth, then the total reduction ratio (engine shaft to rear wheels) for this low speed is MOST NEARLY

    A. 3.39   B. 3.90   C. 6.39   D. 9.32

35. In an air brake system, the relay valve is USUALLY installed between the

    A. brake chambers and the compressor
    B. compressor and the reservoir
    C. brake valve and the quick release valve
    D. reservoir and the brake chambers

36. With reference to a vibrating relay voltage regulator, which one of the following statements is TRUE?

    A. With this regulator, the voltage output of the generator is not used for automatic regulation.
    B. The voltage coil is connected across the generator brushes and is wound with heavy wire.
    C. The voltage coil is usually connected in series with the storage battery.
    D. If a break occurs in the voltage regulator circuit at high speeds, an excessive charging rate will result.

37. The object of a vibration damper on the crankshaft of multi-cylinder engines is to

    A. act as a counterweight for the flywheel and absorb the end thrust
    B. maintain the leverage of the crankshaft with respect to the flywheel
    C. resist the sudden movements of the cranks due to torsional twisting of the crankshaft
    D. offset the centrifugal force developed by the rotating crankpins and connecting rods

38. Which one of the following statements concerning hydramatic transmissions is MOST NEARLY CORRECT?

    A. When the clutch is released and the band applied on the front planetary unit, the unit is in reduction.
    B. When the band is released and the clutch applied on the front planetary, the unit is in reduction.
    C. The front planetary unit is for direct drive and the rear planetary unit is for reduction.
    D. The front servo is applied by spring pressure and released by oil pressure.

39. The primary circuit of a typical electric ignition system consists basically of 39.____

    A. condenser, primary element of the distributor, primary winding of the coil, and low voltage current source
    B. low voltage current source, secondary winding of the coil, condenser, and primary element of the distributor
    C. primary element of the distributor, condenser, spark plug, and low voltage current source
    D. low voltage current source, primary winding of the coil, secondary winding of the coil, and condenser

40. Which one of the following statements is MOST NEARLY CORRECT? 40.____

    A. A jack may be used for a load in excess of its rated capacity.
    B. When preparing electrolyte, the water should be poured into the acid.
    C. Gasoline containing tetraethyl lead may be used to clean automobile parts.
    D. For combating electrical fires, CO_2 type extinguishers should be used.

KEY (CORRECT ANSWERS)

1. B	11. A	21. B	31. A
2. A	12. A	22. D	32. C
3. C	13. C	23. C	33. D
4. B	14. D	24. B	34. D
5. D	15. A	25. A	35. D
6. A	16. D	26. B	36. D
7. D	17. C	27. A	37. C
8. B	18. D	28. B	38. A
9. C	19. A	29. D	39. A
10. C	20. D	30. C	40. D

EXAMINATION SECTION
TEST 1

DIRECTIONS: Each question or incomplete statement is followed by several suggested answers or completions. Select the one that BEST answers the question or completes the statement. *PRINT THE LETTER OF THE CORRECT ANSWER IN THE SPACE AT THE RIGHT.*

1. Valve timing in a gasoline engine is the PROPER setting of valve opening and closing with respect to

    A. piston position
    B. distributor position
    C. carburetor mixture setting
    D. connecting rod angularity

    1.____

2. When adjusting the carburetor mixture in order to obtain smooth idling of a gasoline engine, it is BEST to

    A. leave the carburetor air cleaner off while making the adjustment
    B. prime the carburetor before adjusting it
    C. first disconnect the accelerating pump
    D. service the air cleaner and put it in place before making the adjustment

    2.____

3. Combustion leakage into the cooling system of a gasoline engine could be caused by

    A. leakage in the water pump
    B. a defective cylinder head gasket
    C. a leak in the cooling system suction hose
    D. low radiator water level

    3.____

4. In making a vacuum gauge test on a gasoline engine, the gauge is NORMALLY connected to measure _____ pressure.

    A. fuel pump
    B. intake manifold
    C. cylinder compression
    D. oil pump

    4.____

5. On a gasoline vehicle, a dwell angle meter would be USEFUL for adjusting the

    A. carburetor
    B. distributor
    C. fuel pump
    D. automatic transmission

    5.____

6. The MAIN advantage of using an antifreeze such as Prestone instead of alcohol is that the Prestone

    A. has a higher boiling point than the alcohol
    B. seals leaks in the cooling system
    C. mixes better with the water
    D. has a lower boiling point than alcohol

    6.____

7. The fuel tank of an automobile is vented in order to

    A. release fuel fumes
    B. reduce the temperature of the fuel
    C. prevent fuel leaks
    D. prevent a vacuum from forming in the tank

    7.____

8. The number of cells in a 12-volt automobile lead storage battery is   8._____

   A. 3   B. 4   C. 5   D. 6

9. The ignition condenser on a gasoline engine distributor is MAINLY for the purpose of   9._____

   A. decreasing the load on the battery
   B. decreasing interference with radio reception
   C. increasing the spark intensity at the plugs
   D. protecting the ignition coil

10. A trouble which is LIKELY to cause flooding of a gasoline engine carburetor is   10._____

    A. low fuel pump pressure
    B. low cylinder intake suction
    C. dirt in the carburetor
    D. incorrect idle setting

11. The purpose of the dual hydraulic master cylinder which is being used in some new car braking systems is to   11._____

    A. reduce braking wear
    B. reduce evaporation of the braking fluid
    C. provide greater safety
    D. provide for automatic adjustment of the brakes

12. A hydrometer has a scale calibrated to read battery   12._____

    A. power   B. current
    C. voltage   D. specific gravity

13. A LIKELY cause for overheating in a gasoline engine could be   13._____

    A. a leaky exhaust muffler
    B. improper timing
    C. that the cooling system has no thermostat
    D. the use of a high boiling point antifreeze

14. Before adjusting the front wheel bearings of an automobile, it is NECESSARY to   14._____

    A. remove the brake drums
    B. have equal pressure in the tires
    C. make sure the brakes are fully released
    D. loosen the tie rod and drag link ends

15. Leaded gasoline is not recommended for cleaning automobile parts. The MOST important reason for this is that it   15._____

    A. may cause personal illness
    B. leaves a white residue on the parts
    C. does not clean as quickly as non-leaded gasoline
    D. evaporates too quickly

16. The unit designed to store up the energy produced during the power stroke of the gasoline engine is the

    A. flywheel
    B. clutch
    C. automatic transmission
    D. differential

17. Excessive tightening of spark plugs on installation is MOST likely to cause

    A. too hot a spark
    B. a change in the electrode gap
    C. a short-circuit in the ignition coil primary
    D. burnout of the distributor condenser

18. A LIKELY cause for a low battery charging rate would be a(n)

    A. undercut generator commutator
    B. open-circuited generator ground connection
    C. high level of electrolyte in the battery
    D. defective voltage regulator

19. The LOWER the S.A.E. viscosity rating of an engine lubricating oil, the

    A. heavier it is
    B. easier it will flow at low temperatures
    C. fewer the impurities present
    D. harder it will be to start a gas engine

20. A gasoline engine compression test is GENERALLY used to determine

    A. the top speed of the engine
    B. valve and piston ring conditions
    C. if the carburetor is providing the proper fuel mixture
    D. the compression ratio of the engine

21. Piston slap in a gasoline engine is MOST noticeable when

    A. new rings have been installed
    B. the oil has been changed
    C. the engine is cold
    D. the fuel has a low octane rating

22. To check variation in engine cylinder bore, the PROPER instrument to use is a(n)

    A. outside caliper
    B. NO-GO gauge
    C. standard micrometer
    D. dial indicator gauge

23. Engine combustion knock or pinging in a gasoline engine is GENERALLY corrected by

    A. retarding the spark timing
    B. advancing the spark timing
    C. increasing the gap of the distributor points
    D. installing a larger distributor condenser

24. A worn crank pin measures two-thousandths under standard size on its diameter. In this case, the thickness of each replacement bearing shell should exceed the standard size by _____ thousandths.

    A. one B. two C. three D. four

25. Valve tappet clearance is BEST checked by means of a(n)

    A. inside caliper
    B. micrometer
    C. feeler gauge
    D. machinist's scale

26. Reverse flow flushing is a process which is used to clean out a(n)

    A. rear end housing
    B. transmission housing
    C. engine cooling system
    D. engine crankcase

27. Engine cylinder head stud nuts should be tightened

    A. enough to expose a minimum of four threads on each stud
    B. in a definite sequence with a torque wrench
    C. as much as possible
    D. as much as possible and then backed off one turn

28. In making a vacuum gauge test on a gasoline engine, a normal vacuum reading is obtained when the engine is started, but the reading quickly drops to zero. The MOST likely trouble in this case is a

    A. clogged exhaust system
    B. rich carburetor mixture
    C. weak spark
    D. hot spark

29. If the diameter of a shaft is required to be .400 inches plus or minus .003 inches, then a shaft will be satisfactory if it has a diameter of _____ inches.

    A. .370 B. .397 C. .404 D. .430

30. The MAIN reason for not making an engine fan belt too tight is to prevent

    A. excessive pulley wear
    B. hard starting
    C. burning of the belt
    D. premature failure of the fan and generator bearings

31. If the intake screen on the lubricating oil pump on a gasoline engine is clogged, the result is MOST likely to be

    A. high lubricating oil pressure
    B. high lubricating oil consumption
    C. low lubricating oil pressure
    D. excessive crankcase pressure

32. Grease on a brake lining would PROBABLY result in

    A. smooth even braking
    B. reducing brake lining failure
    C. erratic braking
    D. wheel bearing failure

33. If a fellow worker is on fire, he may be BEST helped by 33.____

    A. attempting to beat out the flames with your hands
    B. rolling him on the ground to smother the flames
    C. telling him to pull his clothes off
    D. using an air hose to smother the flames

34. A current of over a hundred amperes is drawn from an automobile storage battery by the 34.____

    A. starting motor   B. ignition system
    C. lights   D. heater system

35. If a starter motor barely turns a gasoline engine over, the cause MAY be that 35.____

    A. winter grade oil is still in the crankcase
    B. the specific gravity of the battery is high
    C. the starter relay has a burned out coil
    D. the battery connections are loose

36. With a standard measuring micrometer, starting with a zero reading, two complete revolutions of the sleeve will give a reading of 36.____

    A. .250"   B. .100"   C. .050"   D. .025"

37. In order to change front wheel toe-in, the adjustment is made on the 37.____

    A. tie rod   B. steering knuckles
    C. king pins   D. stop screws

38. It is generally recommended that the electrical starter motor for a gasoline engine not be operated for more than 30 seconds at a time. 38.____
One reason for this is to prevent

    A. engine flooding
    B. damage to the starter relay
    C. overheating of the starter motor
    D. excessive wear of the starter pinion gear

39. It is NECESSARY to bleed an automobile hydraulic brake system when 39.____

    A. the brakes are adjusted
    B. the master cylinder is replaced
    C. water gets into the brake drums
    D. the brake pedal adjustment is changed

40. Rubber parts of a hydraulic brake system should be cleaned with 40.____

    A. alcohol   B. kerosene
    C. naphtha   D. engine oil

KEY (CORRECT ANSWERS)

1.	A	11.	C	21.	C	31.	C
2.	D	12.	D	22.	D	32.	C
3.	B	13.	B	23.	A	33.	B
4.	B	14.	C	24.	A	34.	A
5.	B	15.	A	25.	C	35.	D
6.	A	16.	A	26.	C	36.	C
7.	D	17.	B	27.	B	37.	A
8.	D	18.	D	28.	A	38.	C
9.	C	19.	B	29.	B	39.	B
10.	C	20.	B	30.	D	40.	A

TEST 2

DIRECTIONS: Each question or incomplete statement is followed by several suggested answers or completions. Select the one that BEST answers the question or completes the statement. *PRINT THE LETTER OF THE CORRECT ANSWER IN THE SPACE AT THE RIGHT.*

1. The voltage drop between the ungrounded battery terminal and the starting motor terminal or stud is checked with the starter motor running in order to determine whether 1.____

    A. the starter drive mechanisms are electrically O.K.
    B. the ground resistance is too high
    C. there is excessive resistance in this circuit
    D. the battery is discharged

2. Wheel bearings are GENERALLY repacked when 2.____

    A. the steering is aligned
    B. lubrication is added to the differential
    C. the brakes are relined
    D. new tires are installed on the wheels

3. If steel particles fall into a mechanic's eye while working under a car and flushing with water does not remove the foreign matter, then the BEST procedure would be to 3.____

    A. rub the eye several times to loosen the particles
    B. use an eye swab to clean the eye
    C. have the eye treated by a doctor
    D. bandage the eye tightly to prevent infection

4. On a hydraulic brake system, if the brake pedal goes to the floor on applying the brakes, then a LIKELY trouble would be 4.____

    A. a sticking wheel brake cylinder
    B. scored front brake drums
    C. high fluid level in the master cylinder
    D. a leak in the hydraulic system

5. On vehicles equipped with alternators, the AC voltage is changed to DC by the 5.____

    A. rectifier
    B. voltage regulator
    C. battery
    D. circuit breaker

6. An air leak on the fuel line from the fuel pump to the carburetor on a gasoline engine would MOST likely cause 6.____

    A. a rich mixture of gasoline and air
    B. hard starting
    C. loss of compression
    D. mechanical failure of the fuel pump

7. When checking the operation of a gasoline engine lubricating oil pump with an oil pressure gauge, it is BEST to make the check with the engine 7.____

    A. cold
    B. at normal operating temperature
    C. at idling speed
    D. stopped

8. The steering of a vehicle is LEAST likely to be affected by a defective   8._____

   A. braking system   B. front axle
   C. front wheel bearing   D. universal joint

9. On many automobile automatic transmissions, a whine or hum in NEUTRAL indicates   9._____

   A. a defective governor   B. the engine is idling too slowly
   C. normal operation   D. a defective throttle valve

10. If on a gasoline engine the installation of a new spark plug in a misfiring cylinder does not   10._____
    correct the trouble, then it would be BEST to check the _____ pressure.

    A. cylinder compression   B. exhaust
    C. crankcase   D. fuel

11. Powdered graphite is a good   11._____

    A. abrasive   B. adhesive   C. lubricant   D. insulator

12. Transistors are coming into use on automobile   12._____

    A. transmission systems   B. braking systems
    C. signal light circuits   D. ignition circuits

13. A tachometer is an instrument used for checking engine   13._____

    A. pressure   B. speed   C. timing   D. noise

14. A *stall test* is made on an automobile to check the performance of the   14._____

    A. engine and transmission B. braking system
    C. electrical system   D. rear axle

15. The BASIC difference between a gasoline engine and a diesel engine is in the method of   15._____

    A. filtering the fuel   B. lubricating the engine
    C. igniting the fuel   D. cranking the engine

16. An overdrive unit is used to secure   16._____

    A. an increase in brake life   B. an increase in clutch life
    C. improved fuel economy   D. reduction of exhaust fumes

17. On an automobile universal joint, usually an arrow is stamped on the splined joint and   17._____
    lined up with another arrow stamped on the propeller shaft.
    This is to insure that on reassembly CORRECT

    A. balance is maintained   B. rotation is secured
    C. lubrication is secured   D. free-play is maintained

18. The setting of a gasoline engine automatic choke when the engine is not is choke _____ and _____ idle.

    A. closed; fast
    B. closed; slow
    C. open; fast
    D. open; slow

19. Slack adjusters are used on the

    A. carburetor
    B. brakes
    C. engine pistons
    D. distributor

20. The upper end of the connecting rod is pivoted to the piston by means of a

    A. crank pin
    B. cam shaft
    C. wrist pin
    D. retainer pin

21. In a gasoline engine cylinder, the spark occurs

    A. at the end of the exhaust stroke
    B. during the admission stroke
    C. just before the end of the compression stroke
    D. at the end of the power stroke

22. In gasoline engines, a COMMON valve seat angle is

    A. 10°   B. 18°   C. 45°   D. 75°

23. On a gasoline engine, vapor lock is MORE likely to occur

    A. when the engine is cold
    B. if dirt is present in the gas tank
    C. if an excessively hot spark is generated
    D. when the engine is hot

24. On a vehicle having mechanical shift, it is recommended that the clutch pedal be pressed down while starting the engine.
    The MAIN reason for this is to

    A. reduce the load on the battery
    B. prevent jamming of the starter pinion
    C. increase clutch life
    D. reduce transmission wear

25. Using tire inflation pressures below those recommended would MOST likely result in

    A. easier steering
    B. greater tendency to skid on icy roads
    C. lower tire temperature
    D. higher tire temperature

26. Use of a high detergent lubricating oil in a gasoline engine will MOST likely result in

    A. harder starting in cold weather
    B. decreasing engine sludge
    C. increasing oil filter life
    D. increased fuel consumption

27. On an automobile, high melting point grease is used for lubricating the

   A. rear axle
   B. wheel bearings
   C. steering knuckles
   D. generator

28. Cross-firing on a gasoline engine is MOST likely to occur when

   A. a lean gasoline mixture is used
   B. the battery is discharged
   C. the distributor points fail to open
   D. the high tension ignition wires are old

29. If the cooling system of an automotive vehicle is operating properly, then when the engine is at normal temperature, the engine radiator should be

   A. hotter at the bottom than at the top
   B. colder at the bottom than at the top
   C. be at the same temperature, top and bottom
   D. cooler with the engine at slow idle than with the engine at fast idle

30. Black exhaust smoke from a gasoline engine would MOST likely indicate

   A. a lean gasoline mixture
   B. a rich gasoline mixture
   C. low exhaust back pressure
   D. a frozen gas line

31. A mechanic finds that a helper assigned to him is so slow in absorbing information and in understanding simple instructions that work delays are being caused.
In this case, the BEST action for the mechanic to take is to

   A. discuss the matter with his foreman
   B. do most of the work himself
   C. tell the helper to take outside courses
   D. find out if the helper has home troubles

32. An accident victim with an injured spine should be

   A. immediately carried to a doctor
   B. turned over on his stomach
   C. moved only if absolutely necessary
   D. given artificial respiration

33. Of the following, the BEST measurement of a mechanic's work performance is

   A. the opinion of his fellow workers
   B. freedom from accidents
   C. speed in doing a job
   D. working properly with little supervision

34. A DESIRABLE safety feature provided on automobiles having automatic shift is that the starter motor   34._____

   A. armature circuit is fused
   B. cannot be operated if the engine is overheated
   C. is inoperative if the transmission is leaking
   D. can be operated only with the shift lever in NEUTRAL or PARK positions

35. The PRINCIPAL reason for not cranking a gasoline engine with one or more plugs removed and the ignition switch on is that   35._____

   A. poisonous fumes will result
   B. the engine may kick back
   C. the loose ignition wires may catch in the fan
   D. a fire may result

36. Difficulty in starting a gasoline engine COULD be caused by   36._____

   A. a leaky carburetor float   B. a leaky exhaust manifold
   C. smooth breaker points   D. too hot an ignition spark

37. After starting a cold gasoline engine, it is advisable to increase engine speed to a fast idle.   37._____
   The MOST important reason for doing this is to

   A. prevent harmful deposits from forming on engine parts
   B. increase the cooling system circulation
   C. reset the automatic choke
   D. warm up the voltage regulator

38. Assume your foreman gives you instructions on the procedure to use in performing a special rush job. Unforeseen difficulties arise which force you to change the procedure; and not finding it possible to contact your foreman, you proceed on the new basis. When your foreman appears, he complains that you have not followed orders.   38._____
   In this case, it would be BEST for you to

   A. say nothing and when he leaves, complete the job using your procedure
   B. make a formal complaint to the foreman's superior
   C. tell the foreman he is to blame because he was not around
   D. explain the situation to the foreman

39. A brass drift is used for   39._____

   A. pulling wheels   B. driving a wheel bearing cup
   C. measuring camber   D. checking gear wear

40. Overheating in a gasoline engine will MOST likely result in   40._____

   A. an increase in power   B. a loss of power
   C. damage to the muffler   D. an increase in engine speed

KEY (CORRECT ANSWERS)

1. C	11. C	21. C	31. A
2. C	12. D	22. C	32. C
3. C	13. B	23. D	33. D
4. D	14. A	24. A	34. D
5. A	15. C	25. D	35. D
6. B	16. C	26. B	36. A
7. B	17. A	27. B	37. A
8. D	18. D	28. D	38. D
9. C	19. B	29. B	39. B
10. A	20. C	30. B	40. B

EXAMINATION SECTION
TEST 1

DIRECTIONS: Each question or incomplete statement is followed by several suggested answers or completions. Select the one that BEST answers the question or completes the statement. *PRINT THE LETTER OF THE CORRECT ANSWER IN THE SPACE AT THE RIGHT.*

1. On an engine lathe, the saddle is a part which

   A. is attached to the tailstock
   B. rotates and holds the faceplate
   C. slides along the ways
   D. houses the back gears

2. To facilitate milling cast iron, it is BEST to use

   A. an emulsion of soluble oil and water as a lubricant
   B. an emulsion of soluble oil and water with a small percentage of soda as a lubricant
   C. lard oil as a lubricant
   D. no lubricant

3. When using a milling machine in a machine shop, a MAJOR difference of climb milling as compared to standard milling is that climb milling

   A. uses more power
   B. produces a better finish
   C. uses a downward cut
   D. uses cutters with less rake

4. In an automotive gasoline engine, the camshaft is used PRIMARILY to

   A. drive the transmission
   B. operate the valve lifters
   C. change the reciprocating motion of the pistons to rotary motion
   D. operate the choke mechanism

5. A magnetic motor starter is to be controlled with momentary start-stop pushbuttons at two locations.
   The number of control wires required, respectively, in the conduit between the controller and the first station and in the conduit between the two stations is _____ and _____.

   A. 3;3   B. 4; 4   C. 3; 4   D. 2; 4

6. The type of fitting to use to join a 1 inch branch compressed air, pipe line to a 2 inch main air line is a

   A. reducing valve   B. reducing coupling
   C. reducing tee   D. street elbow

7. If steel weighs 0.30 pounds per cubic inch, then the weight of a 2 inch square steel bar 90 inches long is _____ pounds.

   A. 27   B. 54   C. 108   D. 360

8. In arc welding, the filler metal is provided PRIMARILY by 8._____

   A. the metal to be welded
   B. a second rod of filler metal
   C. the slag
   D. the electrode

9. Oil or grease should NOT be applied to the oxygen valve of an oxyacetylene torch PRIMARILY because this can 9._____

   A. produce an explosion hazard
   B. corrode the valve
   C. give an incorrect pressure reading
   D. make the valve too slippery to handle

10. The PRIMARY function of the thermostat in the cooling system of an automobile engine is to 10._____

    A. control the operating temperature of the engine
    B. keep the operating temperature of the engine as low as possible
    C. provide the proper amount of heat for the heater
    D. retain engine heat when the engine gets hot

11. The PRIMARY purpose of the condenser in the ignition circuit of a gasoline engine is to 11._____

    A. boost the ignition voltage
    B. rectify the ignition voltage
    C. adjust the coil voltage
    D. reduce arcing at the distributor breaker points

12. The PRIMARY purpose of the differential in the rear drive train of an automotive vehicle is to allow each of the rear wheels to 12._____

    A. rotate at different speeds
    B. go in reverse
    C. rotate with maximum torque
    D. absorb road shocks

13. When grinding a fillet weld smooth, it is best NOT to grind 13._____

    A. after the weld has cooled off
    B. slowly
    C. too much of the weld material away
    D. the surface smooth

14. When using a hand file to finish a round piece of wood rod held between lathe centers, it is usually BEST to 14._____

    A. hold the file handle with one hand and to guide the file with the other hand
    B. use the file with the lathe not rotating
    C. hold the file with one hand and guide the workpiece with the other hand
    D. use a file without a handle

15. If the voltage on a 3-phase squirrel case induction motor is reduced to 90% of its rating, the starting current

   A. increases slightly
   B. is unchanged
   C. decreases 10%
   D. decreases 20%

16. If the voltage on a 3-phase squirrel case induction motor is reduced to 90% of its rating, the full load current

   A. decreases slightly
   B. is unchanged
   C. increases 10%
   D. increases 20%

17. When laying brick, the PRIMARY reason for wetting the brick before laying it is that

   A. the brick will absorb less water from the mortar and form a better bond
   B. wet bricks are easier to position
   C. wet bricks take less time to form a bond to mortar
   D. less cement is needed in the mortar

18. Concrete is a mixture that NORMALLY consists of cement,

   A. sand, and water
   B. sand, mortar, and water
   C. gravel, and water
   D. sand, gravel, and water

19. A type of rivet which can be put in place even when a worker does NOT have access to the back side of the work is known as a _____ rivet.

   A. *bucking*
   B. *double-head*
   C. *pop*
   D. *side*

20. The fraction which is equal to 0.875 is

   A. 7/16
   B. 5/8
   C. 3/4
   D. 7/8

21. When fabricating forms for pouring concrete, the MAIN advantage of using plywood sheets over sheets made of pine boards is that plywood

   A. doesn't splinter
   B. is lighter
   C. is less expensive
   D. resists warping better

22. When chipping concrete with a pneumatic hammer, the MOST important safety item that a man should wear is

   A. goggles
   B. gloves
   C. a hard hat
   D. rubber boots

23. It is considered POOR practice to paint a wooden ladder PRIMARILY because the

   A. paint will wear off in time
   B. rails will become susceptible to damage
   C. paint will shorten the life of the rungs
   D. paint can hide serious defects

24. A concrete wall is 36' long, 9' high, and 1 1/2' thick. The number of cubic yards of concrete that were needed to make this wall is

   A. 14
   B. 18
   C. 27
   D. 36

25. Before disassembling a complex mechanical machine, a mechanic may use a center punch to make adjacent punch marks on two or more of the parts in the machine in order to

    A. mark each part as he removes it
    B. check the hardness of the parts
    C. loosen the parts
    D. give himself a guide for correct reassembly

25.____

26. From among the following tools, the BEST one to use in cutting off a section of 4-inch cast iron pipe would be a

    A. hammer and chisel   B. pneumatic hammer
    C. hammer and star drill   D. hacksaw

26.____

27. The MOST important reason for removing pressure from an air hose before breaking a hose connection is to avoid

    A. damage to the air compressor
    B. losing air
    C. damage to the hose connection
    D. personal injury

27.____

28. When using a rope fall to lower a heavy load vertically, the strain on the hand line can be reduced and the load lowered more safely if the

    A. rope is wound three or four times around a fixed post
    B. rope is lightly greased
    C. rope is held very tightly in the sheaves of the fall
    D. sheaves of the fall are small in diameter

28.____

29. Oil is frequently applied to the inside of forms prior to pouring concrete in them in order to

    A. make the concrete flow better
    B. make stripping easier
    C. keep the moisture in the concrete
    D. protect the forms

29.____

30. The instrument generally used to determine the specific gravity of a lead-acid storage battery is the

    A. ammeter   B. voltmeter   C. ohmmeter   D. hydrometer

30.____

31. A tachometer is an instrument that is used to measure

    A. horizontal distances
    B. radial distances
    C. current in electric circuits
    D. motor speed

31.____

32. If the centers of a lathe are out of line when turning a cylindrical piece, it will cause

    A. the centers to be damaged
    B. a spiral groove to be cut on the piece

32.____

C. the cutting tool to be damaged
D. the piece to have a taper

33. A low reading on the oil pressure gauge of a gasoline engine may mean that the

    A. engine bearings are too tight
    B. crankcase oil level is too low
    C. transmission oil level is too low
    D. transmission oil needs changing

33._____

34. Although cloth tapes are used for taking measurements in many kinds of work, they should NOT be used when taking accurate measurements PRIMARILY because

    A. small changes in the amount of pull on these tapes can make a big difference in the reading
    B. the numbers become worn easily and are thus difficult to read
    C. small temperature changes cause large changes in readings
    D. there are too few subdivisions of each inch on these tapes

34._____

35. When painting walls with two coats of paint, a different color is used for each coat PRIMARILY to

    A. check for full coverage by the second coat
    B. provide a better appearance
    C. lower the painting cost
    D. allow the painter to use any color paint for the first coat

35._____

36. To drill a hole in the same place on a number of identical steel parts, it is BEST to use a

    A. blanking tool   B. punch press
    C. counterbore   D. jig

36._____

37. The MAIN purpose of a chuck on a lathe is to

    A. hold the workpiece
    B. hold the cutting tool
    C. allow speed changes to be made
    D. allow screw threads to be turned

37._____

38. The metal which has the GREATEST resistance to the flow of electricity is

    A. steel   B. copper   C. silver   D. gold

38._____

39. Tinning a soldering iron means

    A. applying flux to the tip
    B. cleaning the tip to make it bright
    C. applying a coat of solder to the tip
    D. heating the iron to the proper temperature

39._____

40. A protractor is an instrument that is used to 40._____
    A. measure the thickness of shims
    B. drill blind holes
    C. measure angles
    D. drill tapped holes

KEY (CORRECT ANSWERS)

1. C	11. D	21. D	31. D
2. D	12. A	22. A	32. D
3. C	13. C	23. D	33. B
4. B	14. A	24. B	34. A
5. C	15. C	25. D	35. A
6. C	16. C	26. A	36. D
7. C	17. A	27. D	37. A
8. D	18. D	28. A	38. A
9. A	19. C	29. B	39. C
10. A	20. D	30. D	40. C

TEST 2

DIRECTIONS: Each question or incomplete statement is followed by several suggested answers or completions. Select the one that BEST answers the question or completes the statement. *PRINT THE LETTER OF THE CORRECT ANSWER IN THE SPACE AT THE RIGHT.*

1. Common nail sizes are designated by   1.____

    A. penny size
    B. weight
    C. head size
    D. shank diameter

2. Toggle bolts should be used to fasten conduit clamps to a _____ wall.   2.____

    A. concrete
    B. hollow tile
    C. brick
    D. solid masonry

3. Backlash in a pair of meshed gears is defined as the   3.____

    A. distance between the gear centers
    B. gear ratio of the pair
    C. wear of the teeth
    D. *play* between the gear teeth

4. Relief valves on an air supply reservoir are used for the purpose of   4.____

    A. protecting the reservoir against excessively high pressures
    B. compensating for air leakage from the reservoir
    C. retaining the air in the reservoir
    D. draining moisture from the reservoir

5. Of the following, the BEST tool to use for securely tightening a one-inch standard hexagonal nut is a(n)   5.____

    A. monkey wrench
    B. open-end wrench
    C. Stillson wrench
    D. pair of heavy duty pliers

6. The type of pipe which is MOST likely to be broken by careless handling is one made of   6.____

    A. copper   B. steel   C. brass   D. cast iron

7. Open-end wrenches are usually made with the sides of the jaws at about a 15 degree angle to the centerline of the handle.   7.____
The PURPOSE of this type of design is that it

    A. increases the leverage of the wrench
    B. enables the wrench to lock on to the bolt head
    C. is useful when using the wrench in close quarters
    D. prevents extending the handle with a piece of pipe

8. The type of tool which is used with a portable electric drill to cut 2-inch diameter circular holes in wood is the   8.____

    A. reamer
    B. twist drill
    C. hole saw
    D. circular saw

9. For a certain job, you will need 25 steel bars 1 inch in diameter and 4'6" long. If these bars weigh 3 pounds per foot of length, then the TOTAL weight for all 25 bars is _____ pounds.

   A. 13.5   B. 75.0   C. 112.5   D. 337.5

10. If the allowable load on a wooden scaffold is 60 pounds per square foot and the scaffold surface area is 3 feet by 12 feet, then the MAXIMUM total distributed load that is permitted on the scaffold is _____ pounds.

    A. 720   B. 1800   C. 2160   D. 2400

11. If the floor area of one shop is 15' by 21'3" and the size of an adjacent shop is 18' by 30'6", then the TOTAL floor area of these two shops is _____ square feet.

    A. 1127.75   B. 867.75   C. 549.0   D. 318.75

12. To make certain that two points separated by a vertical distance of 8 feet are in exact vertical alignment, it would be BEST to use a

    A. plumb bob
    B. spirit level
    C. protractor
    D. mason's line

13. An offset screwdriver is MOST useful for turning a wood screw when

    A. the screw is large
    B. space above the screw is limited
    C. the screw is the Phillips type
    D. the screw must be tightened very securely

14. If an 8-32 x 11" machine screw is not available, the screw which could MOST easily be modified to use in an emergency is the

    A. 8-36 x 1"
    B. 10-32 x 1"
    C. 6-32 x 1 1/2"
    D. 8-32 x 1 1/2"

15. After a file has been used on soft material, the BEST way to clean the file is to use

    A. a file card
    B. fine emery cloth
    C. a bench brush
    D. a cleaning solution

16. The type of wrench that should be used to tighten a nut or bolt to a specified number of foot-pounds is a _____ wrench.

    A. torque   B. spanner   C. box   D. lug

17. When a hacksaw blade is turned at right angles to its holding frame, it is done PRIMARILY to

    A. increase the accuracy of cutting
    B. reduce the strain on the frame
    C. cut more rapidly
    D. make cuts which are deeper than the frame

18. The PRIMARY purpose of galvanizing steel is to

    A. increase the strength of the steel
    B. provide a good base for painting

C. prevent rusting of the steel
D. improve the appearance of the steel

19. When installing a heavy new machine in a shop, the BEST way to level the machine on the shop floor is to

   A. use steel shims under the feet
   B. use a thin layer of cement under the feet
   C. grind the feet of the machine to suit
   D. install adjustable shock mounts

20. The type of valve that permits fluid to flow in one direction ONLY in a pipe run is a _____ valve.

   A. check   B. gate   C. globe   D. cross

21. If the scale on a shop drawing is 1/2 inch to the foot, then the length of a part which measures 4 1/4 inches long on the drawing has a length of APPROXIMATELY _____ feet.

   A. 2 1/8   B. 4 1/4   C. 8 1/2   D. 10 3/4

22. It is important to use safety shoes PRIMARILY to guard the feet against

   A. tripping hazards   B. heavy falling objects
   C. shock hazards   D. mud and dirt

23. When using a wrench to tighten a bolt, it is considered BAD practice to extend the handle of the wrench with a pipe for added leverage PRIMARILY because

   A. the pipe may break
   B. the bolt head may be broken off
   C. more space will be needed to turn the wrench with the pipe on it
   D. no increase in leverage is obtained in this manner

24. To accurately measure the small gap between relay contacts, it is BEST to use a(n)

   A. depth gauge   B. GO-NO GO gauge
   C. feeler gauge   D. inside caliper

25. The plumbing symbol shown on the right represents a
   A. steam trap
   B. coupling
   C. cross fitting
   D. valve

26. On oxyacetylene welding equipment, the feed pressure of the gases is reduced by means of

   A. tip valves   B. regulator valves
   C. relief valves   D. nozzle size

27. The purpose of the ignition coil in a gasoline engine is PRIMARILY to

   A. smooth the voltage   B. raise the voltage
   C. raise the current   D. smooth the current

28. The weight per foot of length of a 2" x 2" square steel bar as compared to a 1" x 1" square steel bar is _____ times as much.

   A. two   B. four   C. six   D. eight

29. Electric arc welding is COMMONLY done using _____ amperage and _____ voltage.

   A. low; low
   B. low; high
   C. high; low
   D. high; high

30. Creosote is COMMONLY used

   A. to preserve wood
   B. to produce a good finish on wood
   C. as a primer coat of paint on wood
   D. to fireproof wood

31. The term *shipping* when applied to rope means

   A. coiling the rope in a tight ball
   B. lubricating the strands with tallow
   C. wetting the rope with water to make it easier to coil
   D. binding the ends with cord to prevent unraveling

32. Many portable electric power tools, such as electric drills, which operate on 110V A.C., have a third conductor in the power cord.
    The reason for this extra conductor is to

   A. prevent overheating of the power cord
   B. provide a spare conductor
   C. make the power cord stronger
   D. ground the case of the tool

33. The sum of 4 feet 3 1/4 inches, 7 feet 2 1/2 inches, and 11 feet 1/4 inch is _____ feet _____ inches.

   A. 21; 6 1/4   B. 22; 6   C. 23; 5   D. 24; 5 3/4

34. The number 0.038 is read as

   A. 38 tenths
   B. 38 hundredths
   C. 38 thousandths
   D. 38 ten-thousandths

35. Assume that an employee is paid at the rate of $5.43 per hour with time and a half for overtime past 40 hours in a week.
    If he works 43 hours in a week, his gross weekly pay is

   A. $217.20   B. $219.20   C. $229.59   D. $241.64

36. Vapor lock in a vehicle with a gasoline engine is caused by excessive heat.
    To prevent vapor lock, it may be necessary to relocate the(a)

   A. ignition system
   B. cooling system
   C. starter motor
   D. part of the fuel line

37. An ohmmeter is an instrument for measuring electrical

   A. voltage   B. current   C. power   D. resistance

38. A thermal overload device on a motor is used to protect it against

   A. high voltage
   B. over-speeding
   C. excessively high current
   D. low temperatures

39. A union is a pipe fitting that is used to join together

   A. two pipes of different diameters
   B. two pipes of the same diameter
   C. a threaded pipe to a sweated pipe
   D. two sweated pipes of the same diameter

40. If a 30 ampere fuse is placed in a fuse box for a circuit requiring a 15 ampere fuse,

   A. serious damage to the circuit may result from an overload
   B. better protection will be provided for the circuit
   C. the larger fuse will tend to blow more often since it carries more current
   D. it will eliminate maintenance problems

KEY (CORRECT ANSWERS)

1.	A	11.	B	21.	C	31.	D
2.	B	12.	A	22.	B	32.	D
3.	D	13.	B	23.	B	33.	B
4.	A	14.	D	24.	C	34.	C
5.	B	15.	A	25.	D	35.	D
6.	D	16.	A	26.	B	36.	D
7.	C	17.	D	27.	B	37.	D
8.	C	18.	C	28.	B	38.	C
9.	D	19.	A	29.	C	39.	B
10.	C	20.	A	30.	A	40.	A

MECHANICAL APTITUDE EXAMINATION SECTION
TEST 1

MECHANICAL COMPREHENSION

DIRECTIONS: Questions 1 through 4 test your ability to understand general mechanical devices. Pictures are shown and questions asked about the mechanical devices shown in the picture. Read each question and study the picture. Each question is followed by four choices. For each question, choose the one BEST answer (A, B, C, or D). Then, *PRINT THE LETTER OF THE CORRECT ANSWER IN THE SPACE AT THE RIGHT.*

1.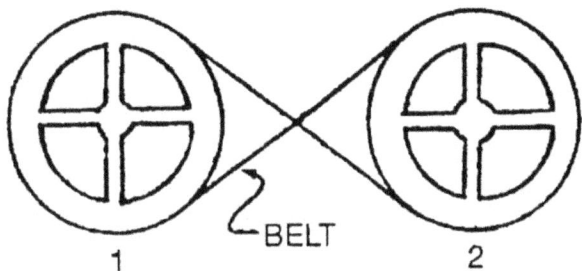

   The reason for crossing the belt connecting these wheels is to
   A. make the wheels turn in opposite directions
   B. make wheel 2 turn faster than wheel 1
   C. save wear on the belt
   D. take up slack in the belt

1.____

2.

   The purpose of the small gear between the two large gears is to
   A. increase the speed of the larger gears
   B. allow the larger gears to turn in different directions
   C. decrease the speed of the larger gears
   D. make the larger gears turn in the same direction

2.____

3.

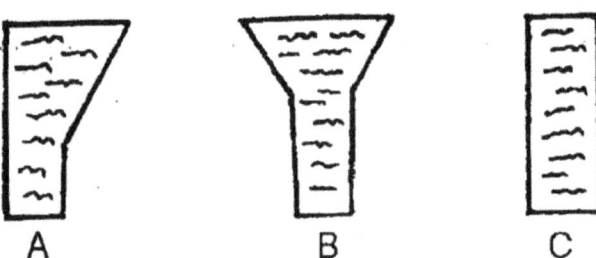

Each of these three-foot-high water cans have a bottom with an area of one square foot.
The pressure on the bottom of the cans is
   A. least in A   B. least in B   C. least in C   D. the same in all

3.____

4.

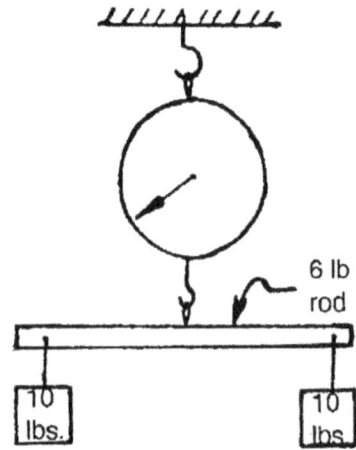

The reading on the scale should be
   A. zero   B. 10 pounds   C. 13 pounds   D. 26 pounds

4.____

KEY (CORRECT ANSWERS)

1. A
2. D
3. D
4. D

TEST 2

DIRECTIONS: Questions 1 through 6 test knowledge of tools and how to use them. For each question, decide which one of the four things shown in the boxes labeled A, B, C, or D normally is used with or goes best with the thing in the picture on the left. *PRINT THE LETTER OF THE CORRECT ANSWER IN THE SPACE AT THE RIGHT.*

NOTE: All tools are NOT drawn to the same scale.

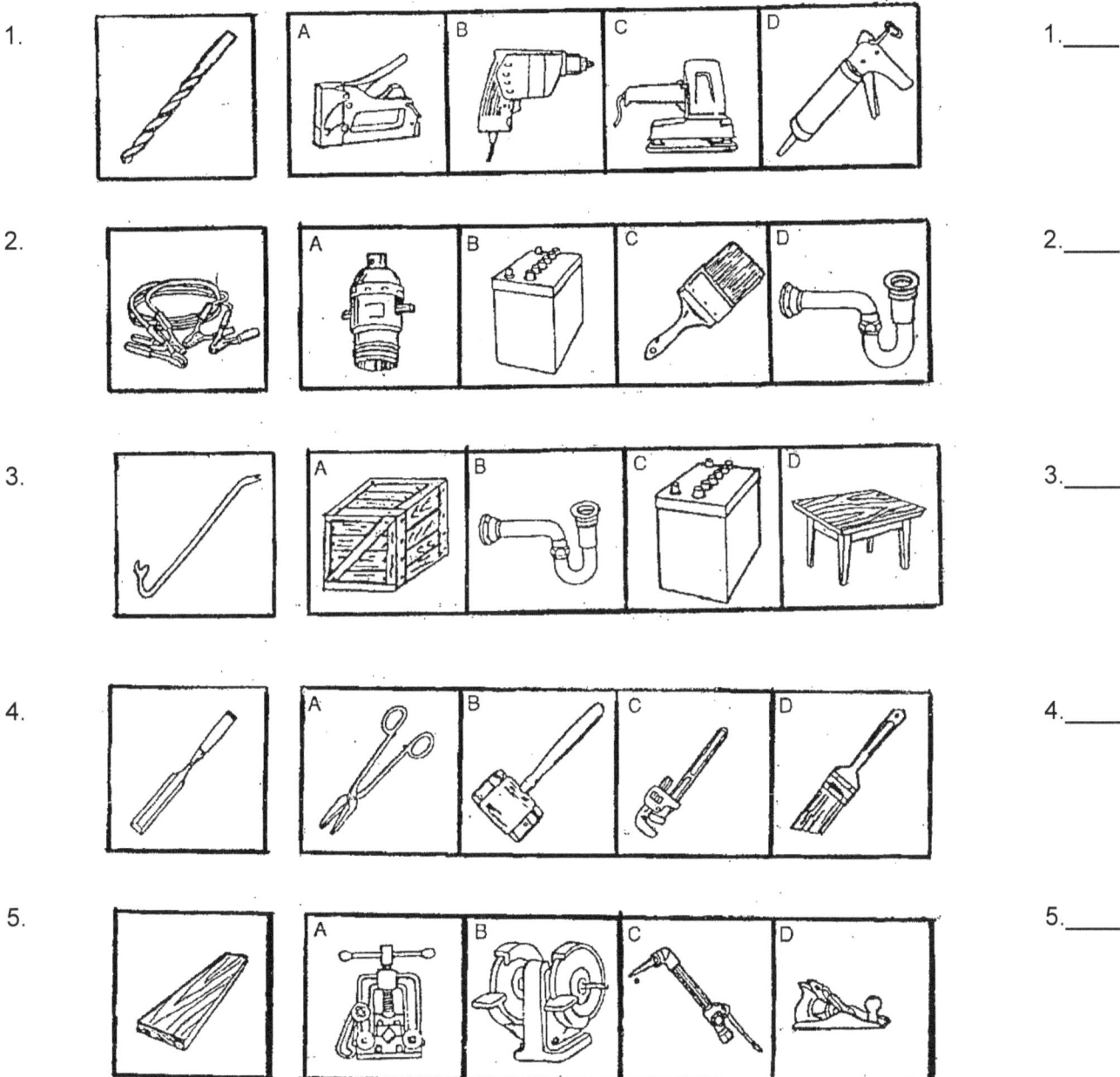

6.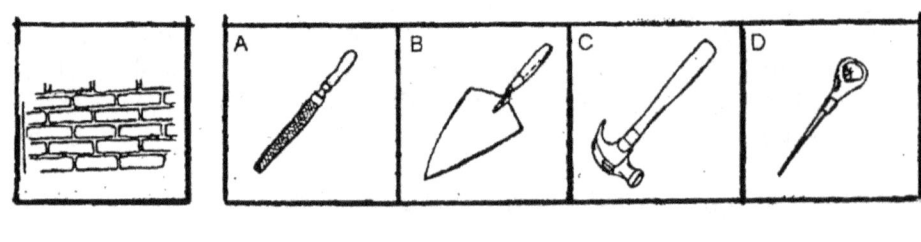

KEY (CORRECT ANSWERS)

1.	B	4.	B
2.	B	5.	D
3.	A	6.	B

READING COMPREHENSION
UNDERSTANDING AND INTERPRETING WRITTEN MATERIAL

EXAMINATION SECTION

TEST 1

DIRECTIONS: Each question or incomplete statement is followed by several suggested answers or completions. Select the one that BEST answers the question or completes the statement. *PRINT THE LETTER OF THE CORRECT ANSWER IN THE SPACE AT THE RIGHT.*

Questions 1-2.

DIRECTIONS: Questions 1 and 2 are to be answered in accordance with the following paragraph.

    Steam cleaners get their name from the fact that steam is used to generate pressure and is also a by-product of heating the cleaning solution. Steam itself has little cleaning power. It will melt some soils, but it does no dissolve them, break them up, or destroy their clinging power. Rather surprisingly, good machines generate as little steam as possible. Modern surface chemistry depends on a chemical solution to dissolve dirt, destroy its clinging power, and hold it in suspension. Steam actually hinders such a solution, but heat helps its physical and chemical action. Cleaning is most efficient when a hot solution reaches the work in heavy volume.

1. In accordance with the above paragraph, for MOST efficient cleaning,   1.____
    A. a heavy volume of steam is needed
    B. hot steam is needed to break up the soils
    C. steam is used to dissolve the surface dirt
    D. a hot chemical solution should always be used

2. With reference to the above paragraph, the steam in a steam cleaner is used to   2.____
    A. generate pressure
    B. create b-product chemicals
    C. slow down the chemical action of the cleaning solution
    D. dissolve accumulations of dirt

Questions 3-5.

DIRECTIONS: Questions 3 through 5 are based on the information given in the following paragraphs. Use ONLY the information given in these paragraphs in answering these questions.

    METHOD A: Move voltmeter lead from BAT to GEN terminal of regulator. Retard generator speed until generator voltage is reduced to 2 volts on a 6-volt system or 4 volts on a 12-volt system. Move voltmeter lead back to BAT terminal of regulator. Bring generator back to specified speed and note voltage setting.

METHOD B: Connect a variable resistance into the field circuit. Turn out all resistance. Operate generator at specified speed. Slowly increase (turn in) resistance until generator voltage is reduced to 2 volts on a 6-volt system or 4 volts on a 12-volt system. Turn out all resistance again, and note voltage setting. Regulator cover must be in place. To adjust voltage setting, turn adjusting screw. Turn clockwise to increase setting and counterclockwise to decrease voltage setting.

3. According to the instructions given in the paragraphs, when taking readings, 3.____
   A. a variable resistance is to be connected into the generator armature circuit
   B. the generator voltage on a 12-volt system is reduced to 2 volts
   C. the cover is to be in place
   D. the voltmeter lead should be continuously connected to the BAT terminal

4. In following the instructions given in the paragraphs, the one of the following statements that is MOST NEARLY correct is: 4.____
   A. The adjusting screw must be turned clockwise to increase the voltage setting
   B. Method B makes use of a fixed resistor
   C. Method A makes use of a variable resistor
   D. The generator voltage is reduced by decreasing the resistance

5. The above instructions pertain MOST likely to a(n) 5.____
   A. voltage regulator   B. starting regulator
   C. amperage regulator   D. circuit breaker

Questions 6-7.

DIRECTIONS: Questions 6 and 7 are based upon the following paragraph. Use ONLY the information contained in this paragraph in answering these questions.

With the engine running at normal idling speed and the engine hood open, attach the vacuum gauge to the intake manifold. The vacuum gauge should read about 18 to 21 inches, and the pointer should be steady. A needle fluctuating between 10 and 15 inches may indicate a defective cylinder-head, gasket, or valve. An extremely low reading indicates a leak in the intake manifold or gaskets. Accelerate the engine with full throttle momentarily. Notice if the gauge indicator fails to drop to approximately 2 inches as the throttle is opened, and recoil to at least 24 inches as the throttle is closed. If so, this may be an indication of diluted oil, poor piston-ring sealing, or an abnormal restriction in the exhaust, carburetor, or air cleaner. The above reading apply to sea level. There will be approximately a 1inch drop for each 1,000 feet of altitude.

6. If a vacuum test is made on a properly operating engine at an altitude of 3,000 feet, the vacuum gauge should read MOST NEARLY 6.____
   A. 12"   B. 15"   C. 13"   D. 24"

7. If a vacuum test is made on an engine which has an abnormal restriction in the exhaust, this will be evidenced by
   A. a leak in the intake manifold
   B. the gauge indicator failing to drop to approximately 3 inches on opening the throttle
   C. the gauge fluctuating around 12 inches
   D. a steady high gauge reading

7.____

Questions 8-10.

DIRECTIONS: Questions 8 through 10 are to be answered in accordance with the information in the following paragraph.

The following is a set of instructions on engine shut-down procedure: When an engine equipped with an electric shut-down valve is used, the engine can be shut down completely by turning off the switch key on installations equipped with an electric shut-down valve, or by turning the manual shut-down valve lever. Turning off the switch key which controls the electric shut-down valve always stops the engine unless the override button on the shutdown valve has been locked in the open position. If the manual override on the electric shut-down valve is being used, turn the button full counterclockwise to stop the engine.

CAUTION: Never leave the switch key or the override button in the valve open or run position when the engine is not running. With overhead tanks, this would allow fuel to drain into the cylinder, causing hydraulic lock.

8. According to the above paragraph, it becomes apparent that if an engine does not stop when the electric shut-down valve switch key is shut off,
   A. an open manual switch is present
   B. the override button is locked in the closed position
   C. a closed manual switch is functioning
   D. the override button is locked in the open position

8.____

9. When using an engine equipped with an electric shut-down valve,
   A. no alternate method is available
   B. a manual method is not present
   C. a manual override can shut the engine down
   D. a manual override will not work

9.____

10. As a matter of caution, the switch key in the closed position or the override button in the stop position will
    A. assist in keeping fuel in the cylinders
    B. prevent fuel from flooding the cylinder cavities
    C. assist in producing hydraulic lock
    D. aid fuel dilution

10.____

Questions 11-12.

DIRECTIONS: Questions 11 and 12 are to be answered according to the information given in the following paragraph.

You have been instructed to expedite the fabrication of four special salt spreader trucks using chassis that are available in the shop. All four trucks must be delivered before the opening of business on December 1. Based on workload and available hours, the foreman of the body shop indicates that he could manufacture one complete salt spreader body in five weeks, with one additional week required for mounting and securing each body to the available chassis. No work could begin on the body until the engines and hydraulic component, which would have to be purchased, were available for use. The Purchasing Department has promised delivery of engines and hydraulic components three months after the order is placed. (Assume that all months have four weeks, and the same crew is doing the assembling and manufacturing.)

11. With reference to the above paragraph, assuming that the Purchasing Department placed the order at the beginning of the first week in February and ultimate delivery of the engines and components was delayed by six weeks, the date of completion of the first salt spreader truck would be CLOSEST to the end of the _____ week in _____.   11._____
   A. fourth; July
   B. second; August
   C. fourth; August
   D. first; September

12. With reference to the above paragraph, the LATEST date that the engines and associated hydraulic components could be requisitioned in order to meet the specified deadline would be CLOSEST to the beginning of the _____ week in _____.   12._____
   A. first; February
   B. first; March
   C. third; March
   D. first; April

Questions 13-20.

DIRECTIONS: Questions 13 through 20 are based on the paragraph on JACKS shown below. When answering these questions, refer to this paragraph.

JACKS

When using a jack, a workman should check the capacity plate or other markings on the jack to make sure the device is heavy enough to support the load. Where there is no plate, capacity should be determined and painted on the side of the jack. The workman should see that jacks are well lubricated, but only at points where lubrication is specified, and should inspect them for broken teeth or faulty holding fixtures. A jack should never be thrown or dropped upon the floor; such treatment may crack or distort the metal, thus causing the jack to break when a load is lifted. It is important that the floor or ground surface upon which the jack is placed be level and clean, and the safe limit of floor loading is not exceeded. If the surface is earth, the jack base should be set on heavy wood blocking, preferably hardwood, of sufficient size that the blocking will not turn over, shift, or sink. If the surface is not perfectly level, the jack may be set on blocking, which should be leveled by wedges securely placed so that they cannot be brushed or forced out of place. Extenders of wood or metal, intended to provide a higher rise where a jack cannot reach up to load or lift it high enough, should never be used. Instead, a larger jack should be obtained or higher blocking which is correspondingly wider and longer should be placed under the jack. All lifts should be vertical with the jack correctly centered for the lift. The base of the jack should be on a perfectly level surface, and the jack head, with its hardwood shim, should bear against a perfectly level meeting surface.

13. To make sure the jack is heavy enough to support a certain load, the workman should
    A. lubricate the jack   B. shim the jack
    C. check the capacity plate   D. use a long handle
13.____

14. A jack should be lubricated
    A. after using   B. before painting
    C. only at specified points   D. to prevent slipping
14.____

15. The workman should inspect a jack for
    A. manufacturer's name   B. broken teeth
    C. paint peeling   D. broken wedges
15.____

16. Metal parts on a jack may crack if
    A. the jack is thrown on the floor   B. the load is leveled
    C. blocking is used   D. the handle is too short
16.____

17. It would not be a safe practice for a workman to
    A. center the jack under the load   B. set the jack on a level surface
    C. use hardwood for blocking   D. use extenders to reach up to the load
17.____

18. Wedges may safely be used to
    A. replace a broken tooth   B. prevent the overloading of a jack
    C. level the blocking under a jack   D. straighten distorted metal
18.____

19. Blocking should be
    A. made of a soft wood
    B. placed between the jack base and the earth surface
    C. well lubricated
    D. used to repair a broken tooth
19.____

20. A hardwood shim should be used
    A. between the head and its meeting surface
    B. under the jack
    C. as a filler
    D. to level a surface
20.____

Questions 21-22.

DIRECTIONS: Questions 21 and 22 are to be answered ONLY on the basis of the information contained in the following paragraph.

Many experiments have been made on the effects of alcoholic beverages. These studies show that alcohol decreases alertness and efficiency. It decreases self-consciousness and, at the same time, increases confidence and feelings of ease and relaxation. It impairs attention and judgment. It destroys fear of consequences. Usual cautions are thrown to the winds. Habit systems become disorganized. The driver who uses alcohol tends to disregard his usual safety practices. He may not even be aware that he is disregarding them. His reaction time slows down; normally quick reactions are not possible for him. To make matters worse, he may not realize he is slower. His eye muscles may be so affected that his vision is not normal. He cannot correctly judge the speed of his car or of any other car. He cannot correctly estimate distances being covered by each. He becomes a highway menace.

21. The paragraph states that the drinking of alcohol makes a driver
    A. *more* alert
    B. *less* confident
    C. *more* efficient
    D. *less* attentive

21.____

22. From the above paragraph, it is reasonable to assume that a driver may overcome the bad effects of drinking alcohol by
    A. being more cautious
    B. relying on his good driving habits to a greater extent than normally
    C. watching the road more carefully
    D. waiting for the alcohol to wear off before drinking

22.____

Questions 23-25.

DIRECTIONS: Each question consists of a statement. You are to indicate whether the statement is TRUE (T) or FALSE (F). PRINT THE LETTER OF THE CORRECT ANSWER IN THE SPACE AT THE RIGHT.

When in use, the storage battery becomes hot, and water evaporate from the cells of the battery, so clean water preferably distilled, must be added at frequent intervals. This action keeps the level of the battery liquid above the top of the battery plates.

23. All water loss from a storage battery occurs when the battery is in use.

23.____

24. The water added to a storage battery does not have to be distilled.

24.____

25. Water in the storage battery must be kept level with the top of the battery plates.

25.____

KEY (CORRECT ANSWERS)

1.	D	11.	A
2.	A	12.	B
3.	C	13.	C
4.	A	14.	C
5.	A	15.	B
6.	B	16.	A
7.	B	17.	D
8.	D	18.	C
9.	C	19.	B
10.	B	20.	A

21. D
22. F
23. F
24. T
25. F

TEST 2

DIRECTIONS: Each question or incomplete statement is followed by several suggested answers or completions. Select the one that BEST answers the question or completes the statement. *PRINT THE LETTER OF THE CORRECT ANSWER IN THE SPACE AT THE RIGHT.*

Questions 1-2.

DIRECTIONS: Questions 1 and 2 are based on the following paragraph

Because electric drills run at high speed, the cutting edges of a twist drill are heated quickly. If the metal is thick, the drill point must be withdrawn from the hole frequently to cool it and clear out chips. Forcing the drill continuously into a deep hole will heat it, thereby spoiling its temper and cutting edges. A portable electric drill has the advantage that it can be taken to the work and used to drill holes in material too large to handle in a drill press.

1. According to the above paragraph, overheating of a twist drill will 1.____
   A. slow down the work
   B. cause excessive drill breakage
   C. dull the drill
   D. spoil the accuracy of the work

2. According to the above paragraph, one method of preventing overheating of 2.____
   a twist drill is to
   A. use cooling oil
   B. drill a smaller pilot hole first
   C. use a drill press
   D. remove the drill from the work frequently

Questions 3-5.

DIRECTIONS: Questions 3 through 5, inclusive, are to be answered in accordance with the paragraph below.

A steam heating system with steam having a pressure of less than 10 pounds is called a low-pressure system. The majority of steam-heating systems are of this type. The steam may be provided by low-pressure boilers installed *expressly* for the purpose, or it may be generated in boiler at a higher pressure and reduced in pressure before admitted to the heating mains. In other instances, it may be possible to use exhaust steam which has been made to run engines and other machines and which still contains enough heat to be utilized in the heating system. The first case represents the system of heating used in the ordinary residence or other small building; the other two represent the systems of heating employed in industrial buildings where a power plant is installed for general power purposes.

3. According to the above paragraph, whether or not a steam heating system is 3.____
   considered a low pressure system is determined by the pressure
   A. generated by the boiler
   B. in the heating main
   C. at the inlet side of the reducing valve
   D. of the exhaust

4. According to the above paragraph, steam used for heating is sometimes obtained from steam
   A. generated principally to operate machinery
   B. exhausted from larger boilers
   C. generated at low pressure and brought up to high pressure before being used
   D. generated by engines other than boilers

5. As used in the above paragraph, the word *expressly* means
   A. rapidly   B. specifically   C. usually   D. mainly

Questions 6-7.

DIRECTIONS: Questions 6 and 7 are to be answered in accordance with the following paragraph.

When one is making the selection of grinding wheel specifications, the first variable factor to consider is the wheel speed, which influences the grade and the bond of the wheel. It is recommended that the grade should be determined in this way: the higher the wheel speed with relation to work speed, the softer the wheel should be. When, for any reason, the wheel speed is reduced, then it may be expected that the wheel will wear faster, but this can be overcome by choosing a wheel of a harder grade, assuming that the grade was correct for the initial speed.

6. It can be said that the MOST important piece of information in the above paragraph is:
   A. The higher the relative wheel speed, the softer should be the wheel
   B. Wheel speed is a variable factor
   C. At low speeds wheels wear rapidly
   D. When a wheel slows down, it should be replaced by a harder grade

7. According to the above paragraph, no indication is made that
   A. there are other factor too be considered beside speed
   B. hard wheels at low speed wear faster than soft wheels at high speed
   C. the lower the speed, the harder should be the grade
   D. the selection of the bond of the wheel is affected by speed

Questions 8-9.

DIRECTIONS: Questions 8 and 9 are to be answered ONLY according to the information in the following paragraph.

Metal spraying is used for many purposes. Worn bearings on shafts and spindles can be readily restored to original dimensions with any desired metal or alloy. Low-carbon steel shafts may be supplied with high-carbon steel journal surfaces, which can then be ground to size after spraying. By using babbitt wire, bearings can be lined or babbitted while rotating. Pump shafts and impellers can be coated with any desired metal to overcome wear and corrosion. Valve seats may be re-surfaced. Defective castings can be repaired by filling in blow-holes and checks. The application of metal spraying to the field of corrosion resistance is growing, although the major application in this field is in the use of sprayed zinc. Tin, lead, and aluminum have been used considerably. The process is used for structural and tank applications in the field as well as in the shop.

8. According to the above paragraph, worn bearing surfaces on shafts are metal-sprayed in order to
    A. prevent corrosion of the shaft
    B. fit them into larger-sized impellers
    C. return them to their original sizes
    D. replace worn babbitt metal

8._____

9. According to the above paragraph, rotating bearings can be metal-sprayed using
    A. babbitt wire
    B. high-carbon steel
    C. low-carbon steel
    D. any desired metal

9._____

Questions 10-11.

DIRECTIONS: Questions 10 and 11 are to be answered ONLY according to the information in the following paragraph.

The wheels used for internal grinding should general be softer than those used for other grinding operations because the contact area between the wheel and work is comparatively large. A soft wheel that will cut with little pressure should be used to prevent springing the spindle. The grade of the wheel depends upon the character of the work and the stiffness of the machine; and where a large variety of work is being ground, it may not be practicable to have an assortment of wheels adapted to all conditions. By adjusting the speed, however, a wheel not exactly suited to the work in hand can often be used. If the wheel wears too rapidly, it should be run faster; and if it tends to glaze, the speed should be diminished.

10. On the basis of the above passage only, it may BEST be said that
    A. the type and grade of wheel are independent of the sturdiness of the machine
    B. by increasing the wheel speed, parts can easily be internally ground
    C. wheels used for outside grinding usually have a smaller contact area between the wheel and work
    D. to carry on hand an assortment of wheels for all conceivable internal grinding jobs is economical

10._____

11. On the basis of the above passage only, it may BEST be said that
    A in general, if a wheel wears too rapidly, the speed should be decreased
    B. by decreasing the wheel speed, a wheel not quite appropriate for the job may sometimes be used
    C. where a large variety of work is being ground, the grade of wheel depends on the diameter of the wheel
    D. if a wheel tends to glaze, it should run faster

11._____

Questions 12-15.

DIRECTIONS: Questions 12 through 15, inclusive, are to be answered ONLY in accordance with the following paragraph.

Cylindrical surfaces are the most common form of finished surface found on machine parts, although flat surfaces are also very common; hence, many metal-cutting *processes* are for the purpose of producing either cylindrical or flat surfaces. The machines used for cylindrical or flat shapes may be, and often are, utilized also for forming the various irregular or special shapes required on many machine parts. Because of the prevalence of cylindrical and flat surfaces, the student of manufacturing practice should learn first about the machines and methods employed to produce these surfaces. The cylindrical surfaces may be internal as in holes and cylinders. Any one part may, of course, have cylindrical sections of different diameters and lengths and include flat end or shoulders; and frequently there is a threaded part or possibly some finished surface that is not circular in cross-section. The prevalence of cylindrical surfaces on machine parts explains why lathes are found in all machine shops. It is important to understand the various uses of the lathe because many of the operations are the same fundamentally as those performed on other types of machine tools.

12. According to the above paragraph, the MOST common form of finished surfaces found on machine parts is
    A. cylindrical   B. elliptical   C. flat   D. square

13. According to the above paragraph, any one part of cylindrical surface may have
    A. chases   B. shoulders   C. keyways   D. splines

14. According to the above paragraph, lathes are found in all machine shops because cylindrical surfaces on machine parts are
    A. scarce   B. internal   C. common   D. external

15. As used in the above paragraph, the work *processes* means
    A. operations   B. purposes   C. devices   D. tools

Questions 16-17.

DIRECTIONS: Questions 16 and 17 are to be answered ONLY in accordance with the following paragraph.

The principle of interchangeability requires manufacture to such specification that component parts of a device may be selected at random and assembled to fit and operate satisfactorily. Interchangeable manufacture, therefore, requires that parts be made to definite limits of error and to fit gages instead of mating parts. Interchangeability does not necessarily involve a high degree of precision; stove lids, for example, are interchangeable but are not particularly accurate, and carriage bolts and nuts are not precision products but are completely interchangeable. Interchangeability may be employed in unit production as well as mass production systems of manufacture.

16. According to the above paragraph, in order for parts to be interchangeable, they must be
    A. precision-machined
    B. selectively-assembled
    C. mass-produced
    D. made to fit gages

    16.____

17. According to the above paragraph, carriage bolts are interchangeable because they are
    A. precision-made
    B. sized to specific tolerances
    C. individually matched products
    D. produced in small units

    17.____

Questions 18-22.

DIRECTIONS: Questions 18 through 22 are to be answered in accordance with the following passage.

TITANIC AIR COMPRESSOR

Valves: The compressors are equipped with Titanic plate valves which are automatic in operation. Valves are so constructed that an entire valve assembly can readily be removed from the head. The valves provide large port area with short lift and are accurately guided to insure positive seating.

Starting Unloader: Each compressor (or air end) is equipped with a centrifugal governor which is bolted directly to the compressor crankshaft. The governor actuates cylinder relief valves so as to relieve pressure from the cylinders during starting and stopping. The motor is never required to start the compressor under load.

Air Strainer: Each cylinder air inlet connection is fitted with a suitable combination air strainer and muffler.

Pistons: Pistons are lightweight castings, ribbed internally to secure strength, and are accurately turned and ground. Each piston is fitted with four (4) rings, two of which are oil control rings. Piston pins are hardened and tempered steel of the full floating type. Bronze bushings are used between piston pin and piston.

Connecting Rods: Connecting rods are of solid bronze designed for maximum strength, rigidity, and wear. Crank pins are fitted with renewable steel bushings. Connecting rods are of the one-piece type, there being no bolts, nuts, or cotter pins which can come loose. With this type of construction, wear is reduced to a negligible amount, and adjustment of wrist pin and crank pin bearings is unnecessary.

Main Bearings: Main bearings are of the ball type and are securely held in position by spacers. This type of bearing entirely eliminates the necessity of frequent adjustment or attention. The crankshaft is always in perfect alignment.

Crankshaft: The crankshaft is a one-piece heat-treated forging of best quality open-hearth steel, of rugged design, and of sufficient size to transmit the motor power and any additional stresses which may occur in service. Each crankshaft is counter-balanced (dynamically balanced) to reduce vibration to a minimum, and is accurately machined to properly receive the ball bearing races, crank pin bushing, flexible coupling, and centrifugal governor. Suitable provision is made to insure proper lubrication of all crankshaft bearings and bushings with the minimum amount of attention.

    Coupling: Compressor and motor shafts are connected through a Morse Chain Company all-metal enclosed flexible coupling. This coupling consists of two sprockets, one mounted on, and keyed to, each shaft; the sprockets are wrapped by a single Morse Chain, the entire assembly being enclosed in a split aluminum grease packed cover.

18. The crank pin of the connecting rod is fitted with a renewable bushing made of
    A. solid bronze
    B. steel
    C. slight-weight casting
    D. ball bearings

19. When the connecting rod is of the one-piece type,
    A. the wrist pins require frequent adjustment
    B. the crank pins require frequent adjustment
    C. the cotter pins frequently will come loose
    D. wear is reduced to a negligible amount

20. The centrifugal governor is bolted DIRECTLY to the
    A. compressor crankshaft
    B. main bearing
    C. piston pin
    D. muffler

21. The number of oil control rings required for each piston is
    A. one
    B. two
    C. three
    D. four

22. The compressor and motor shafts are connected through a flexible coupling. These couplings are _____ to the shafts.
    A. keyed
    B. brazed
    C. soldered
    D. press fit

Questions 23-25.

DIRECTIONS: Questions 23 through 25, inclusive, are to be answered in accordance with the following paragraph.

    Wherever a soil pipe has to be provided for in a partition, special care must be taken that the hubs do not project beyond the finish face of the plaster. Before framing a building, it is desirable to ascertain where the stacks are and to provide for them. Building regulations require the stacks to be of 4-inch cast-iron even in small dwellings. With a 4-inch stack, the hub is 6 1/8 inches in diameter; and, therefore, 2 by 6 studs must be used. Special care should be taken that no plaster comes in contact with a soil pipe for *subsequent* settlement may cause cracking.

23. As used in the above paragraph, *subsequent* means MOST NEARLY
    A. heavy
    B. sudden
    C. later
    D. soon

24. According to the above paragraph, 4" cast-iron soil pipes are used because
    A. they will not project beyond the face of the plaster
    B. it is easier to plaster over 4" pipe
    C. they can be located easier
    D. they are required by law

25. According to the above paragraph, the reason plaster should NOT be in direct contact with soil pipe is because
    A. the plaster would be damaged by moisture
    B. rust will bleed through the plaster
    C. of the possibility of cracks due to settlement
    D. it is harder to plaster over 4" pipe

KEY (CORRECT ANSWERS)

1.	C		11.	B
2.	D		12.	A
3.	B		13.	B
4.	A		14.	C
5.	B		15.	A
6.	A		16.	D
7.	B		17.	B
8.	C		18.	B
9.	A		19.	D
10.	C		20.	A

21.	B
22.	A
23.	C
24.	D
25.	C

BASIC FUNDAMENTALS OF ENGINES

CONTENTS

		Page
I.	Engine Construction	1
II.	Engine Operation	2
III.	Comparison of Engine Types	5
IV.	Engine Measurements	10
V.	Timing	14
VI.	Engine Output	16
VII.	Engine Efficiency	20
VIII.	Advantages of Multicylinder Engines	22
IX.	Classification of Engines	23

BASIC FUNDAMENTALS OF ENGINES

I. ENGINE CONSTRUCTION

The first step in understanding automotive engine construction and operation is to understand what goes on inside the engine. No matter how many cylinders an engine has, whether 1, 2, 6, or 12, the same actions take place in each cylinder. Since the diesel engine is mechanically similar to the gasoline engine, we can learn about engine construction and operation by studying a single-cylinder engine (Fig. 1). This engine is a 4-stroke cycle (Fig. 2), internal combustion, gasoline engine; these terms are explained in subsequent paragraphs.

    A. Cylinder and Piston. A cutaway of a single cylinder gasoline engine is shown in Figure 1. The upper, or head end, is closed by a cylinder head, but the lower end is open. The piston is a hollow metal tube with the top end closed. It is a close-sliding fit in the cylinder, which means it can move up and down in the cylinder. This up-and-down movement, produced by the burning of fuel in the cylinder, results in the production of power from the engine.

    B. Connecting Rod and Crank. The up-and-down movement of the piston is called *reciprocating motion*. This reciprocating motion must be changed to rotary motion so the wheels of the vehicle can be made to rotate. The change is accomplished by a crank on the crankshaft and a connecting rod which connects between the piston (Fig. 3) and the crank. The connecting rod is connected to the piston by a piston pin. The pin passes through bearing surfaces in the piston and the connecting rod. The lower end of the connecting rod is attached to the crankpin on the crankshaft. As the piston moves up and down in the cylinder, the upper end of the connecting rod moves up and down with it. The lower end of the connecting rod also moves up and down but, because it is attached to the crankpin on the crankshaft (Fig. 3), it must also move in a circle with the crankpin. Each movement of the piston from top to bottom or from bottom to top is called a *stroke*. The piston takes two strokes as the crankshaft makes one complete revolution, an upstroke and a downstroke. When the piston is at the top of a stroke, it is said to be at top dead center (TDC). When the piston is at the bottom of a stroke, it is said to be at bottom dead center (BDC). These positions are called rock position (par. VC).

    C. Valves. There are two valves (Fig. 1) at the top of the cylinder. A valve is an accurately machined plug that fits into a machined opening at the top of the cylinder. When the valve is resting in this opening, it is said to be *seated*. When a valve is so positioned, it is *closed* and the opening is sealed off. When the valve is pushed off its seat, it is *opened*. The two valves in the cylinder are closed part of the time and opened part of the time. The valve mechanism that causes the valves to open and close is discussed in paragraph IIC. One of the valves, called the *intake valve*, opens to admit a mixture of fuel and air into the cylinder. The other valve, called the *exhaust valve*, opens to allow the escape of burned gases after the fuel-and-air mixture has burned.

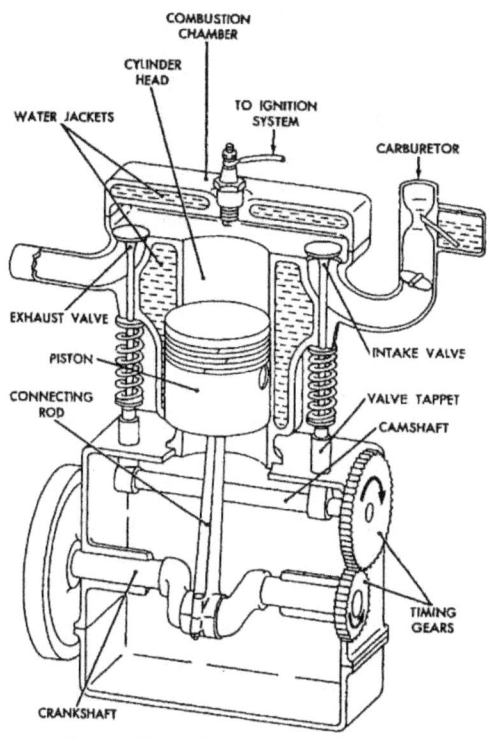

Figure 1. Single-cylinder, 4-stroke cycle, internal combustion, gasoline engine, cutaway view.

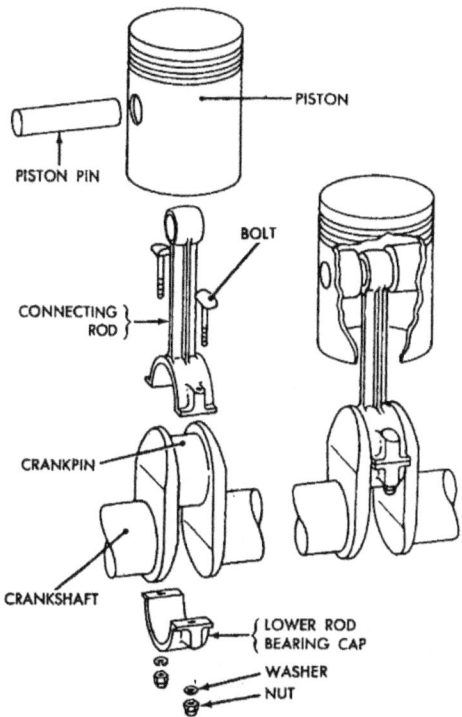

Figure 2. Piston, connecting rod, and piston pin.

II. ENGINE OPERATION

  A. Intake Stroke: The actions that take place within the engine cylinder may be divided into four basic parts, which are called *strokes*. The first stroke in the sequence is called the *intake* stroke (Fig. 4). During this stroke, the piston is moving downward and the intake valve is open. This downward movement of the piston produces a partial void, or vacuum, in the cylinder, and air rushes into the cylinder past the opened intake valve. This is somewhat the same effect as when drinking through a straw. A partial vacuum is produced in the mouth and the liquid moves up through the straw to fill the vacuum (Fig. 5). In the engine, the inrushing air passes through the carburetor before it enters the cylinder. The carburetor charges the air with gasoline vapor to produce a combustible mixture.

Figure 5. Partial vacuum produced by suction.

B. Compression Stroke. When the piston reaches bottom dead center at the end of the intake stroke and is therefore at the bottom of the cylinder, the intake valve closes. This seals the upper end of the cylinder. As the crankshaft continues to rotate, it pushes up, through the connecting rod, on the piston. The piston is therefore pushed upward and compresses the combustible mixture in the cylinder; this is called the *compression* stroke. The mixture is compressed to about a sixth or a seventh of its original volume. This is the same as taking a gallon of air and compressing it until a little more than a pint of air is left. Compressing the mixture in this way makes it still more combustible; the energy in the fuel is concentrated into a smaller space.

C. Power Stroke: As the piston reaches top dead center at the end of the compression stroke and therefore has moved to the top of the cylinder, the compressed fuel-air mixture is ignited. This ignition is produced by the ignition system. The ignition system causes an electric spark to occur suddenly in the cylinder. The spark sets fire to the fuel-air mixture. The mixture burns so rapidly that it might be said to explode. The pressure in the cylinder goes up to as much as 400 psi. This means that the force pushing on the end of a 3-inch piston would be more than 2,500 pounds. This force, or thrust, pushed the piston down. The thrust is carried through the connecting rod to the crankpin on the crankshaft. The crankshaft is given a powerful twist. This is called the *power* stroke. This turning effort, rapidly repeated in the engine and carried through gears and shafts, will turn the wheels of a vehicle and cause it to move along the highway.

D. Exhaust Stroke: After the fuel-oil mixture has burned, it must be cleared from the cylinder. This is done by opening the exhaust valve just as the power stroke is finished and the piston starts back up on the *exhaust* stroke. The piston forces the burned gases out of the cylinder past the opened exhaust valve. The four strokes (intake, compression, power, and exhaust) are continuously repeated as the engine runs.

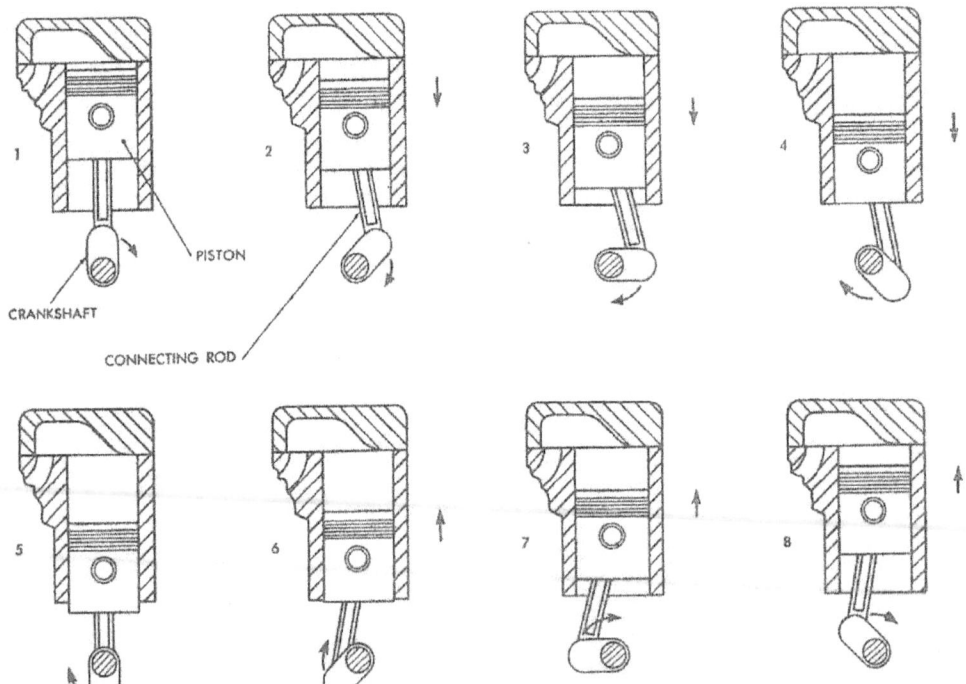

Figure 3. Relationship of piston, connecting rod, and crank on crankshaft as crankshaft turns one revolution.

E. **Valve Mechanism Action.** There are various ways of causing the intake and exhaust valves to open and close. One method is shown in Fig. 1. Here, a gear on the crankshaft is meshed with a second gear on another shaft. When the crankshaft turns, the other shaft must also turn. This second shaft is called the *camshaft* because it has a number of *cams* on it. These cams are simply raised sections, or collars, with high spots on them. When the camshaft rotates, the high spots (called *lobes*) move around and push away anything they are in contact with. Riding on each cam is a cylindrical valve tappet. As the lobe moves up under the valve tappet, the valve tappet is raised. This upward movement causes the valve above it to be raised also. Thus, the valve is raised up off its seat in the cylinder so that the valve opens. When the lobe on the cam moves on around out of the way, the pressure of the spring under the valve forces the valve to move down and reseat. At the same time, the valve tappet is also forced downward so that it remains in contact with the cam. The gear on the crankshaft is twice as large (has twice the number of teeth) as the gear on the crankshaft. This means that the camshaft will revolve half as fast as the crankshaft. In other words, the crankshaft must turn twice for the camshaft to turn once. Thus, the valves are opened only once every two crankshaft revolutions. This is the way it should be, since there is only one intake stroke (intake valve open) and only one exhaust stroke (exhaust valve open) every two crankshaft revolutions.

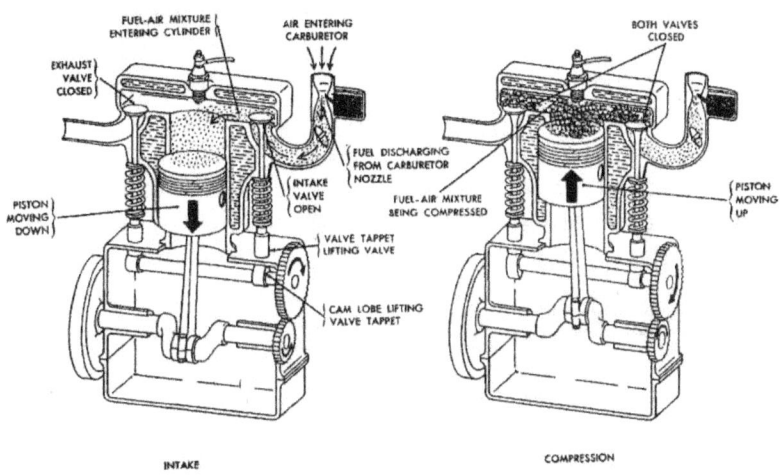

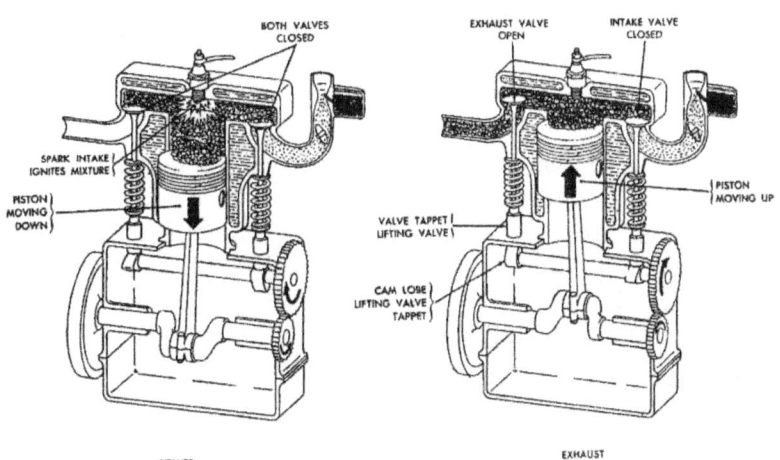

Figure 4. The four strokes in the 4-stroke cycle, gasoline engine.

F. Engine Accessory Systems. We have mentioned the carburetor which supplies vaporized fuel to the air passing into the engine cylinder on the intake stroke (A above). The carburetor is a unit in the fuel system. Another accessory system is the ignition system which ignites the compressed fuel-air mixture in the cylinder at the end of the compression stroke. A third accessory system is the lubrication system; this supplies lubricating oil to the various moving parts in the engine. The oil lubricates all parts, such as the piston, bearings, crankpin, and valve stems, that rotate or slide in or on other parts. This oil permits the parts to move easily so that little power is lost and wear of parts is kept to a minimum. A fourth system is the cooling system. In the simple engine shown in Fig. 1, water is used as the cooling medium. Water circulates in jackets around the cylinder and in the cylinder head. This water removes part of the heat produced by the combustion of the fuel-air mixture. This action prevents the engine from overheating and thereby being damaged. All these accessor systems are described in detail in following chapters.

III. COMPARISON OF ENGINE TYPES

A. Internal and External Combustion Engines. In the internal combustion engine, the combustion of the fuel takes place inside the engine cylinder. This is in contrast to external combustion engines, such as steam engines, where the combustion takes place outside of the engine. Fig. 6 shows in simplified form an internal and an external combustion engine. The external combustion engine requires a boiler in which a fuel is burned. This combustion causes water to boil to produce steam. The steam passes into the engine cylinder under pressure and forces the piston to move downward. With the internal combustion engine, the combustion taking place inside the cylinder is directly responsible for forcing the piston to move downward. In both types of engine, valving is arranged to permit the piston to move back upward as the spent steam (external combustion engine) or burned gas (internal combustion engine) is exhausted.

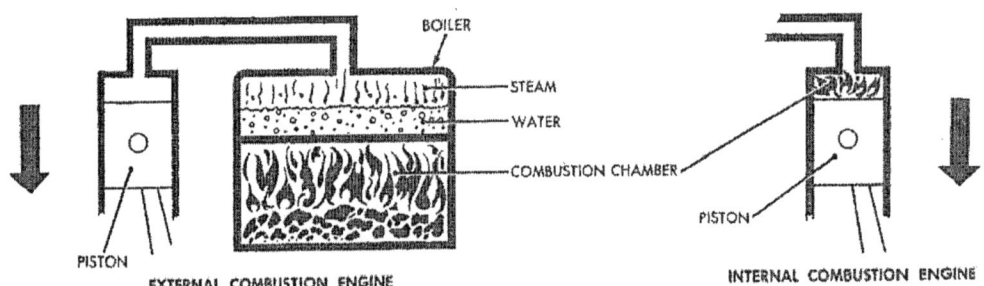

Figure 6. Comparison of internal and external combustion engines.

B. Four-Stroke-Cycle and Two-Stroke-Cycle Engines. The engine described in Paragraph VIII and illustrated in Figs. 1 and 4 is a four-stroke cycle engine. Four strokes of the piston, with two revolutions of the crankshaft and one revolution of the camshaft, are required for the complete cycle of events. This type of engine is also called a four-stroke-Otto-cycle engine because it was Dr. N.A. Otto who, in 1876, first applied the principals of this engine. In the two-stroke-cycle engine, the entire cycle of events (intake, compression, power, and exhaust) takes place in two piston strokes. This is accomplished by combining the four events so that they take place in two instead of four strokes, as explained in 1 and 2 below.

1. Two-stroke Cycle. A two-stroke cycle engine is shown in Figure 7. Every other stroke on this engine is a power stroke. Each time the piston moves down, it is on the power stroke. Intake, compression, power, and exhaust still take place, but they are completed in just two strokes. Intake and exhaust ports are cut into the cylinder wall instead of being placed at the top of the combustion chamber as in the four-stroke cycle engine. As the piston moves down on its power stroke, it first uncovers the exhaust port to let burned gases escape and then uncovers intake port to allow a new fuel-air mixture to enter the combustion chamber. Then, on the upward stroke, the piston covers both ports and, at the same time, compresses the new mixture in preparation for ignition and another power stroke. In the engine shown in Fig. 7, the piston is so shaped that the incoming fuel-air mixture is directed upward, thereby sweeping out ahead of it the burned exhaust gases. Also, there is an inlet into the crankcase through which the fuel-air mixture passes before it enters the cylinder. This inlet is opened as the piston moves upward, but it is sealed off as the piston moves downward on the power stroke. The downward moving piston slightly compresses the mixture in the crankcase, thus giving the mixture sufficient pressure to pass rapidly through the intake port as the piston clears this port. This improves the "sweeping out," or scavenging, effect of the mixture as it enters and clears the burned gases from the cylinder through the exhaust port.

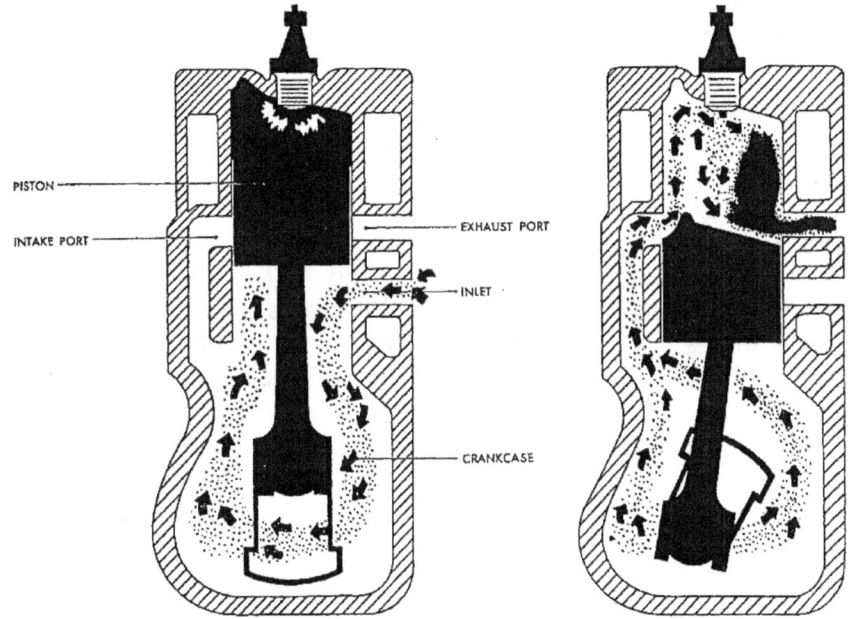

Figure 7. Events in a two-stroke-cycle, internal combustion engine.

2. Comparison of Two-stroke Cycle and Four-stroke-Cycle Engines. It might appear that a two-stroke cycle engine could produce twice as much horsepower as a four-stroke-cycle engine of the same size, operating at the same speed. However, this is not the case. In order to scavenge the burned gases at the end of the power stroke and during the time both the intake and exhaust ports are open, the fresh fuel-air mixture rushes into and through the cylinder. A portion of the fresh fuel-air mixture mingles with the burned gases and is carried out the exhaust port. Also, due to the much shorter period the intake port is open (as compared to the period the intake valve in a four-stroke-cycle engine is open), a

relatively smaller amount of fuel-air mixture is admitted. Hence, with less fuel-air mixture, less power per power stroke is produced as compared to the power produced in a four-stroke-cycle engine of like size operating at the same speed, and with other condition being the same. To increase the amount of fuel-air mixture, auxiliary devices are used with two-stroke-cycle engine to assure delivery of greater amounts of fuel-air mixture into the cylinder. Fig. 7 shows one device which utilizes compression in the crankcase (1 above). Other engines may use a blower or supercharger.

C. Diesel Engines. The diesel engine bears the name of Dr. Rudolph Diesel, a German engineer. He is credited with constructing, in 1897, the first successful diesel engine using liquid fuel. His objective was an engine with greater fuel economy than the steam engine, which used only a small percentage of the energy contained in the coal burned under its boilers. Dr. diesel originally planned to use pulverized coal as fuel, but his first experimental engine in 1893 was a failure. After a second engine also failed, he changed his plan and used liquid fuel. The engine then proved successful.

D. Diesel Engines Compared to Gasoline Engines

1. General Mechanical Construction. The diesel engine is mechanically similar to the gasoline engine but is somewhat heavier in construction. Both engine types utilize air, fuel, compression, and ignition. Intake, compression, power, and exhaust occur in the same sequence; arrangements of pistons, connecting rods, and crankshafts are similar. Both are internal combustion engines; that is, they extract energy from a fuel-air mixture by burning the mixture inside the engine.

2. Fuel Intake and Ignition of Fuel-Air Mixture. In principles of operation, the main difference between gasoline and diesel engines (Figs. 8 and 9) is the two different methods of introducing the fuel into the cylinder and of igniting the fuel-air mixture. Fuel and air are mixed together before they enter the cylinder of a gasoline engine. The mixture is compressed by the upstroke of the piston and is ignited within the cylinder by a spark plug. (Devices other than spark plugs, such as "firing tubes," are sometimes utilized.) Air alone enters the cylinder of a diesel engine. The air is compressed by the upstroke of the piston and the diesel fuel is injected into the combustion chamber near the top of the upstroke (compression stroke). The air becomes greatly heated during compression and the diesel fuel ignites and burns as it is injected into the heated air. No spark plug is used in the diesel engine; ignition is by contact of the fuel with the heated air, although "glow plugs" are used in some models of diesel engines to assist in starting. Pressure developed by the compression stroke is much greater in the diesel engine, in which pressures as high as 500 psi are common. For each pound of pressure exerted on the air, there will be a temperature increase of about 2°F. At the top of the compression stroke (when pressure is highest), the temperature in the chamber will be about 1,000°F. This heat ignites the fuel almost as soon as it is injected into the cylinder, and the piston, actuated by the expansion of burning gases, then moves down on the power stroke. In a gasoline engine, the heat from compression is not enough to ignite the fuel-air mixture and a spark plus is therefore necessary.

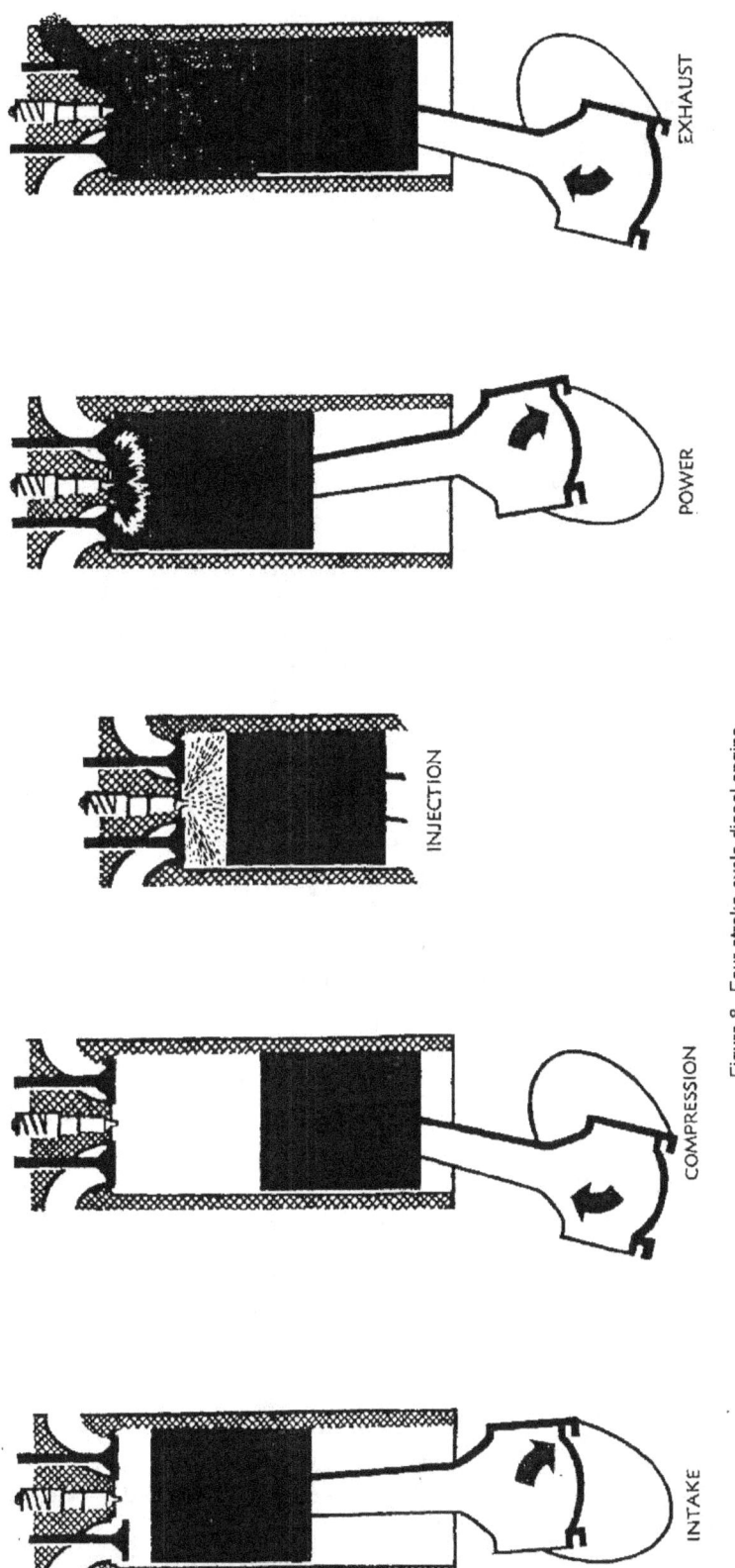

Figure 8. Four-stroke-cycle diesel engine.

GASOLINE	INTAKE STROKE	DIESEL
ON DOWNWARD STROKE OF PISTON, INTAKE VALVE OPENS AND ATMOSPHERIC PRESSURE FORCES AIR THROUGH CARBURETOR WHERE IT PICKS UP A METERED COMBUSTIBLE CHARGE OF FUEL. THE MIXTURE GOES PAST THE THROTTLE VALVE INTO CYLINDER SPACE VACATED BY THE PISTON	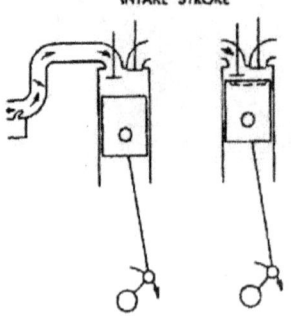	ON DOWNWARD STROKE OF PISTON, INTAKE VALVE OPENS AND ATMOSPHERIC PRESSURE FORCES PURE AIR INTO THE CYLINDER SPACE VACATED BY THE PISTON, THERE BEING NO CARBURETOR OR THROTTLE VALVE. CYLINDER FILLS WITH SAME QUANTITY OF AIR, REGARDLESS OF LOAD ON THE ENGINE.
	COMPRESSION STROKE	
ON UPSTROKE OF PISTON, VALVES ARE CLOSED AND MIXTURE IS COMPRESSED, USUALLY FROM 70 TO 125 PSI, DEPENDING ON COMPRESSION RATIO OF ENGINE.	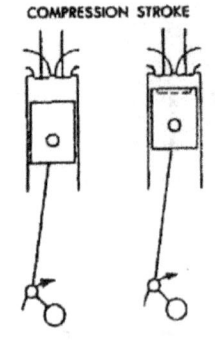	ON UPSTROKE OF PISTON, VALVES ARE CLOSED AND AIR IS COMPRESSED TO APPROXIMATELY 500 PSI.
	POWER STROKE	
COMPRESSED FUEL-AIR MIXTURE IS IGNITED BY ELECTRIC SPARK. HEAT OF COMBUSTION CAUSES FORCEFUL EXPANSION OF CYLINDER GASES AGAINST PISTON, RESULTING IN POWER STROKE.	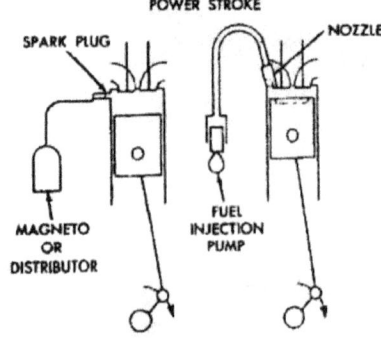	HIGH COMPRESSION PRODUCES HIGH TEMPERATURE FOR SPONTANEOUS IGNITION OF FUEL INJECTED NEAR END OF COMPRESSION STROKE. HEAT OF COMBUSTION EXPANDS CYLINDER GASES AGAINST PISTON, RESULTING IN POWER STROKE.
	EXHAUST STROKE	
UPSTROKE OF PISTON WITH EXHAUST VALVE OPEN FORCES BURNED GASES OUT, MAKING READY FOR ANOTHER INTAKE STROKE.	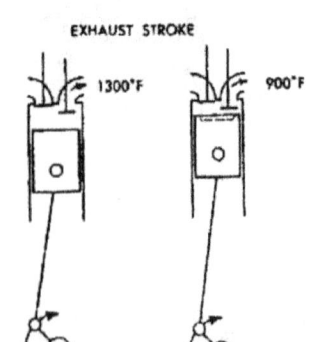	UPSTROKE OF PISTON WITH EXHAUST VALVE OPEN FORCES BURNED GASES OUT, MAKING READY FOR ANOTHER INTAKE STROKE.

Figure 9. Comparison of sequence of events in diesel and gasoline engines.

3. Control of Speed and Power. The speed and power output of diesel engines are controlled by the quantity of fuel injected into the cylinder. This is opposed to the common gasoline engine, which controls speed and power output by limiting the amount of air admitted to the carburetor. The difference is that the diesel engine controls the quantity of fuel, whereas the gasoline engine regulates the quantity of air. In the diesel engine, a varying amount of fuel is mixed with a constant amount of compressed air inside the cylinder. A full charge of air enters the cylinder on each intake stroke. Because the quantity of air is constant, the amount of fuel injected determines power output and speed. As long as the amount of fuel is injected is below the maximum established by the manufacturer in designing the engine, there is always enough air in the cylinder for complete combustion. A device in the carburetor of the gasoline engine controls the amount of air admitted. The amount of air and its velocity, in turn, control the quantity of fuel that is picked up and mixed with air to be admitted to the cylinder. The amount of mixture available for combustion determines power output and speed. It is apparent, therefore, that the controlling factor is the quantity and velocity of air passing through the carburetor.

4. Combustion Process. In the diesel engine, there is continuous combustion during the entire length of the power stroke, and pressure resulting from combustion remains approximately constant throughout the stroke. In the gasoline engine, however, combustion is completed while the piston is at the upper part of its travel. This means that the volume of the mixture stays about the same during most of the combustion process. When the piston does move down and the volume increases, there is little additional combustion to maintain pressure. Because of these facts, the cycle of the gasoline engine is often referred to as having *constant-volume* combustion while the diesel cycle is said to have *constant-pressure* combustion.

IV. ENGINE MEASUREMENTS

A. Bore and Stroke. The size of an engine cylinder is usually indicated in terms of bore and stroke (Fig. 10). *Bore* is the diameter of the cylinder. *Stroke* is the distance the piston moves in the cylinder, or the distance between top dead center and bottom dead center. When reference is made to these two measurements, the bore is always given first. For example, a 3 5/8 x 4 cylinder means that the cylinder bore, or diameter, is 3 5/8 inches and the length of the stroke is 4 inches.

B. Piston Displacement. Piston displacement is the volume of space that the piston displaces as it moved from bottom dead center to top dead center. The volume is figured by multiplying the length of stroke by the area of a circle having the diameter of the cylinder bore. Thus, a 5/8-inch-diameter circle has an area of 10.321 square inches, and, therefore, this times 4 inches (length of stroke) equals 41.284 cubic inches, the piston displacement, that is, the number of cubic inches the piston displaces as it moves from bottom dead center to top dead center.

C. Vacuum in Cylinder on Intake Stroke. The piston in moving down on the intake stroke, produces a partial vacuum in the cylinder. It is this vacuum that is responsible for air rushing in to fill the vacuum. A vacuum can be defined as an absence of air or other substances. It may be hard to think of air as a substance because it does not seem substantial, but it can be felt as a breeze or wind when it is moving.

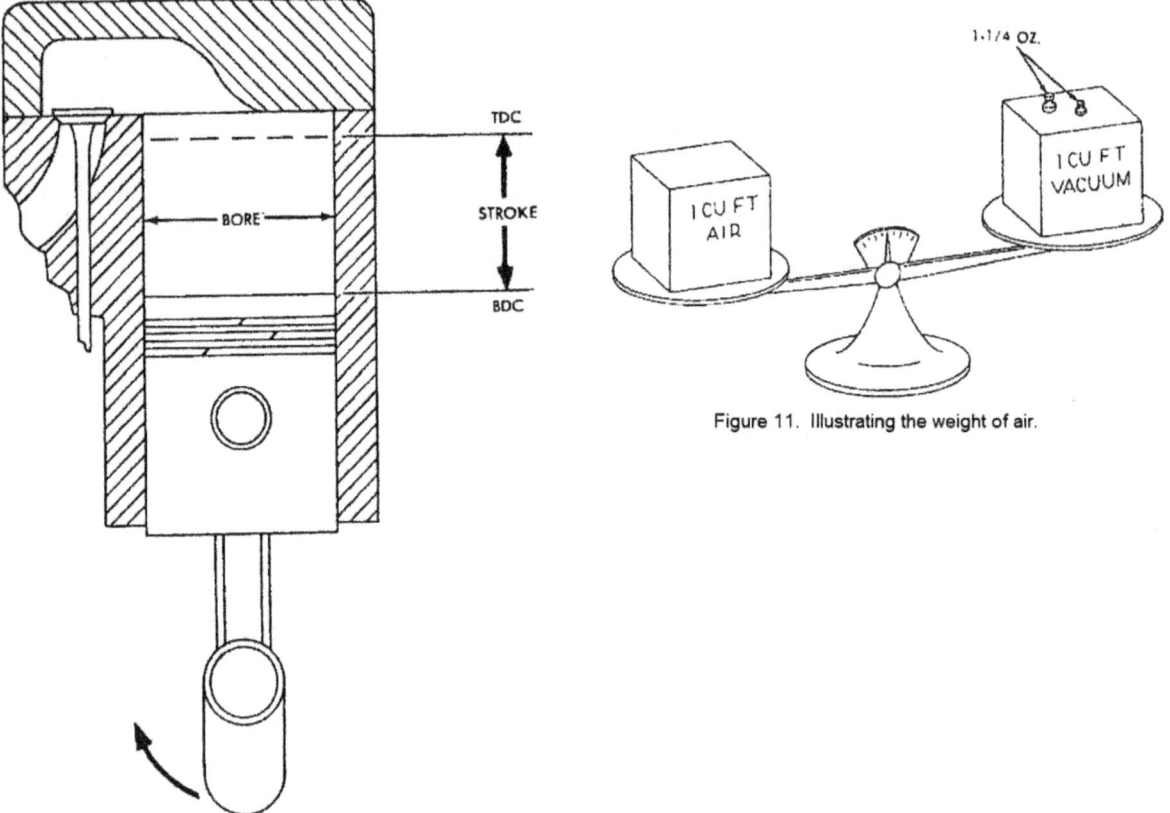

Figure 10. Bore and stroke of an engine cylinder.

Figure 11. Illustrating the weight of air.

1. The Atmosphere. Air does have weight, as can be proven with a balance scale and two 1-cubic-foot containers (Fig. 11). If all air was drawn from one container so that it would be really empty (a vacuum), then it would weigh less than the other container. In fact, to balance the scales, 1¼ ounces would have to be placed on the empty container. At sea level, the weight of the air, pressing downward on the ground, produces a pressure of about 14.7 psi. This amount of pressure means there is a great deal of air above us and there is a great amount of air surrounding the earth. This air, called the *atmosphere*, extends many miles above the earth. The atmosphere is a great ocean of air, and we live at the bottom of it, on the ground.

2. Atmospheric Pressure. The miles and miles of air extending above presses downward, or exerts pressure. Ordinarily this pressure is not noticed because we are accustomed to it. If the air was removed from a container and then the container was opened, this pressure would push air back into the container. This might be compared to what happens when an empty bottle is held under water and the cork is removed. The pressure of the water pushes water into the bottle. The higher we go into the air, as for instance when in an airplane, the less pressure is found. The reason for this is that as we ascend there is less air above us; we climb toward the top of the atmosphere. This means there is less

air to press down on us and therefore the pressure is less. Six miles above the earth, for example, the pressure is only about 4.4 psi. Returning to earth, the air pressure increases. The nearer earth is approached, or the bottom of the ocean of air, the greater the pressure of the air. At sea level, this pressure is about 14.7 psi (1 above).

3. Vacuum in the Cylinder. When the piston starts to move downward in the cylinder on the intake stroke, it produces a vacuum in the cylinder. If both the intake and exhaust valves were closed, then no substance could enter to fill this vacuum. The cylinder would remain empty. However, at the same time that the piston starts to move down, the intake valve is opened. Now, atmospheric pressure pushes air past the intake valve and into the cylinder. The cylinder, therefore, becomes filled with air (or with fuel-air mixture in gasoline engines).

D. Volumetric Efficiency. Although the atmosphere exerts considerable pressure and rapidly forces air into the cylinder on the intake stroke, it does take time for the air to flow through the carburetor and past the intake valve. If given enough time, enough air will flow into the cylinder to "fill it up." However, the air is given very little time to do this. For example, when the engine is running at 1,200 rpm, the intake stroke lasts only 0.025 second. In this very brief period, all the air that could enter does not have time to flow into the cylinder. The intake stroke ends too quickly. Nevertheless, engine design has taken this factor into consideration so that good operation will result even at high engine speed.

1. Measuring Volumetric Efficiency. This measure of the amount of fuel-air mixture that actually enters the cylinder is referred to in terms of *volumetric efficiency*. Volumetric efficiency is the ratio between the amount of fuel-air mixture that actually enters the cylinder and the amount that could enter under ideal conditions. The greater the volumetric efficiency, the greater the amount of fuel-air mixture entering the cylinder. And the greater the amount of fuel-air mixture, the more power produced from the engine cylinder. At low speeds, more fuel-air mixture can get into the cylinder, and therefore the power produced during the power stroke is greater. Volumetric efficiency is high. But at high speeds, the shorter time taken by the intake stroke reduces the amount of fuel-air mixture entering the cylinder. Volumetric efficiency then is lower. In addition, the air is heated as it passes through hot manifolds on its way to the cylinder, and it therefore expands. This further reduces the amount of fuel-air mixture entering the cylinder and further reduce volumetric efficiency.

2. Increasing Volumetric Efficiency. Volumetric efficiency is higher at low engine speed because more fuel-air mixture gets into the cylinder ((1) above). Volumetric efficiency can also be improved by use of a blower, or air-compressing, device. On gasoline engines, this device is called a *supercharger*. It raises the air pressure above atmospheric pressure so that the air is pushed harder on its way into the cylinder. The harder push, or higher pressure, insures that more air will enter the cylinder. In a supercharged engine, the volumetric efficiency can run well over 100 percent. Since 100 percent efficiency means that the pressure inside the cylinder equals atmospheric pressure, a volumetric efficiency of more than 100 percent means the pressure inside the cylinder would be greater than atmospheric pressure at the end of the intake stroke. This

increased volumetric efficiency increases engine power output. A supercharger is very important on airplane engines because the lowered air pressure (about 4.4 psi at a height of 6 miles) must be greatly increased if engine power output is to be maintained at high altitudes. Also, on two-stroke-cycle engines, some form of device is required to increase the pressure of the ingoing fuel-air mixture (par. III.B.

E. Compression Ratio. The compression ratio of an engine (Fig. 12) is the volume in one cylinder with the piston at bottom dead center (displacement volume plus clearance volume) divided by the volume with the piston at top dead center (clearance volume). This figure indicates the actual amount that the air drawn into the cylinder will be compressed. For example, suppose that an engine cylinder has an air volume of 63 cubic inches with the piston at bottom dead center and a volume of 10 cubic inches with the piston at top dead center. This gives a compression ratio of 63 divided by 10 or 6.3:1. That is, the air is compressed from 64 to 10 cubic inches, or to 1/63 of its original volume, on the compression stroke.

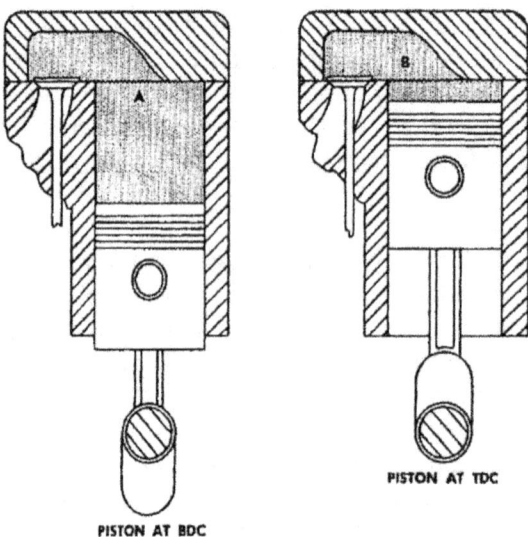

Figure 12. Compression ratio between "A" and "B".

F. Effect of Increasing Compression Ratio. As compression ratio is increased, the fuel-air mixture drawn into the cylinder is compressed into a smaller space. This means a higher initial pressure at the start of the power stroke. It also means that the burning gases can expand a greater amount. Thus, there are higher pressures for a longer period on the power stroke. More power is obtained with each power stroke. Therefore, increasing compression ratio increases power output of an engine. Racing-car builders machine off cylinder heads so as to reduce the volume of the combustion chamber and thereby increase compression ratios. By this one act, the power output of an engine can be increased several horsepower. One important problem brought about by increasing compression ratios is to find a fuel that will not cause difficulty from detonation.

V. TIMING

In a gasoline engine, the valves must open and close at the proper times with regard to piston position and stroke. In addition, the ignition system must produce the sparks at the spark plugs at the proper time so the power strokes can start. Both valve and ignition system action must be properly timed if good engine performance is to be obtained.

A. **Valve Timing.** A new mixture must be trapped in the cylinder at the proper time during each cycle and, after combustion, the exhaust gases must be allowed to flow out of the cylinder. This means that the intake and exhaust valves must open and close in step with the piston movement. The opening and closing of the valves is controlled by the camshaft. The position of the piston is related to the position of the crankshaft since they are connected by the connecting rod. Thus, the crankshaft and camshaft must be in the proper relationship for correct valve timing. Figure 1 shows one method of driving the camshaft; a gear on the crankshaft drives a gear on the camshaft. These gears are called *timing gears*. The camshaft gear has twice as many teeth as the crankshaft gear (par. IIC). Thus, the camshaft turns once for every two crankshaft revolutions. As long as the relationship between the gears is not changed, the timing of the valve action will be in correct relationship to the piston movement. Figure 13 illustrates a valve timing diagram on one engine. Valve timing varies for different engines.

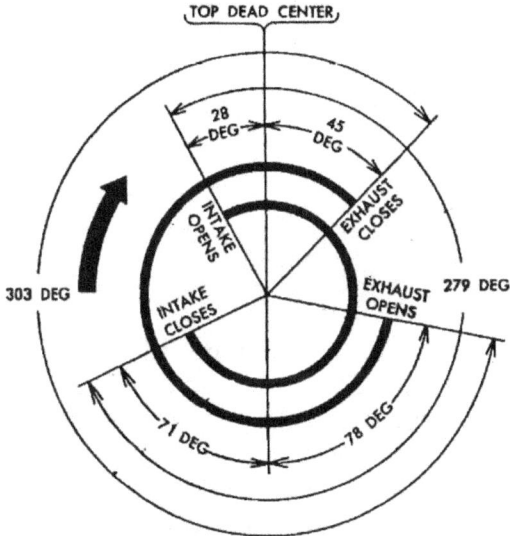

Figure 13. Valve timing diagram on one engine.

B. **Exhaust Valve Timing.** The exhaust valve opens before the piston reaches the end of the power stroke so that the pressure remaining in the cylinder will cause the exhaust gases to start rushing from the cylinder. If the valve did not open until the end of the power stroke, then there would be pressure in the cylinder at the start of the exhaust stroke that would impede the upward piston movement. Opening the exhaust valve well before bottom dead center on the power stroke causes some loss of pressure on the piston at the end of the power stroke. However, it does insure better removal of the burned gases which, plus the reduced pressure on the piston at the start of the exhaust stroke, more than balances this small loss.

C. Rock Positions. When the piston is at top dead center, the crankshaft can move 15° to 20° without causing the piston to move up or down any perceptible distance. This is one of the two rock positions (Fig. 14). When the piston moves up on the exhaust stroke, considerable momentum is imparted to the exhaust gases as they pass out through the exhaust valve port, but if the exhaust valve closes at top dead center, a small amount of the gases will be diluted. Since the piston has little downward movement while in the rock position, the exhaust valve can remain open during scavenging of the exhaust gases.

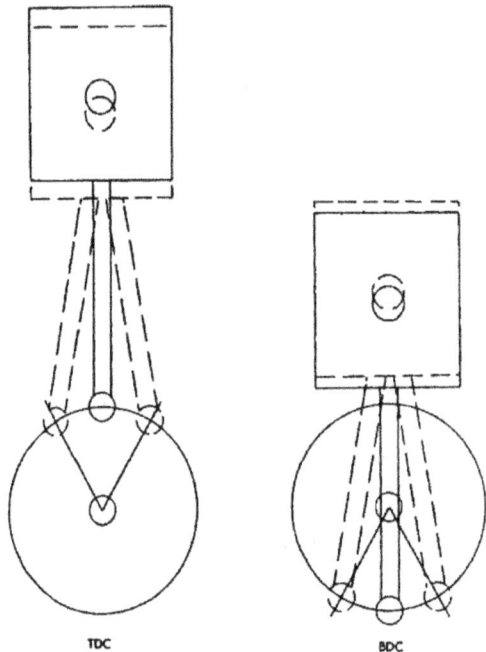

Figure 14. Rock positions.

D. Intake Valve Timing. Very little vacuum is produced in the cylinder as the piston passes through the rock position at top dead center. The exhaust gases, however, because of their momentum in passing through the exhaust valve port, produce an air current in the chamber. This air current is sufficient to cause a new mixture to start moving into the cylinder if the intake valve is open. For this reason, the intake valve is opened slightly before the piston reaches top dead center. As the piston goes down on the intake stroke, the rapid decrease in pressure in the cylinder enables atmospheric pressure to impart considerable momentum to the incoming mixture. If the piston were to move slowly, the mixture would be able to enter fast enough to keep the pressure in the cylinder equal to that outside. But ordinarily, the piston will be moving so fast that it will reach the end of its downward stroke before a complete change has had time to enter. That is, the pressure in the cylinder will be below that of the atmosphere. The intake valve therefore remains open a number of additional degrees of crankshaft rotation pat bottom dead center (or through the lower rock position). This allows additional time for fuel-air mixture to flow into the cylinder.

E. Ignition Timing. Ignition timing refers to the timing of the spark at the spark plug gap with relation to the piston position during the compression and power strokes. Even though the compressed fuel-air mixture burns very rapidly, almost explosively, it does take some time for the mixture to burn and for the pressure increase from combustion to take place. Therefore, it is common for the ignition system to be so timed that the spark occurs before the piston reaches top dead center on the compression stroke. This gives the mixture sufficient time to ignite and start burning. If this time were not provided, that is, if the spark occurred at or after top dead center, then the pressure increase would not keep pace with the piston movement. The piston would be moving down on the power stroke as the mixture started to burn. The pressure, therefore, would not go very high and power would be lost. This power loss is avoided by timing the spark to occur before top dead center.

F. Ignition Advance. At the higher speeds, there is still less time for the fuel-air mixture to ignite and burn. In order to compensate for this, and thereby avoid power loss, the ignition system includes an advance mechanism that functions on speed. As engine speed increases, the advance mechanism causes the spark to occur earlier in the cycle. Thus, at high speed, the spark may occur as much as 30° before top dead center on the compression stroke. This means that the fuel-air mixture is ignited and starts to burn well before the power stroke actually starts. However, the piston is up over top dead center and moving down on the power stroke before the pressure rises to any great extent. This extra time gives the mixture ample time to burn well and deliver maximum push to the downward-moving piston. On most distributors, there is also a vacuum-advance mechanism which functions on intake-manifold vacuum. At part throttle, there is a partial vacuum in the intake manifold, and less fuel-air mixture is getting into the cylinder. With less fuel-air mixture, the mixture is less highly compressed and burns more slowly. Therefore, the vacuum-advance mechanism provides a spark which gives the mixture ample time to burn and increase pressure in the cylinder in the early part of the power stroke.

VI. ENGINE OUTPUT

Engines vary in size and output. To compare engines, compare not only their size, but also the work they can do. These functions are explained in A through J below.

A. Work. Work is the movement of a body against an opposing force. When a weight is lifted from the ground, work is done on the weight. It is moved upward against the force of gravity. When a tank pushes over a tree, it does work on the tree as it forces it to the ground. If a 1-pound weight is lifted one foot, one *foot-pound* of work is done.

B. Energy. Energy is the ability to do work. As the speed of a tank is increased, the energy of movement of the tank is increased. It can thereby knock over a tree more easily. The higher a weight is lifted from the ground, the more energy is stored in the weight. Then, when it falls, it will strike the ground harder; that is, it will do more work on the ground. Suppose a stake is being driven in the ground. The greater the distance the weight falls, the more work it does on the stake and the farther it drives it into the ground.

C. Power. Power is the rate of work. It takes more power to work fast than to work slowly. Engines are rated in terms of the amount of work they can do per minute. A large engine that can do more work per minute is more powerful than a small engine which cannot work so hard. The work capacity of engines is measured in *horsepower*. A horsepower is a definite amount of power. Actually, it is the amount of power that an average horse was found to develop when working hard in tests made many years ago at the time steam engines were being developed. It was found that an average horse could lift a weight of 200 pounds a distance of 165 feet in 1 minute. The amount of work involved here is 33,000 foot-pounds (165 times 200). If 100 pounds were lifted 330 feet, or if 330 pounds were lifted 100 feet, the amount of work would be the same, 33,000 foot-pounds. When this amount of work is done in 1 minute, then 1 horsepower is required. If it took 2 minutes to do this amount of work, then 16,500 foot-pounds per minute, or ½ hp, would be required. Or, if 33,000 foot-pounds of work were done in ½ minute, or 2 hp, would be required.

D. Prony Brake. A prony brake may be used to measure the actual horsepower that an engine can deliver. This device usually makes use of a series of wooden blocks fitted around a special flywheel that is driven by the engine (Fig. 15). A tightening device is arranged so the blocks can be tightened on the flywheel. In addition, an arm is attached to this tightening device and one end of the arm rests on a scale. In operation, the wooden blocks are tightened on the flywheel. This loads up the engine and works it harder. Also, the pressure on the blocks tends to cause the arm to turn so that force is exerted on the scales. The length of the arm times the force exerted on the scales gives the engine torque in pound-feet (F below). The results of the prony brake test can be converted into brake horsepower by using the formula:

Bhp = $\frac{2\pi lnw}{33,000}$ where l is length of the arm in feet, n is the speed in rpm, and w is the load in pounds on the scale. For example, suppose the arm is 3 feet long, the load on the scale is 50 pounds, and the speed is 1,000 rpm. Substituting in the formula gives:

Bhp = $\frac{2 \times 3.1416 \times 3 \times 1,000 \times 50}{33,000}$ = 28.56 brake horsepower.

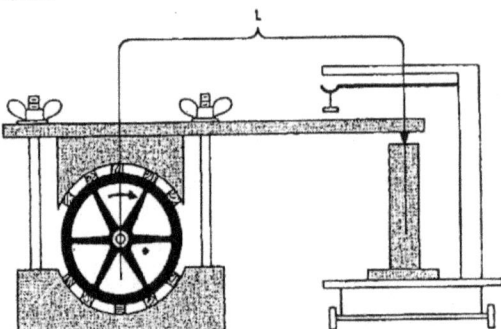

Figure 15. Simplified drawing of a prony brake.

E. Dynamometer. The dynamometer is essentially a dynamo of a special type which can be driven by an engine. This special dynamo can absorb all the power the engine can produce and indicate this power on dials or gages. Although the dynamometer is more complicated than a prony brake, it is generally considered to be more flexible and accurate. In addition to measuring engine power output, the dynamometer can also be used to drive the engine for purposes of measuring the friction of the engine itself or of the various accessories.

F. Torque Effect.

1. Torque is twisting, or turning, effort. When the lid on a jar is loosened, a twisting force, or torque, is applied to it (Figure 16). Torque is measured in *pound-feet*

(not too be confused with work, which is measured in foot-pounds). For instance, suppose a wrench is used to tighten a nut on a stud (Fig. 17). If the handle of the wrench were 1-foot long and a 10-pound fore is put on its end, 10 pound-feet of torque would be applied on the nut. If the handle were 2 feet long and 10-pound force is put on its end, 20 pound-feet of torque would be applied. Torque can be converted into work with the formula ft-lb (work) = 2π n × lb-ft (torque) = 6.2832n × lb-ft where n is the speed in revolutions per minute. For example, if an engine were checked on a prony brake and found to be delivering 100 pound-feet torque at 1,000 rpm then it would be doing 628,320 foot-pounds of work every minute. This can be converted into horsepower by dividing it by 33,000 (D above). An illustration of a torque wrench in use is shown in Fig. 18.

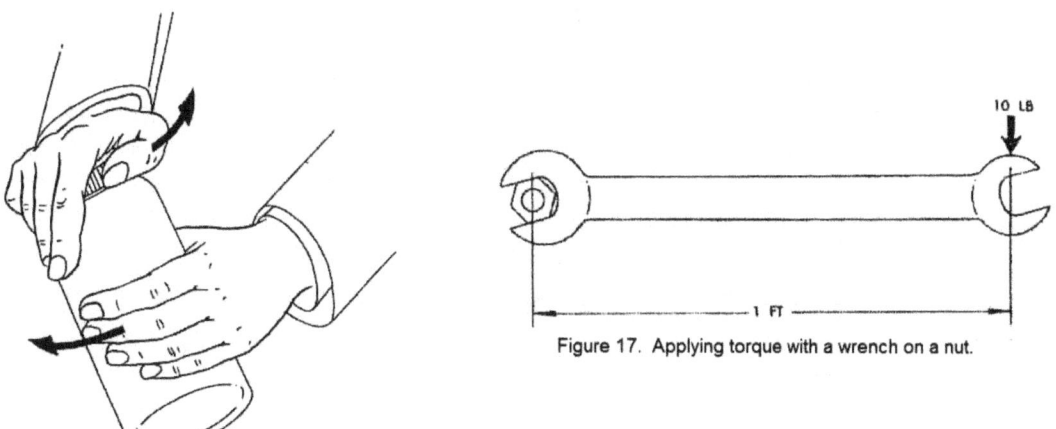

Figure 17. Applying torque with a wrench on a nut.

Figure 16. Applying twisting effort, or torque, on can lid.

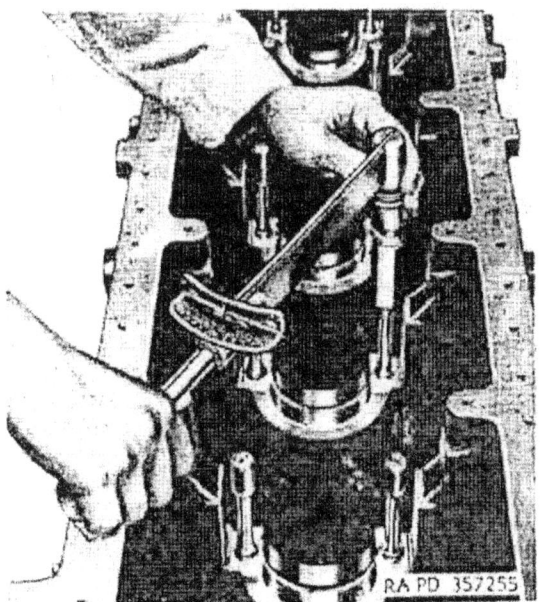

Figure 18. Torque wrench in use, tightening main bearing studs of an engine.

2. The engine exerts torque through gears and shafts connected to the wheels so that the wheels turn and the vehicle moves. The amount of torque that an engine produces varies with engine speed (Fig. 19). Note that torque increases and then, at an intermediate speed, falls off. The reason for this variation is that, with increasing speed, the engine is turning faster and is thus capable of supplying a greater twisting effort, or torque. However, with further speed increases, volumetric efficiency falls off. Less fuel-air mixture gets to the cylinders each intake stroke and thus the power strokes are not as powerful; torque falls off.

G. Torque-Horsepower-Speed (RPM) Relationship

1. Figure 20 shows the comparison between the horsepower and torque of an engine. Torque increases with speed (up to rated speed) as shown in Fig. 19. Horsepower also shows a change with speed, and this is more marked than with torque. Horsepower is directly related to both torque and to speed. When both torque and speed are on the increase, as in the speed range of 1,200 to 1,600 rpm, then horsepower goes up sharply. When torque reaches maximum and then begins to taper off, the horsepower curve starts to drop. Finally, in the higher speed ranges, where torque falls off sharply, horsepower also falls off. The horsepower formula (Hp = $\frac{2\pi l w}{33,000}$ given in D above shows that horsepower depends on both speed and torque, since torque equals lw and n is speed. Substituting in the formula and dividing 2π (or 6.2832) into 33,000 gives Hp = $\frac{\text{torque} \times \text{rpm}}{5,252}$, which shows the relationship between horsepower, torque, and speed more directly.

2. A *rated speed* is indicated in Figs. 19 and 20. This is the speed at which the governor is usually set in military vehicles. The rated speed is selected because, at higher engine speeds, wear on the engine increases rapidly and a disproportionate amount of fuel is used. Overspeeding, or driving the engine above rated speed, allows but a slight increase of horsepower.

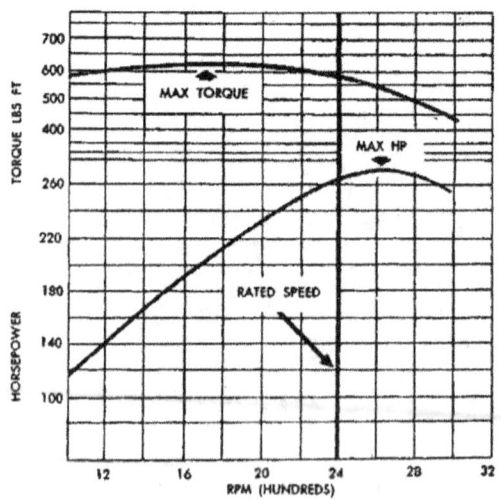

Figure 20. Relationship between torque and horsepower.

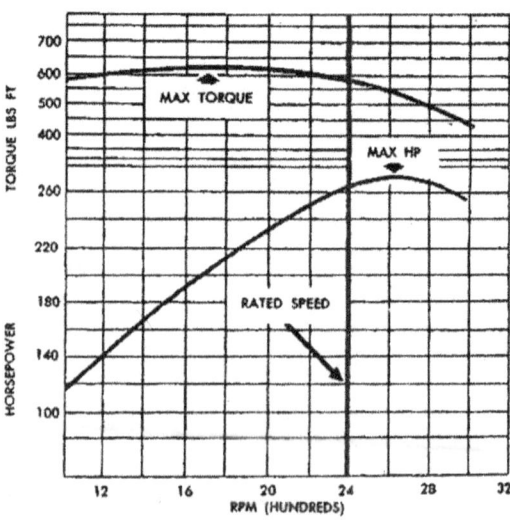

Figure 20. Relationship between torque and horsepower.

H. Gross and Net Horsepower. The gross horsepower of an engine is the amount of power the engine delivers after it has been stripped of muffler, fan, generator, pump, and other accessories that require power to operate. Net horsepower is the power remaining and actually available to drive the vehicle. Net horsepower is the power available at the flywheel after the accessories have detracted from the gross horsepower.

I. Indicated Horsepower. Indicated horsepower is the horsepower actually developed inside the engine cylinders. It is called "indicated" horsepower because an indicating device is required to measure this horsepower. This device measures the pressure developed in the engine cylinders and, by a series of steps, translates this data into indicated horsepower is always considerably greater than horsepower delivered by the engine because power is lost from the engine in a number of ways (friction, heat-loss, etc.).

J. SAE Horsepower. The Society of Automotive Engineers (SAE) developed a simplified method of calculating horsepower, based on engine dimensions. This rating was used only for commercial licensing of vehicles. The formula is: $Hp = \frac{DN}{2.5}$ where D is the cylinder diameter and N is the number of cylinders.

VII. ENGINE EFFICIENCY

The term *efficiency* means the relationship between results obtained and the effort required to obtain those results. It is expressed as: efficiency = $\frac{output}{input}$. Suppose, for example, a set of pulleys were used to raise a 450-pound weight 2 feet and this required a 100-pound pull for 10 feet (Fig. 21). It would take 1,000 foot-pounds to get out 900 foot-pounds. The ratio would be $\frac{900}{1,000}$ or 0.90. In other words, the efficiency of the pulleys would be 90 percent. There was a loss of 10 percent of the work put in. The system of pulleys shows a loss (or is only 90 percent efficient) because of friction. No machine or engine is 100 percent efficient; all lose energy, as explained in A, B, and C below.

A. Friction Loss. Friction is source of energy loss in any mechanical system. If a heavy plank is dragged across a rough floor, it offers some resistance to the movement. This resistance to movement would be less if the plank and floor were polished smooth. Resistance would be still less if the plank floated in water. This resistance to movement is called *friction*. Friction can be visualized as being caused by tiny irregularities, or high points, on the surfaces of the moving objects. These catch on each other and particles are torn off. All this requires force to overcome. If the plank and floor are made smooth, then the projecting points are much smaller and have less tendency to catch and tear off. Therefore, less force is required to pull the plank across the floor. And if the plank is floated in water, the surfaces can no longer rub against each other. There is, however, still some friction in the liquid. In the engine, friction occurs at all moving parts, even though the parts are, in effect, floated in films of oil.

B. Mechanical Efficiency. The mechanical efficiency of the engine is the relationship between the power produced in the engine cylinders indicated horsepower) and the power delivered by the engine (brake horsepower). Internal engine losses from friction and other factors always prevent brake horsepower from equaling indicated horsepower. A typical engine, for example, might develop 200 indicated horsepower as against an actual brake horsepower of 180. This engine would have a mechanical efficiency of: $\frac{\text{Brake Horsepower}}{\text{Indicated Horsepower}} = \frac{180}{200} = 90$ percent.

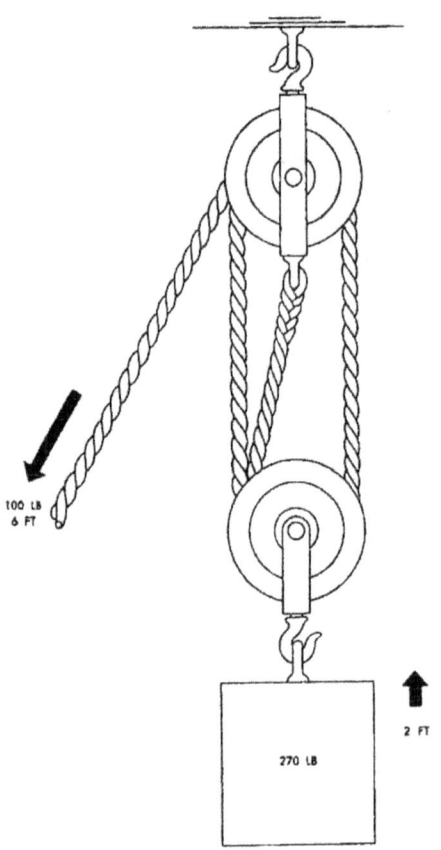

Figure 21. System of pulley in which 1,000 foot-pounds must be expended to realize 900 foot-pounds of work.

C. Thermal Efficiency.

1. Thermal efficiency is the relationship between the heat energy in the fuel and the engine power output (thermal means of or pertaining to heat). The term *thermal efficiency* relates the heat energy of the fuel and the work output. The heat energy is the amount of heat the fuel will produce as it burns. Much of this heat is lost to the cylinder walls and cooling system. Still more is lost in the hot exhaust gases as they pass out of the cylinder. This heat that is lost cannot do anything to cause the engine to produce power. Therefore, only a relatively small part of the heat in the burning fuel can contribute anything toward pushing down on the pistons and thereby causing the engine to produce power. In actual practice, because of the great amount of heat lost to the cooling water, lubricating oil, and in the exhaust gases, thermal efficiency may be as low as 20 percent. In other words, as much as 80 percent of the energy in the fuel is lost. However, the remaining 20 percent is sufficient to operate the engine normally. Practical limitations prevent thermal efficiencies of much above 25 percent.

2. The overall thermal efficiency of an engine is the relationship between the fuel input and the power output. This relationship is commonly expressed in heat units called *British thermal units* (Btu). One Btu is equal to 778 ft.-lb. of work; therefore, the horsepower output of an engine can be readily converted into Btu per unit of time. The source of power in an engine is fuel, and the Btu content of regularly-used fuels has been determined by laboratory analysis: Thermal efficiency = $\frac{\text{power output in Btu}}{\text{fuel input in Btu}}$. Example: An engine delivers 85 bhp for a period of 1 hour and in that time consumes 50 pounds (approx. 7½ gals) of gasoline. Assuming that the gasoline has a value of 18,800 Btu per lb., we find the thermal efficiency of the engine:

Power delivered by engine is 85 bhp for 1 hour, or 85 hp-hours.

1 hp hour = $\frac{33{,}000 \text{ ft–lb per min} \times 60 \text{ min}}{778 \text{ ft–lb per Btu}}$ = 2,545 Btu.

88 bhp × 2,545 Btu = 216,325 Btu output.

50 lb. × 18,800 Btu per lb = 940,000 Btu input per hour

Overall thermal efficiency = $\frac{216{,}325}{940{,}000}$ = 0.230, or 23 percent.

VIII. ADVANTAGES OF MULTICYLINDER ENGINES

A. Power Increase. In early automotive vehicles, 1-cylinder and some 3-cylinder engines were used, but the many advantages of a larger number of cylinders soon led to the adoption of 4-, 6-, 8-, 12-, and 16-cylinder engines. Although the power stroke of each piston theoretically continues for 180° of crankshaft rotation, best results can be obtained if the exhaust valve is opened when the power stroke has completed about four-fifths of its travel. Therefore, the period that power is delivered during 720° of crankshaft rotation, or one 4-stroke cycle, will be 145° multiplied by the number of cylinders in the engine. If an engine has two cylinders, power will be transmitted for 290° of the 720° of travel necessary to complete the four events of the cycle. The flywheel (Par 29) must supply power for the remaining 430° of crankshaft travel.

B. Power Overlap. As cylinders are added to an engine, each one must complete the four steps of the cycle during two revolutions of the crankshaft. The number of power impulses for each revolution also increases, producing smoother operation. If there are more than four cylinders, the power strokes overlap as shown in Fig. 22. The length of overlap increases with the number of cylinders. The diagram for the 6-cylinder engine shows a new power stroke starting each 120° of crankshaft rotation and lasting for four-fifths of a stroke, or 145°. This provides an overlap of 25°. In the 8-cylinder engine, a power stroke starts every 90° and continues for 145°, resulting in a 55° overlap of power. Because the cylinders fire at regular intervals, the power overlap will be the same regardless of firing order, and will apply to either in-line or V-type engines.

23

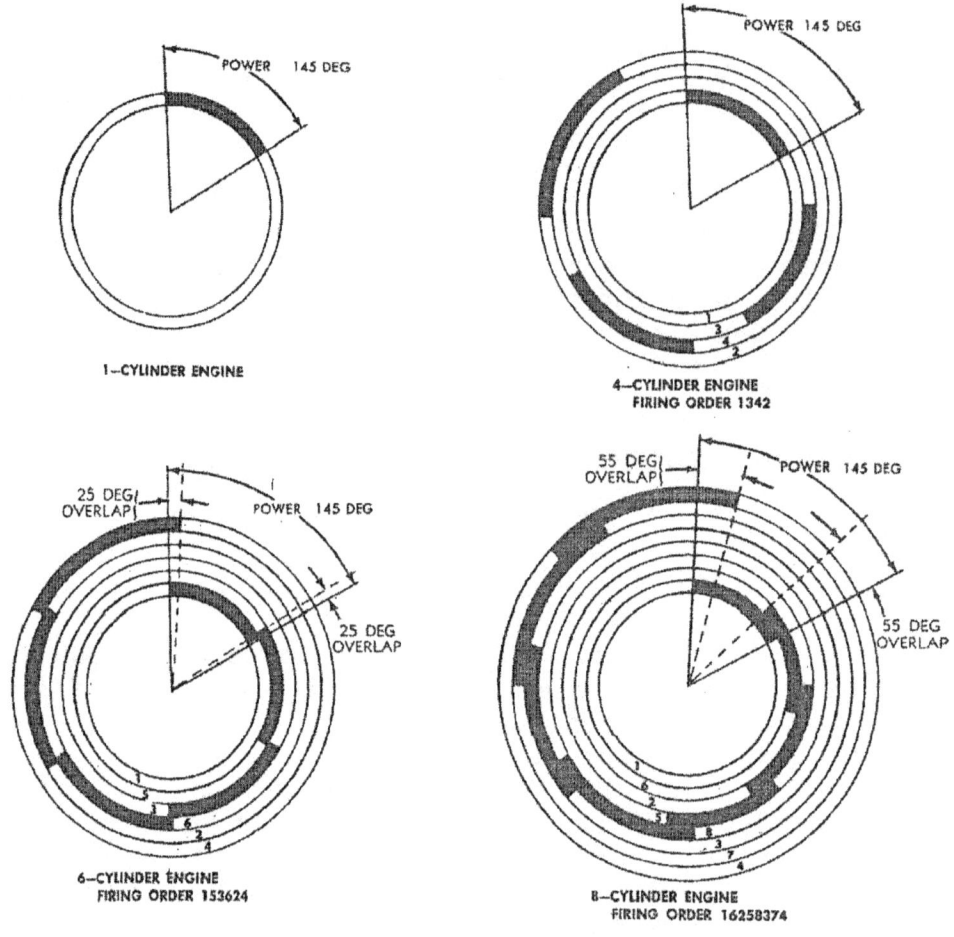

Figure 22. Power in 1-, 4-, 6-, and 8-cylinder engines.

IX. CLASSIFICATION OF ENGINES

Automotive engines may be classified according to the type of fuel they use, type of cooling employed, or valve and cylinder arrangement. They all operate on the internal combustion principle, and the application of basic principles of construction to particular needs or systems of manufacture has caused certain designs to be recognized as conventional. The most common method of classification is by type of fuel used, that is, whether the engine burns gasoline or diesel fuel.

A. Cooling. Engines are classified as to whether they are air- or liquid-cooled. All engines are cooled by air to some extent, but air-cooled engines are those in which air is the only external cooling medium. Lubricating oil and fuel helps somewhat to cool all engines, but there must be an additional external means of dissipating the heat absorbed by the engine during the power stroke.

1. Air-cooled. Although air-cooled engines are not normally used in passenger cars and commercial trucks, they are used extensively in military vehicles as well as in aircraft. This type of engine is used where there must be an economy of space and weight. It does not require a radiator, water jacket, coolant, or a pump to circulate the coolant. The cylinders are cooled by conducting the heat to metal fins on the outside of the cylinder wall and head. To effect the cooling, air is circulated between the fins. When possible, the engine is installed so that it is exposed to the air stream of the vehicle; the baffles direct the air to the fins. If the engine cannot be mounted in the air stream, a fan is employed to force the air through the baffles.

2. Water-cooled. Water-cooled engines require a water jacket to hold the coolant around the valve ports, combustion chambers, and cylinders; a radiator to dissipate the heat from the coolant to the surrounding air; and a pump to circulate the coolant through the engine. Water-cooled engines also require a fan to pass air through the radiator because the speed of the vehicle does not always force enough air through the radiator to provide proper dissipation of heat.

B. Valve Arrangement. Engines may be classified according to the position of the intake and exhaust valves, that is, whether they are in the cylinder block or in the cylinder head. Various arrangements have been used, but the most common are L-head, I-head, and F-head (Fig. 23). The letter designation is used because the shape of the combustion chamber resembles the form of the letter identifying it.

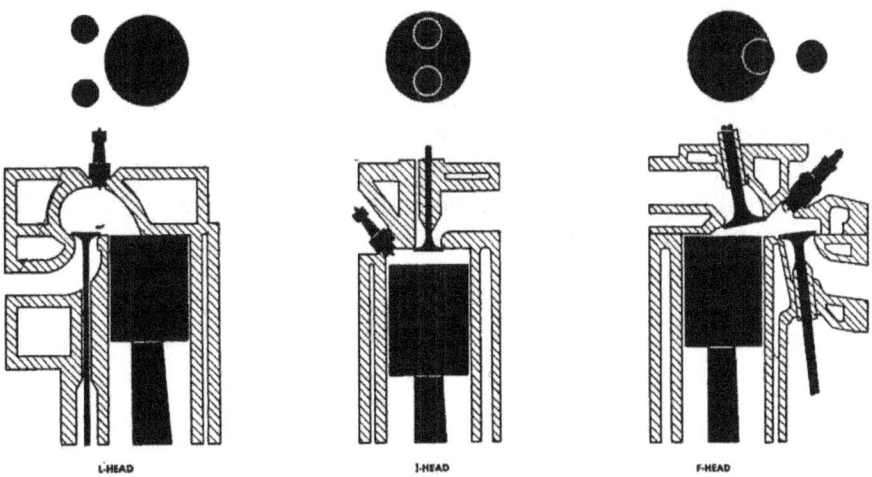

Figure 23. L-, I-, and F-head valve arrangements.

1. L-head. In the L-head engines both valves are placed in the block on the same side of the cylinder. The valve-operating mechanism is located directly below the valves, and one camshaft actuates both the intake and exhaust valves. This type has supplanted the T-head, in which both valves were in the block but on opposite sides of the cylinder. The disadvantage of the T-head was that it required two complete valve-operating mechanisms.

2. I-head. Engines using the I-head construction are commonly called *valve-in-head* or *overhead valve* engines, because the valves are mounted in the cylinder head above the cylinder. This arrangement requires a tappet, a push rod, and a rocker arm above the cylinder to reverse the direction of valve movement, but only one camshaft is required for both valve. Some overhead valve engines make use of an overhead camshaft. This arrangement eliminates the long linkage between the camshaft and valve.

3. F-head. In the F-head engine, the intake valves normally are located in the head, while the exhaust valves are located in the engine block. This arrangement combines, in effect, the L-head and the I-head valve arrangements. The valves in the head are actuated from the camshaft through tappet, push rods, and rocker arms (I-head arrangement), while the valves in the block are actuated directly from the camshaft by tappets (L-head arrangement).

C. Cylinder Arrangement. Automotive engines also vary in the arrangement of cylinders in the block, depending on the engine use. Cylinder arrangement in liquid-cooled engines is usually in-line or V-type; in air-cooled engines, it is V-type, radial, or horizontal-opposed.

1. In-line. The vertical in-line cylinder arrangement is one of the most common used types. All the cylinders are cast or assembled in a straight line above a common crankshaft which is immediately below the cylinders. A variation is the inverted in-line type.

2. V-type. In the V-type engine, two "banks" of in-line cylinders are mounted in a V-shape above a common crankshaft. This type is designated by the number of degrees in the angle between the banks of cylinders. Usually the angle of the V is 90° for 8-cylinder engines; 75°, 60°, or 45° for 12-cylinder engines; and 45° or 135° for 16-cylinder engines. Crankshafts for V-type engines generally have only half as many throws as there are cylinders, a two connecting rods (one from each bank) are connected to each throw.

3. Radial. The radial engine has cylinders placed in a circle around the crankshaft. The crankshaft has only one throw, and one piston is connected to this throw by a *master rod*. The connecting rods from the other pistons are fastened to the master rod, making the power flow first to the master rod and then to the crankshaft. The result is the same as if each rod were connected directly to the crankshaft. High-powered radial engines may have two rows of cylinders in which each row operates on its own throw of the crankshaft.

4. Horizontal-opposed. The horizontal-opposed engine has its cylinders laid on their sides in two rows, with the crankshaft in the center. Because of its low overall height, much less headroom is required for mounting the engine. It can be put under the body of a bus, for example, or can be so mounted in a tank as to provide additional interior space in the tank. This engine is often called a *pancake* engine, because it is relatively flat like a pancake.

5. Horizontal-opposed With Vertical Crankshaft. In this engine, the cylinders are horizontal and opposed to each other, but the crankshaft is set vertically. This is the same type of engine mentioned in 4 above, except that the engine has been set up on end so that the crankshaft is vertical rather than horizontal.

FUNDAMENTALS OF AUTOMOTIVE POWER TRAINS AND CHASSIS

CONTENTS

		Page
I.	POWER TRAIN COMPONENTS	1
II.	BRAKE SYSTEMS	12
III.	SUSPENSION SYSTEMS	19
IV.	FRAME	22

BASIC FUNDAMENTALS OF AUTOMOTIVE POWER TRAINS AND CHASSIS

The mechanism that transmits the power of a vehicle's engine to the wheels and accessory equipment is called the power train. In a simple situation, a set of gears or a chain and sprocket could perform this task, but automotive vehicles are not designed for simple operating conditions. They are designed to have pulling power as well as to move at high speeds, to travel in reverse as well as forward, and to operate on rough terrain as well as on smooth roads. To meet these varying demands, a number of units have been added including clutches, transmissions, propeller shafts, universal joints, differentials, and live axles.

The chassis is the assembly of mechanisms that make up the major operating part of the vehicle. It usually includes everything except the vehicle body. This assembly includes the engine, the frame which supports the engine and the power train, the steering and braking systems, and the suspension system.

This chapter provides information on the various components, or subassemblies, that make up the automotive power train and chassis. In effect, it establishes the relationship between these various parts and shows how they work together in the automotive vehicle. To maintain and service these components, or subassemblies, you must know where to find them on a vehicle. You must also understand their purpose and how they operate. This chapter contains a general discussion of these subject; the operation and maintenance manuals which accompany each piece of equipment will give you more detailed information.

I. POWER TRAIN COMPONENTS

The common elements of the power train system assembled in a typical vehicle are shown in the following figure. The main components of the power train are described as follows:

CLUTCH.
By means of the clutch, the operator can disconnect the engine from the remainder of the power train. This is essential when starting the engine, thus allowing the vehicle to stand motionless while the engine is running. It also allows gradual engagement of the engine to the power train and gear ratio changing to meet varying road conditions.

TRANSMISSION.
An internal combustion engine cannot develop appreciable torque at low speeds; it develops maximum torque only at one speed, and the crankshaft of an engine must always rotate in the same direction. Because of these limitations, a transmission is necessary in automotive vehicles. The transmission provides the mechanical advantage that enables the engine to propel the vehicle under adverse conditions of the load. It also provides the operator with a selection of vehicle speeds while the engine is held at speeds within the effective torque range, and it allows disengaging and reversing the flow of power from the engine to the wheels.

PROPELLER SHAFT.
A propeller shaft is used to transfer the power from the transmission located near the front of the vehicle to the differential near the rear.

UNIVERSAL JOINTS.

It is necessary to provide flexibility in the power train if springs are to be used on the vehicle. As the load is increased or decreased, and as the vehicle travels over uneven surfaces, the vertical distance between the transmission output shaft and the axle will change. This flexibility is provided by the use of universal joints which permit transfer of torque at an angle.

SLIP JOINTS.

As the load is changed, and as the vehicle travels over uneven ground, the distance from the axle to the transmission varies. Slip joints allow for this variation.

DIFFERENTIAL.

A differential is required to compensate for the difference in distance the rear wheels travel when the vehicle rounds a turn. The differential permits application of power to the rear wheels while allowing each wheel to turn at a different speed when the vehicle is rounding a curve.

AXLES.

An axle is a shaft supporting a vehicle on which the wheels turn. A *live axle* is one that supports part of the weight of a vehicle and also drives the wheels connected to it. A *dead axle* is one that carries part of the weight of a vehicle, but does not drive the wheels. The usual front axle of a vehicle is a dead axle and the rear axle is a live axle. In four-wheel drive vehicles, both front and rear axles are live axles, and in six-wheel drive vehicles, all three axles are live axles.

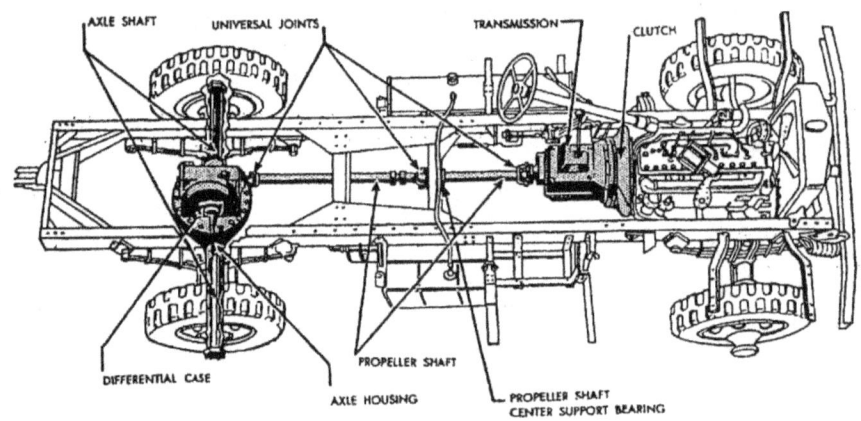

TYPICAL POWER TRAIN

THE CLUTCH

A clutch in an automotive vehicle is the mechanism in the power train that connects the engine crankshaft to, or disconnects it from, the transmission and thus the remainder of the power train. Since the internal combustion engine does not develop a high starting torque, it must be disconnected from the power train and allowed to operate without load until it develops enough torque to overcome the inertia of the vehicle when starting from rest. The application of the engine power to the load must be gradual to prove smooth engagement and to lessen the shock on the driving parts. After engagement, the clutch must transmit all the engine power to the transmission without slipping. Further, it is desirable to disconnect the engine from the power train during the time the gears in the transmission are being shifted from one gear ratio to another.

Clutches are located in the power train between the engine and the transmission assembly.

Clutches transmit power from the clutch driving plate to the driven member by friction. In the disk clutch, the driving plate or member, which is secured to the engine flywheel, is gradually brought into contact with the driven member (disk), which is attached to the transmission input shaft. The contact is made and held by strong spring pressure controlled by the operator with the clutch pedal. With only light spring pressure, there is little friction between the two members and the clutch is permitted to slip. As the spring pressure increases, friction also increases, and less slippage occurs. When the operator removes his foot from the clutch pedal and full spring pressure is applied, the speed of the driving plate and driven disk is the same, and all slipping stops. There is then a direct connection between the flywheel and transmission input shaft.

Malfunction Detection. Several types of clutch troubles that may be encountered during vehicle operation are: slipping, chattering or grabbing when engaging, spinning or dragging when engaged, and clutch noises. As an operator, you would explain the malfunction on the Operator's Trouble Report and turn the report into the maintenance shop for corrective action.

Clutch Lubrication. Although some clutches do not require lubrication, there are other types of clutches that require it at periodic intervals. The clutch-pedal control shaft and clutch linkage are among some of the lubricating points that would be greased at normal regular servicing intervals in accordance with the manufacturer's lubrication manual.

MANUAL TRANSMISSIONS

The transmission is part of the power train. It is located in the rear of the engine between the clutch housing and the propeller shaft. The transmission transfers engine power from the clutch shaft to the propeller shaft, and allows the operator a means of varying the gear ratio between the engine and the rear wheels.

Dual ratio, or two-speed, rear axles are sometimes used on trucks. They contain two different gear ratios which can be selected at will by the driver, usually by a manual-control lever. A dual-ratio rear axle serves the same purpose as the auxiliary transmission, and like the latter, it doubles the number of gear ratios available for driving the vehicle under the various loads and road conditions.

Operator's Maintenance. It is the operator's responsibility to check with the manufacturer's instruction manual for instruction on the proper type and amount of recommended lubricant to be used in the transmission case. You must maintain the lubricant at the proper level. The normal level of lubricant to be placed in a transmission is usually at the bottom of the filler plug opening. By maintaining the proper level, gear teeth are protected, foaming is reduced, and thus the transmission will continue to perform properly.

Malfunction Detection. Several types of transmission troubles that may be encountered in vehicle operation are: hard shifting into gears, transmission slips out of *first* or *reverse*, transmission slips out of *second*, transmission slips out of high, no power through transmission, transmission noisy in gear, gear clash in shifting, and oil leaks. As an operator, you would explain the malfunction on the Operator's Trouble Report enabling the mechanic to check out the possible cause of trouble reported.

AUTOMATIC TRANSMISSION

The transmissions described previously are manual transmissions; that is, they require a clutch and a lever for shifting gears. The automatic transmission is used in almost all types of automotive and construction equipment. Automatic transmissions are composed of a fluid coupling or hydraulic torque converter and a system of planetary gears controlled automatically.

<u>Fluid Couplings</u>. Fluid couplings are widely used with automatic transmissions. By slipping at idling speeds and by holding to increase power as engine speed increases, fluid couplings act as a sort of automatic clutch. There is no mechanical connection between the engine and transmission, but power is transmitted through the use of oil.

The principle of fluid drive can best be illustrated through the use of a pair of electric fans facing each other. If one fan is operated with power, the air blast from this fan will cause the other fan to rotate.

There is considerable power loss through slippage at low speeds, but at intermediate or high driving speeds the power loss is very small. It ranges from 1 percent at 25 miles per hour to one-quarter percent at 60 miles per hour.

<u>Torque Converters</u>. A torque converter is a special form of fluid coupling. It is one of the most common types of automatic transmissions and is widely used in the latest models of automotive and construction equipment.

The torque converter consists of three basic elements: the pump (driving member), the turbine (driven member), and the stator (reaction member). All of these members have curved vanes. The stator is placed between the load and the power source to act as a fulcrum and is secured to the torque converter housing. The pump throws out oil in the same direction in which the pump is turning. As the oil strikes the turbine blade, it forces the turbine to rotate, and the oil is directed toward the center of the turbine. Then the oil leaves the turbine and moves in a direction opposite to that of the pump. As the oil strikes the stator, it is redirected to flow in the same direction as the pump, thereby adding its force to that of the pump. Torque is multiplied by the velocity and direction given to the oil by the pump, plus the velocity and direction of the oil entering the pump from the stator.

<u>Planetary Gears</u>. Automatic transmissions use a system of planetary gears to enable the torque from the torque converter or fluid coupling to be used as efficiently as possible.

Planetary units are the heart of the modern automatic transmission. An understanding of the power flow through the planetary units is essential to an understanding of the operation of the automatic transmission.

Four basic parts make up the planetary gear system. These basic parts are the sun gear, the ring (or internal) gear, the planet pinions, and the planet carrier.

The sun gear is so named because it is the center of the system. The term *planet* is used to describe these pinions and gears because they rotate around the sun gear. The ring gear, or internal gear, is so called because of its shape and because it has internal teeth.

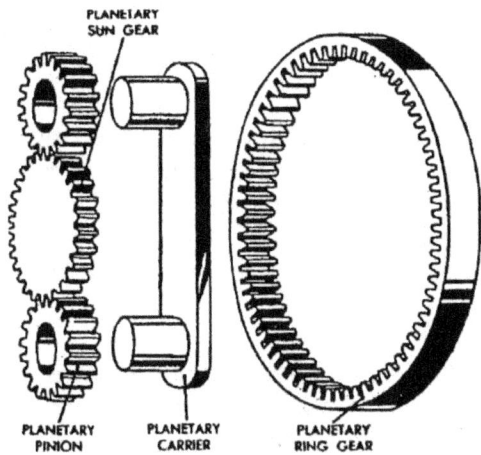

There are several advantages inherent in the planetary gear system. One of the advantage is the compactness of the system. Another advantage is that there is more tooth contact to carry the load, in that each gear of the planetary system is usually in contact with at least two other gears of the system. The gears are always in mesh. There can be no tooth damage due to tooth clash or partial engagement. The big advantage is the one which makes it so popular: namely, the ease of shifting gears. Planetary gear sets in automatic transmissions are shifted without any skill on the part of the driver.

There are various ways in which power may be transmitted through the planetary gear set. shaft from the engine may be connected to drive the sun gear, it may be connected to drive the planet carrier, or it may be connected to drive the ring gear. The propeller shaft also may be connected to any of these members. However, only power can be transmitted in the planetary gear system when (1) the engine is delivering power to one of the three member, (2) the propeller shaft is connected to one of the other members, and (3) the remaining member is held against rotation. All three conditions must be satisfied for power to be transmitted in the system. Automatic transmissions provide the means for holding a member through hydraulic servos or spring pressure.

Operation. Most automatic transmissions are basically the same. They combine a fluid torque converter with a planetary gear set, and control the shifting of the planetary gears with an automatic hydraulic control system.

To start the engine, the selector lever must be in the Neutral or Park position. It is good practice to apply the service brakes before starting the engine and keep them applied after the engine is running. In the automatic transmission, the fluid torque converter is attached to the engine crankshaft and serves as the engine flywheel. This means that whenever the engine runs, engine power flows into the converter and drives the converter output (turbine) shaft. There is no neutral in the torque converter. Neutral is provider in the planetary gear set by the release of bands and clutches.

With the engine running, you can *feel* the transmission go into gear and into neutral as the selector level is moved from Park or Neutral to Drive, Low, or Reverse. If the engine is running at fast (cold) idle, the vehicle will start to move as soon as the transmission goes into gear, unless the parking or service brakes are applied. If the engine is idling at normal (hot) idle, the vehicle will not move. You can, however, *feel* the transmission go into gear. Part of this *feel* is the audible decrease in engine rpm. The engine is now running under a load. The torque converter and the planetary gear set are actually transmitting engine torque to the driveshaft. The torque applied, however, is not sufficient to move the vehicle.

For all normal forward driving, the selector is moved to Drive. As the throttle is advanced from the idle position, the vehicle will start off smoothly and accelerate steadily. The transmission is designed to operate at a steady-throttle position. Most drivers depress the accelerator pedal to definite position and hold it there steadily until the desired speed is attained. Depending on the accelerator pedal position, the transmission will upshaft automatically to intermediate and then to high.

The transmission automatically multiplies and/or transmits engine torque to the driveshaft as driving conditions demand. The speeds at which the coupling point and the gear shifts occur are controlled partially by the driver. The driver has only a partial control in the Drive position, because the transmission in the Drive position will shift the planetary gear set into the higher gear to prevent engine overspeeding regardless of throttle position.

The transmission can multiply engine torque as much as 5.4 times. The torque converter can multiply engine torque as much as 2.2 times. The planetary gear set in low gear multiplies the torque converter output torque 2.46 times. The maximum engine torque multiplication in the transmission is 2.2 x 2.46 or 5.41 times. This means that the transmission can receive an engine output torque of 100 ft-lbs and deliver 541 ft-lbs torque to the driveshaft. Of course, frictional losses have to be subtracted from the 541 ft-lbs.

The driver can force downshaft the transmission from high to intermediate at speed up to about 65 mph. A detent on the downshift linkage warns the driver when the carburetor is wide open. Accelerator pedal depression through the detent will bring in the downshift.

With the throttle closed, the transmission will downshift automatically as the vehicle speed drops to about 10 mph. With the throttle open at any position up to the detent, the downshifts will come in automatically at speeds about 10 mph and in proportion to throttle opening. This prevents engine lugging on steep hill climbing.

When the selector lever is moved to L (low) with the transmission in high, the transmission will downshift to intermediate or to low depending on the road speed. At speeds below about 25 mph, the downshift will be from high to low.

With the selector in Low position, the transmission cannot upshift. On some vehicles the Low position is called Hill Control, since low gear provides maximum engine braking. When maximum engine braking is desired, the transmission must not upshift, because an upshift will reduce engine braking effort. When the selector is moved to Reverse, the hydraulic control system shifts the planetary gear set to reverse. When the selector lever is moved to Park, a spring force is applied against a pawl to engage the parking pawl with a parking gear on the output shaft. When the pawl is engaged, the transmission output shaft (and, therefore, the rear wheels) is mechanically locked to the transmission main case.

In summary:
1. An automatic transmission has the torque converter to act as an automatic clutch. This automatic clutch permits the vehicle to stand still at engine idle, but automatically

goes to work at a full-throttle start so that the transmission can take maximum engine torque, multiply it more than four times and deliver it to the driveshaft.
2. It is practically impossible to *kill* the engine under any driving condition.
3. At a start, engine speed is fast and vehicle speed is slow. With a steady throttle, engine speed remains fairly constant while vehicle speed increases to 65 mph. You found that the torque converter and planetary gear set *know* when engine torque should be multiplied, how much to multiply it, and when to transmit it to the driveshaft.
4. The ratio changes (shifts) occur at full-engine torque within a fraction of a second and without extreme harshness.

Operator's Maintenance. Periodic service by the operator includes checking the transmission oil level when the engine is idling and at normal operating temperature, the vehicle is level, and the transmission control lever is in Park. Remove dipstick and note oil level. If it is low, and sufficient transmission fluid (the oil used in all automatic transmission is special and is composed of mineral oil and additives). In the transmission, it is used as a combination power-transmission medium, hydraulic control fluid, heat transfer medium, bearing surface lubricant, and gear lubricant. In all cases, the manufacturer's recommendations should be followed when servicing and filling the transmission with transmission fluid.

Caution: Do not overfill the transmission because overfilling will cause foaming and shifting troubles.

Malfunction Detection. Several types of automatic transmission troubles that may be encountered during vehicle operation are: No drive in any selected position; engine speed accelerates on standstill starts but vehicle acceleration lags; engine speed accelerates during upshifts; transmission will not upshift; upshift harsh; closed throttle (coast) downshift harsh; will not downshift; vehicle creeps excessively in drive; vehicle creeps in neutral; no drive in reverse, improper shift points; unusual transmission noise; and oil leaks. As an operator, you must explain the malfunction on the Operator's Trouble Report and turn the report into the maintenance shop for corrective action.

AUXILIARY TRANSMISSIONS

Auxiliary transmissions are mechanisms mounted in the rear of the regular transmission to provide an increased number of gear ratios. The types most commonly used, normally have only a low and a high (direct) range, incorporated into a transfer assembly. The low range provides an extremely low gear ratio on hard pull. At all other times, the high range is used, and the power passes through the main shaft. Gears are shifted by a separate gearshift lever in the driver's cab.

Transfer Cases. Transfer cases are placed in the power trains of vehicles driven by all wheels. Their purpose is to provide the necessary offsets for additional propeller shaft connections to drive the wheels.

Transfer cases in heavier vehicles have two speed positions and a declutching device for disconnecting the front driving wheels. Two speed transfer cases serve also as auxiliary transmissions.

Some transfer cases are quite complicated. When they have speed changing gear, declutching device, and attachment for three or more propeller shafts, they are even larger than the main transmission.

Some transfer cases contain an overrunning sprag unit (or units) on the front output shaft. (A sprag unit is a form of overrunning clutch; power can be transmitted through it in one direction but not in the other.) On these transfer cases, the transfer is designed to drive the front axle slightly slower than the rear axle. During normal operation, when both front and rear wheels turn at the same speed, only the rear wheels drive the vehicle. However, if the rear wheels should lose traction and begin to slip, they tend to turn faster than the front wheels. As this happens, the sprag unit automatically engages so that the front wheels also drive the vehicle. The sprag unit simply provides an automatic means of engaging the front wheels in drive whenever additional tractive effort is required. There are two types of sprag-unit-equipped transfers: a single-sprag-unit transfer and a double-sprag unit transfer. Essentially, both types work in the same manner.

Power Takeoffs. Power takeoffs are attachments in the power train used for obtaining power to drive auxiliary accessories. They are attached to the transmission, auxiliary transmission, or transfer case.

Malfunction detection and operator maintenance for auxiliary transmissions are similar to those for the manual transmission.

PROPELLER SHAFT ASSEMBLY

The propeller shaft assembly consists of a propeller shaft, a slip joint, and one or more universal joints. This assembly provides a flexible connection through which power is transmitted from the transmission to the live axles.

The propeller shaft may be solid or tubular. A solid shaft is somewhat stronger than the hollow or tubular shaft of the same diameter, but the hollow shaft is stronger than a solid shaft of the same weight. Hollow shafts are used in the open.

A slip joint is provided at one end of the propeller shaft to take care of end play. The driving axle, being attached to the springs, is free to move up and down while the transmission is attached to the frame and cannot move. Any upward or downward movement of the axle, as the spring are flexed, shortens or lengthens the distance between the axle assembly and the transmission. To compensate for this changing distance, the slip joint is provided at one end of the propeller shaft.

The usual type of slip joint consists of a splined stub shaft, welded to the propeller shaft, which fits into a splined sleeve in the universal joint.

A universal joint is a connection between two shafts that permits one to drive the other at an angle. Passenger vehicles and trucks usually have universal joints at both ends of the propeller shaft.

Universal joints normally do not require any maintenance other than lubrication. Some universal joints (U-joints) have grease fittings and should be lubricated when the vehicle has a preventive maintenance inspection. Others may require disassembly and lubrication periodically. When lubricating U-joints that have grease fittings, use a low pressure grease gun to avoid damaging seals.

FINAL DRIVES

A final drive is that part of the power train that transmits the power delivered through the propeller shaft to the drive wheels or to sprockets, in the case of tracklaying equipment. Because it is encased in the rear axle housing, the final drive is usually referred to as a part of the rear axle assembly. It consists of two gears called the ring gear and pinion. These are beveled gears, and they may be spur, spiral, or hypoid.

The function of the final drive is to change by 90 degrees the direction of the power transmitted through the propeller shaft to the driving axles. It also provides a fixed reduction between the speed of the propeller shaft and the axle shafts and wheels. In passenger car this reduction varies from about 3 to 1 to 5 to 1. In trucks, it can vary from to 1 to as much as 11 to 1.

The gear ratio of a final drive having bevel gears is found by dividing the number of teeth on the driven or ring gear by the number of teeth on the pinion. In a worm gear final drive, the gear ratio is found by counting the number of revolutions of the worm gear required for one revolution of the driven gear.

Most final drives are of the gear type. Hypoid gears are used in passenger cars and light trucks to eliminate the rear seat propeller shaft tunnel or to permit a lower body design. They permit the bevel driven pinion to be placed below the center of the ring gear, thereby lowering the propeller shaft. Worm gears allow a large speed reduction and are used to a limited extent on larger trucks. Spiral bevel gears are similar to hypoid gears. They are used in both passenger cars and trucks to replace spur gear that are considered too noisy.

DIFFERENTIALS

Associated with the final drive and contained in the rear axle housing is the differential. The purpose of the differential is easy to understand when you compare a vehicle to a company of men marching in mass formation. When the company makes a turn, the men in the inside file must take short steps, almost marking time, while men in the outside file must take long steps and walk a greater distance to make the turn. When a motor vehicle turns a corner, the wheels on the outside of the turn must rotate faster and travel a greater distance than the wheels on the inside. This causes no difficulty for front wheels of the usual passenger car because each wheel rotates independently. However, in order to drive the rear wheels at different speeds, the differential is needed. It connects the individual axle shaft for each wheel to the bevel drive gear. Therefore, each shaft can turn at a different speed and still be driven.

To overcome the situation where one spinning wheel might be undesirable, some trucks are provided with a *differential lock*. This is a simple dog clutch, controlled manually or automatically which locks one axle shaft to the differential case and bevel drive gear. Although this device forms a rigid connection between the two axle shafts and makes both wheels rotate at the same speed, it is used, very little. Too often the driver forgets to disengage the lock after using it. There are, however, automatic devices for doing almost the same thing. One of these, which is rather extensively used today, is the high-traction differential. This does not work, however, when one wheel loses traction completely. In this respect, it is inferior to the differential lock.

With the no-spin differential, one wheel cannot spin because of loss of tractive effort and thereby deprive the other wheel of driving effort. For example, one wheel is on ice and the other wheel is on dry pavement. The wheel on ice is assumed to have no traction. However, the wheel on dry pavement will pull to the limit of its tractional resistance at the pavement. The wheel on ice cannot spin because wheel speed is governed by the speed of the wheel applying tractive effort.

AXLES

A live axle is one that supports part of the weight of a vehicle and also drives the wheels connected to it. A dead axle is one that carries part of the weight of a vehicle but does not drive the wheels.

In 4-wheel drive vehicles, both front and rear axles are live axles, and in 6-wheel drive vehicles, all three axles are live axles. The third axle, part of a *bogie drive* is joined to the rearmost axle by a trunnion axle. The axle trunnion is attached rigidly to the frame. Its purpose is to help in distributing the load on the rear of the vehicle to the two live axles which it connects.

There are four types of live axles used in automotive and construction equipment. They are: plain, semifloating, three-quarter floating, and full floating.

The plain live axle, or nonfloating rear axle, is seldom used in construction equipment today. The axle shafts in this assembly are called nonfloating because they are supported directly in bearings located in the center and ends of the axle housing. In addition to turning the wheels, these shafts carry the entire load of the vehicle on their outer ends. Plain axles also support the weight of the differential case.

The semifloating axle that is used on most passenger cars and light trucks has its differential case independently supported. The differential carrier relieves the axle shafts from the weight of the differential assembly and the stresses caused by its operation. For this reason, the inner ends of the axle shafts are said to be floated. The wheels are keyed or bolted to outer ends of axle shafts and the outer bearings are between the shafts and the housing. The axle shafts, therefore, must take the stresses caused by turning or skidding of the wheels. The axle shaft in a semifloating live axle can be removed after the wheel and brake drum have been removed.

The axle shafts in a three-quarter floating axle may be removed with the wheels, which are keyed to the tapered outer ends of the shafts. The inner ends of the shafts are carried as in semifloating axle. The axle housing, instead of the shafts, carries the weight of the vehicle because the wheels are supported by bearings on the outer ends of the housing. However, axle shafts must take the stresses caused by the turning, or skidding, of the wheels. Three-quarter floating axles are used in some trucks but in very few passenger cars.

The full floating axle is used in most heavy trucks. These axle shafts may be removed and replaced without removing the wheels or disturbing the differential. Each wheel is carried on the end of the axle tube on two ball bearings or roller bearings and the axle shafts are bolted to the wheel hub. The wheels are driven through a flange on the ends of the axle shaft which is bolted to the outside of the wheel hub. The bolted connection between axle and wheel does not make this assembly a true full floating axle, but nevertheless, it is called a floating axle. A true full floating axle transmits only turning effort, or torque.

MAINTENANCE

There are very few adjustments that must be made to the power train during normal operations. As an operator, your primary duties will be limited to lubrication of the power train. You can reduce repairs by proper lubrication and periodic inspection of these power train units.

Proper lubrication depends upon the use of the right kind of lubricants which must be put in the right places in the amounts specified by the lubrication charts. The charts provided with the vehicle will show what units in the power train will require lubrication, and where they are located.

In checking the level of the lubricant in gear cases, keep these two important points in mind:

First, always carefully wipe the dirt away from around the inspection plug and then use the proper size wrench to remove the inspection plugs. A wrench too large will round the corners and prevent proper tightening of the plug. For the same reason, never use a pipe wrench or a pair of pliers for removing plugs.

Secondly, be sure the level of the lubricant is right—usually just below or on a level with the bottom of the inspection hole. Before checking the level, allow the vehicle to stand for a while on a level surface so the gear oil can cool and find its own level. Gear oil heated and churned by revolving gears expands and forms bubbles. Although too little gear oil in the gear boxes is responsible for many failures of the power train, do not add too much gear lubricant. Too much oil causes extra maintenance.

Excessive oil or grease can find its way past the oil seals or gear cases. It may be forced out of a transmission into the clutch housing and result in a slipping clutch; or it may get by the rear wheel bearings from the differential housing to cause brakes to slip or grab. Always clean differential and live axle housing vents to prevent leaking seals.

Universal joints and slip joints at the ends of propeller shafts are to be lubricated if fittings are provided. Some of these joints are packed with grease when assembled, others have grease fittings. Do not remove these plugs until you consult the manual or your chief for instructions.

Some passenger cars and trucks have a leather boot or shoe covering the universal and slip joints. The boot prevents grease from being thrown from the joints and it also keeps dirt from mixing with the grease. A mixture of dirt and grease forms an abrasive that will wear parts in a hurry. Never use so much grease on these joints that the grease will be forced out of the boot. The extra grease will be lost and the added weight of the grease will tend to throw the propeller shaft out of balance.

When you are to give a vehicle a thorough inspection, inspect the power train for loose gear housings and joints. Look for bent propeller shafts that are responsible for vibrations, and examine the gear housing and joints for missing crews and bolts. Check to see that the U-bolts fastening the springs to the rear axle housing are tight. A loose spring hanger can throw the rear axle assembly out of line, and place additional strain on the propeller shaft and final drive. When making these inspections, always check the steel lugs for tightness.

After tightening the gear housing, loose connections, and joints, road test the vehicle to see if the various units in the power train are working properly. Shift the gears into all operating speeds and listen for noisy sounds. Report all improper operation of the power train units on the Operator's Trouble Report enabling the mechanic to check out possible causes.

DRIVING WHEELS

Wheels attached to live axles are the driving wheels. The number of wheels and number of driving wheels is sometimes used to identify equipment. Wheels attached to the outside of the driving wheels make up dual wheels. Dual wheels give additional traction to the driving wheels and distribute the weight of the vehicle over a greater area of road surface. They are considered as single wheels in describing vehicles. For example, a 4x2 (four by two) could be a passenger car or a truck having four wheels with two of them driving. A 4x4 indicates a vehicle having four wheels with all four driving. In some cases, these vehicles will have dual wheels in the rear. You would describe such a vehicle as a 4x4 with dual wheels.

A 6x4 truck, although having dual wheels in the rear, is identified by six wheels, four of them driving. Actually, the truck has ten wheels but the wheel attached to each driving wheel could be removed without changing the identity of the truck. If the front wheels of this truck were driven by a live axle, it would be called a 6x6.

II. BRAKE SYSTEMS

Good brakes are an absolute necessity for the safe operation of a motor vehicle. The modern day vehicle is capable of moving at extremely high speeds, and this results in an ever increasing demand for more efficient braking systems. Braking systems must not only be able to stop the vehicle, but must stop it in as short a distance as possible.

Friction is the resistance to relative motion between two surfaces in contact with each other. Thus, when a stationary surface is forced into contact with a moving surface, the resistance to relative motion or the rubbing action between the two surfaces will slow down the moving surface. In nearly all brake systems, the brake drums provide the moving surface and the brake shoes provide the stationary surface. The friction between the brake drums and the brake shoes slows the drum, wheel, and the friction between the tires and the road surface slows the vehicle, eventually bringing it to a complete stop.

INDIVIDUAL BRAKES

On modern equipment individual service brakes are provided for each wheel and are operated by a foot pedal. The equipment also has an emergency or parking brake. The parking brake is operated by a separate pedal or a hand lever.

Individual brakes are classified into three types: external contracting brake, internal expanding brake, and disk brake.

<u>External Contracting Brakes</u>. External contracting brakes are sometimes used for parking brakes on motor vehicles and for controlling the speed of auxiliary equipment drive shafts.

In operation, the brake band (or shoe) of an external contracting brake is tightened around the rotating drum by moving the brake lever. The brake hand is made of comparatively thin, flexible steel, shaped to fit the drum, with a frictional lining riveted to the inner surface. This flexible brake band cannot withstand the high pressure required to produce the friction that will stop a heavily loaded or fast moving vehicle, but works well as a parking brake.

In an external contracting brake, the brake band is anchored opposite the point where the pressure is applied. In addition to supporting the band, the anchor proves a means for adjusting brake lining clearance. Other adjusting screws and bolts are provided at the ends of the band.

Internal Expanding Brakes. Internal expanding brakes are used almost exclusively as wheel brakes. This type of brake permits a more compact and economical construction. The brake shoe and brake operating mechanism are supported on a backing plate or brake shield which is attached to the vehicle axle. The brake drum, attached to the rotating wheel, acts as a cover for the shoe and operating mechanism and furnishes a frictional surface for the brake shoe.

In operation, the brake shoe of an internal expanding brake is forced outward against the drum to produce the braking action. One end of the shoe is hinged to the backing plate by an anchor pin, while the other end is unattached and can be moved in its support by the operating mechanism. When force from the operating mechanism is applied to the unattached end of the shoe, the shoe expands and brakes the wheel. A retracting spring returns the shoe to the original position when braking action is no longer required.

The brake-operating linkage alone does not provide sufficient mechanical advantage for positive braking. Some means of supplementing the physical application of the braking system has to be used to increase pressure on the brake shoes. A self-energizing action is very helpful in accomplishing this, once setting of the shoes is started by physical effort. While there are variations of this action, it is always obtained by the shoes themselves, which tend to revolve with the revolving drum.

When the brake shoe is anchored (see figure below) and the drum revolves in the direction shown, the shoe will tend to revolve with the drum when it is forced against the drum. As a result, the shoe will exert considerable pressure against the anchor pin. Since the pin is fixed to the brake shield, this pressure will tend to wedge the shoe tightly in between the pin and the drum as shown. As the initial braking pressure is increased on the cam, the wedging action increases and the shoe is forced still more tightly against the drum to increase the friction. This self-energizing results in more braking action than could be obtained with the actuating pressure alone. Brakes making use of this principle to increase pressures on the braking surfaces are known as self-energizing (or servo) brakes.

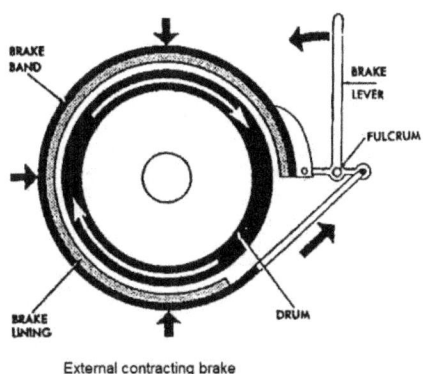

External contracting brake

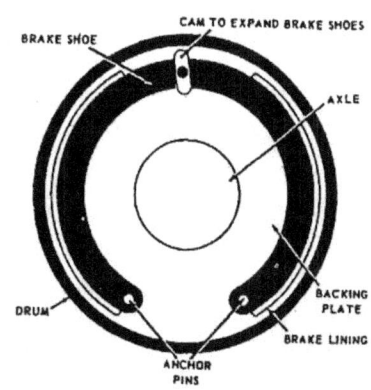

Internal expanding brake

It is most important that the operator control the total braking action at all times; therefore, the self-energizing action should increase only upon application of additional "actuating" pressure at the brake pedal. The amount of self-energizing action available depends mainly on location of the anchor pin. As the pin is moved toward the center of the drum, wedging action increases until a point is reached where the shoe will automatically lock. The pin must be located outside this point so that the operator can control the braking.

When two shoes are anchored on the bottom of the backing plate, self-energizing action is effective on only one shoe. The other shoe tends to revolve away from its pivot, which reduces its braking action. When the wheel is revolving in the opposite direction, the self-energizing action is produced on the opposite shoe.

Two shoes are usually mounted so that self-energizing action is effective on both. This is accomplished by pivoting the shoes to each other and leaving the pivot free of the backing plate. The only physical effort required is for operating the first, or primary, shoe. Both shoes then apply additional pressure to the braking surfaces with no increase in the pressure on the operating linkage. The anchor pins are fitted into slots in the free ends of the brake shoes. This method of anchoring allows the movement of the shoes necessary to expand against the drum when the shoes are forced against the drum, and the self-energizing action of the primary shoe is transmitted through the pivot to the secondary shoe. Both shoes will tend to revolve with the drum and will be wedged against the drum by the one anchor pin. The other anchor pin will cause a similar action when the wheel is revolving in the opposite direction.

The operating mechanism for wheel brakes differs with the brake systems, and so do the brake shoe adjusting devices. The brake drums and brake shoes, however, are similar in all wheel brakes.

Most modern automotive brakes have a self-adjusting feature that automatically adjust the brakes when they need it as a result of brake lining wear.

<u>Disk Brakes</u>. The disk brake has a metal disk instead of a drum, and a pair of flat pads instead of curved brake shoes. The figure below shows a sectional view of a typical disk brake assembly. The two flat pads are located on the two sides of the disk. The assembly in which the flat pads are held is called the caliper assembly. In operation, the pads are forced against the two sides of the disk by the movement of pistons in the caliper assembly. The pistons are actuated by hydraulic pressure from the master cylinder. The effect is to clamp the rotating disk between the stationary pads as illustrated below. This is the same action you get when you pick up a piece of paper; our fingers and thumb clamp on both sides of the paper to hold it. In the same way, the pads apply friction to the disk and attempt to stop its rotation. This provides the braking action.

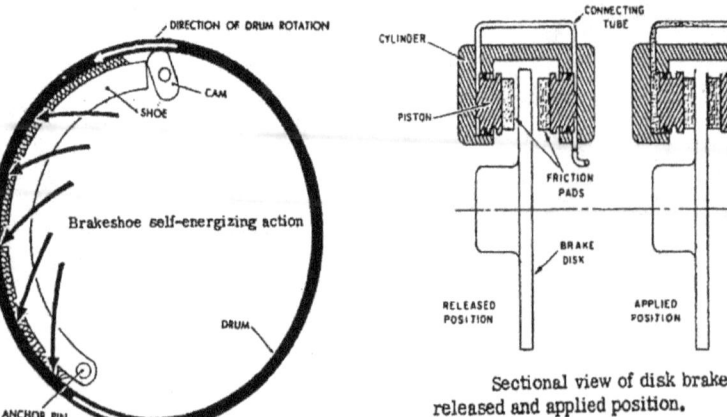

Sectional view of disk brake in released and applied position.

MECHANICAL HANDBRAKES

In most automotive vehicles, the handbrake has its own hookup. Either external contracting brake bands are located on the drive shaft or some type of mechanical linkage operates the rear wheel brakes.

HYDRAULIC BRAKE SYSTEMS

A hydraulic brake system is primarily a liquid connection or coupling between the brake pedal and the individual brake shoes and drums. The system consists of one master cylinder connected by pipes and flexible tubing to the wheel cylinders. The wheel cylinders control the movement of the brake shoes at each wheel.

The brake fluid in hydraulic systems is composed of alcohol and caster oil or glycerin. This liquid neither freezes nor boils at temperatures encountered in year-round operations. When the brake pedal in a hydraulic brake system is depressed, the hydraulic fluid forces the pistons in the wheel cylinder against the brake shoes. The shoes expand against the brake drum and stop the vehicle. Hydraulic brakes are self-equalizing brakes. If the actuating pistons were all the same size, each brake in the hydraulic system would receive an identical hydraulic force when the brakes are applied because a force exerted at any point upon a closed liquid is distributed equally through the liquid in all directions. Some brake systems have larger wheel cylinders in the front than in the rear. This is because, when stopping, more of the vehicle's weight is felt in front and, therefore, more front wheel braking effort is required.

The mechanical advantage of any brake system is the relation between the pressure applied by the operator on the brake pedal to the pressure exerted on the braking surfaces.

The master cylinder has two functions. It is a reservoir for the brake fluid, and it contains the piston and the valves which change mechanical force to hydraulic pressure when the brake pedal is depressed. The pressure on the brake pedal moves the piston within the master cylinder, forcing the brake fluid from the master cylinder through tubing and flexible hose to the wheel cylinders. As pressure on the pedal is increased, greater hydraulic pressure is built up within the brake cylinders, and thus greater force is put forth against the ends of the brake shoes. When pressure on the pedal is released, the springs on the brake shoes return the wheel cylinder pistons to their released positions. This action forces the brake fluid back through the flexible hose and tubing to the master cylinder.

Most older model cars are equipped with the single system master cylinder. This system is, however, being replaced with dual system master cylinders.

The operation of a dual system master cylinder is basically the same as a single master cylinder. The dual system master cylinder, however, has two pistons, two separate fluid reservoirs, and two output ports. Thus, the dual system master cylinder has two separate hydraulic pressure systems. One of the hydraulic systems normally is connected to the front brakes, and the other system is the rear brakes. If either the front or rear hydraulic system fails, the other system remains operational.

The master cylinder, like other parts in the brake system, is subject to wear, leaks, and deposits or corrosion on the cylinder wall and piston. Master cylinder reservoir fluid level should be checked periodically and clean brake fluid added, as needed, to maintain fluid level approximately ½" from the top of the reservoir.

The brake lines transmit fluid and pressure from the master cylinder to the wheel cylinders, which in turn change the hydraulic pressure into mechanical force. The wheel cylinders are mounted on the brake backing plate. Inside each cylinder are two pistons that move in opposite directions by hydraulic pressure, which pushes the brake shoes against the brake drum. The brake shoes are made of iron, steel, or cast aluminum. They support the brake lining and transmit force to the lining, which is attached to the face of the shoe and make contact with the inner surface of the brake drums. During contact with one another the lining and the drum create the frictional surface that gives the braking effect.

AIRBRAKE SYSTEMS

Air, like all gases, is easily compressed. Compressed air exerts pressure and this pressure will be equal in all directions. Air under pressure can be conveniently stored and carried through lines or tubes. Considerable force is available for braking since operating air pressure may be as high as 100 psi. All brakes on a vehicle, and on a trailer (when one is used), are operated together by means of a brake valve.

The compressor is driven from the engine crankshaft or one of the auxiliary shafts. The three common methods of driving the compressor from the engine are gear, belt, and chain.

The compressor may be lubricated from the engine crankcase or be self-lubricated. Cooling may be either by air or liquid from the engine.

The purpose of the compressor governor is to automatically maintain the air pressure in the reservoir between the maximum pressure desired (100-105 psi) and the minimum pressure required for safe operation (80-85 psi) by starting and stopping compression.

The two steel tanks which are components of most air brake systems are called reservoirs. These tanks are used to cool, store, and remove moisture from the air and give a smooth flow of air to the brake system.

A safety valve consists of an adjustable spring-loaded ball check valve in a body. It is used to protect the system against excessive pressures and is usually mounted on a reservoir. The safety valve is normally set at 150 psi but can be varied to suit the vehicle requirements.

A pressure gauge is attached to any line which registers reservoir pressure and is mounted to the dashboard of the vehicle.

The brake valve is the operator's control of the air brake system. When the brake valve is engaged, air from the reservoir flows through the valve to the brakes. The three types of brake valves used in the air brake systems are pedal, treadle, and hand. When you press the pedal of an airbrake system, air under pressure in a reservoir is released to the brake lines by an air valve. This air goes to the brake chambers located close to the wheel brakes, which contain flexible diaphragms. The force of the air admitted to these chambers cause the diaphragms to operate the brake shoes through a mechanical linkage.

An air pressure gage will let you know if you have proper air pressure within the reservoir (60 lbs. pressure is minimum). This gage is usually found on the instrument panel of a truck or bus. If the pressure fails to build up or exceeds the maximum limits after building up, secure the truck until the fault is corrected.

Independent control of trailer brakes is valuable under adverse conditions when it is sometimes desirable to apply the brakes on the trailer without applying the brakes on the truck or tractor. The independent trailer control valve, conveniently located in the cab, provides the operator with perfect control of his trailing load at all times.

VACUUM BRAKES

In the vacuum brake system, depressing the brake pedal opens a valve between the power cylinder, which contains a piston, and the intake manifold to which the power cylinder is connected. To apply the brakes, air is exhausted from the cylinder ahead of the piston, while atmospheric pressure acts on the rear side of the piston to exert a powerful pull on the rod attached to the piston.

When the brake valve is closed, the chamber ahead of the piston is shut off from the intake manifold and is open to the atmosphere. The pressure is then the same on both sides of the piston; therefore, no pull is exerted upon the pull rod. The brake shoe return springs then release the brakes and return the piston to its original position in the power cylinder.

Hydrovac is a trade name for a one-unit vacuum power braking system. It combines into one assembly a hydraulic control valve, a vacuum power cylinder and a hydraulic slave cylinder. This assembly is connected to both the master cylinder and the wheel brakes, eliminating the need for mechanical connections with the brake pedal.

When you press the brake pedal, fluid is forced from the master cylinder through the check valve to the slave cylinder and on to the wheel cylinders. The foot pedal pressure, acting through the master cylinder, acts also against the slave cylinder piston, assisting the vacuum pistons and push rods to press upon the brake shoes.

OPERATOR MAINTENANCE

Periodic brake service by the operator includes the use of proper brake fluid; checking brake fluid level; inflating tires properly; checking for loose connections or parts; checking for leaks in the system; draining air reservoirs daily; and checking the self-contained lubricating oil system of air compressors daily.

MALFUNCTION DETECTION

The types of brake trouble that may be encountered in vehicle operation are: brake pedal goes to the floorboard with no resistance; one brake drags; all brakes drag; vehicle pulls to one side when braking; soft or spongy pedal; excessive pedal effort required; noisy brakes; air in the system; loss of brake fluid; brakes heat up during driving and fail to release; leaky brake cylinder; grabbing brake action; and brake pedal can be depressed without slowing the vehicle. As an operator, you must explain the malfunction on the Operator's Trouble Report and turn it into the maintenance shop for necessary correction.

STEERING MECHANISMS

All steering mechanisms have the same basic parts. The steering linkage ties the front wheels together and connects them to the steering gear case at the lower end of the steering column, which in turn connects the gear case to the steering wheel.

The arms and rods of the steering linkage have ball or ball and socket ends to provide a swivel connection between them. These jointed ends are provided with grease fittings, dust seals or boots, and many of them have end-play adjustment devices. These joints and devices must be adjusted and lubricated regularly.

The tie-rod is usually located behind the axle and keeps the front wheels in proper alignment. To provide for easier steering and maximum leverage, the tie-rod may be separated into two lengths and connected to the steering gear near the center of the vehicle.

The drag link between the steering arm and the pitman arm may be long or short, depending on the installation.

The pitman arm, splined to the shaft extending from the steering gear case, moves in an arc, its position depending on which way the steering wheel is turned. It is approximately vertical when the front wheels are straight ahead. Therefore, the length of the drag link is determined by the distance between the steering arm and the vertical position of the pitman arm. Unlike the tie-rods, the length of the drag link is not adjustable.

The steering gear case contains the gears that control the movement of the pitman arm and steering linkage.

POWER STEERING

Power steering has been used for a number of years on heavy-duty applications, but it is only in recent years that power steering has been applied to any extent on automotive vehicles. The principle of power steering is very simple. A booster arrangement is provided which is set in operation when the steering wheel is turned. The booster then takes over and does most of the work of steering. Power steering has used compressed air, electrical mechanisms, and hydraulic pressure. Hydraulic pressure is used on the vast majority of power-steering mechanisms today.

In the hydraulic power-steering system, a continuously operating pump provides hydraulic pressure. As the steering wheel is turned, valves are operated to admit this hydraulic pressure to a cylinder. Then, the pressure causes a piston to move—and the piston does most of the steering work.

There are actually two general types of power-steering systems. In one, the integral type, the power operating assembly is located in the steering gear case. In the other, the linkage type, the power operating assembly is part of the steering linkage.

In the linkage-type power-steering system, the power cylinder or booster cylinder is not part of the steering gear. Instead, the power cylinder is connected into the steering linkage. In addition, the valve assembly is included in the steering linkage, either as a separate assembly or united with the power cylinder.

WHEEL ALIGNMENT

Steering control depends greatly upon the position of the wheels in relation to the rest of the vehicle and the surface over which it travels. Any changes from the specified setting of the wheels affect steering and the riding control of the vehicle. Therefore, the proper wheel alignment is important for vehicle control.

Steering geometry is the term manufacturers use to describe steering and front wheel alignment. Steering geometry includes pivot inclination, wheel caster, wheel chamber, toe-in and toe-out. These terms refer to angles in the front wheel alignment which may change because of driving over rough terrain, striking stationary objects, and accident damage.

OPERATOR MAINTENANCE
Doing maintenance servicing by the operator, the service that the steering linkage normally requires is periodic lubrication of the connecting joints between the links which contain bushings.

When vehicles are equipped with manually operated steering, check the steering gear housing for sufficient lubrication and add recommended manufacturer's gear lubricant, if necessary. For vehicles equipped with power steering, check belt tension which can cause low oil pressure and hard steering. Check fluid level. If the fluid level is low, add fluid to bring it up to the recommended level. Use only special power steering fluid recommended. If the level is low, the possibility exists that there is a leak. Check all hose and power-steering connections for signs of leaks. Leakage may occur at various points in the power-steering unit if the seals are defective. Report conditions to the maintenance shop for replacement of any defective seal, or it may only be necessary to tighten the connections to eliminate leaks.

MALFUNCTION DETECTION
The types of steering trouble that may be encountered in vehicle operation are: excessive play in the steering system; hard steering; vehicle wanders; vehicle pulls to one side when braking; front wheel shimmy at low speeds; front-wheel tramps (high speed shimmy); steering kickback; tires squeal on turns; improper tire wear; and noises. As an operator, you would explain the malfunction on the Operator's Trouble Report and turn it into the maintenance shop for corrective actions.

III. SUSPENSION SYSTEM

A suspension system is a system of anchoring and suspending the wheels or tracks from the frame by means of springs. The suspension system is an important feature of military vehicles; it supports the weight and allows them to be driven under varying loads and speed conditions over bumpy roads and rough terrain without great risk of damage.

The usual components of a suspension system are the springs and shock absorbers. Some suspension systems also have torsion bars.

SPRINGS
Springs support the frame and the body of the vehicle, as well as the load the vehicle carries. They allow the wheels to withstand the shocks of uneven road surfaces and provide a flexible connection between the wheels and the body. The best spring is the one which absorbs road shock rapidly and returns to its normal position slowly. Such a spring, however, is very rare, if not an impossibility. Extremely flexible, or soft springs, allow too much movement of the vehicle superstructure, while still, hard springs do not allow enough movement.

The springs do no support the weight of the wheels, rims, tires, and axles. These parts make up the unsprung weight of the vehicle. The unsprung weight decreases the action of the springs and is, therefore, kept to a minimum to permit the springs to do the job of supporting the vehicle frame and load.

The three types of spring suspension usually found in vehicles are: the longitudinal, the lengthwise mounting, which is the most common; the independent, which is generally used in front suspensions; and transverse, which is the crosswise mounting.

The multiple leaf spring consists of a number of steel strips or leaves of different lengths, fastened together by a bolt through the center. Each end of the largest or master leaf is rolled in an eye which serves as a means of attaching the spring to the spring hanger and spring shackle. Leaf rebound clips surround the leaves at two or more intervals along the spring to keep them from separating on the rebound after the spring has been depressed. The clips allow the spring leaves to slide but prevent them from separating and throwing the entire rebound stress on the master leaf. Thus, the spring acts as a flexible beam. Leaf springs may be suspended lengthwise (parallel to the frame), or cross-wise.

When installed lengthwise, both ends of the spring are attached to the frame and the center is clamped to the axle or spring seat. In some trucks and cars the rear springs are clamped under the axle, instead of over it to lower the center of gravity. A low center of gravity will help prevent a heavily loaded truck from upsetting.

Springs installed crosswise have the ends attached to the axle, and the frame rests on the center of the spring. Torque arms or radius rods are required with this type of spring suspension to absorb the driving thrust of the wheels. The driving thrust and brake action of wheels tend to twist the springs from the spring hangers and shackles connecting them to the frame or axles.

Spring hangers are fittings to which the spring ends are attached. A bolt or pin passes through the bushing in the spring eye and is secured to the spring hanger on the frame. The bushing and shackle bolt or pin, therefore, provide the bearing surface which supports the load on the spring.

The spring bushings may be made of bronze or rubber. They may be pressed or screwed into the spring eye, depending on the design. The steel bolts or pins that pass through the bushing are also either plain or threaded. Threaded bushings and shackle bolts offer a greater bearing surface and are replaced more easily when they become worn.

When a leaf spring is compressed, it must straighten out or break. Therefore, spring shackles are required at one or both ends of the spring. Spring shackles provide a swinging support and allow the spring to straighten out when compressed. One shackle is used in either the front or rear support of springs installed lengthwise. Two shackles are used in supporting springs installed crosswise.

You will see many types of spring shackles. The link shackle and U-shackle are the most common. Link shackles are used in heavy vehicles, and the U-type is more common for use on passenger cars and light trucks.

You will find link shackles used to support a transverse spring on the dead front axle of some wheeled tractors. Most wheeled tractors do not even have springs, and all load cushioning is obtained through large, low pressure tires.

Track-type tractors are equipped with one large leaf spring supported without spring shackles. It is fastened to the engine support and rests on the frames supporting the tracks and rollers. Brackets on the track frames keep the spring from shifting. The main purpose of the spring is to relieve the running gear of stresses during operation.

Some vehicles are equipped with leaf springs at the rear wheels only; others are so equipped both front and rear.

Coil springs are most generally used on independent suspension systems. They provide a very smooth riding quality. Their use has normally been limited to passenger vehicles. Recently, however, they have been used to a limited extent on trucks. The spring seat and hanger, shaped to fit the coil ends, hold the spring in place. Spacers made of rubberized fabric are placed at each end of the coil to prevent squeaking. The rubber bumper, mounted in the spring supporting member, prevents metal to metal contact when the spring is compressed. Most vehicles are equipped with coil springs at the two front wheels, while some other have them at both front and rear.

SHOCK ABSORBERS

Springs alone are never satisfactory in a light vehicle suspension system. A stiff spring gives a hard ride because it does not flex and rebound when the vehicle passes over a bump. On the other hand, too flexible a spring rebounds too much, and the vehicle rides roughly. To smooth the riding qualities of the vehicle, shock absorbers are used. They prevent excessive jolting of the vehicle by balancing spring stiffness and flexibility. They allow the springs to return to rest slowly after having been compressed. Although single-acting shock absorbers check only spring rebound, double-acting shock absorbers check spring compression as well as spring rebound, permitting the use of the more flexible springs.

FRONT AXLE SUSPENSION

Most passenger car front wheels are individually supported with independent suspension systems. The ones you are likely to encounter are the coil spring and the torsion bar suspension systems. These are used with independent front axles and shock absorbers.

REAR AXLE SUSPENSION

Driving wheels are mounted on a live driving axle that is suspended by springs attached to the axle housing. Leaf springs are generally used for suspending live axles. Coil springs are used on a number of passenger cars with torque tube drive.

OPERATOR MAINTENANCE

Under normal operation, and given proper maintenance, suspension systems would not need adjustments or replacement for many miles. The spring assemblies of the suspension system should be checked regularly to ensure that shackles are tight and that bushings within the shackles are not worn excessively or frozen tight. Occasionally, spraying lubricating oil on the spring leaves helps to prevent squeaking at the ends of the spring leaves. Following the lubrication chart furnished for a particular vehicle, check and lubricate the front suspension system including linkage, kingpin, and ball joints. During your checks you may find shock absorber bushings worn; if so, it is best to have the bushings replaced, or in some instances a complete replacement of the shock absorbers is needed.

MALFUNCTION DETECTION

Some types of suspension troubles that may be encountered in vehicle operation are: hard steering, vehicle wander, vehicular pulls to one side during normal driving, front-wheel shimmy, front-wheel tramp (high speed shimmy), steering kickback, hard or rough ride, sway on turns, spring breakage, sagging springs, and noises. As an operator, you would explain the malfunction on the Operator's Trouble Report and turn the trouble report into the maintenance shop for corrective action.

IV. FRAME

The chassis is the assembly of mechanisms that make up the major operating part of the vehicle. It is usually assumed to include everything except the vehicle body. The individual operating assemblies are mounted on the frame, which must be strong enough to support the weight of the vehicle and its rated load without distortion. The frame must be rigid enough to keep the units of the vehicle in proper alignment and to protect them against the stresses and strains of road and surface shocks.

The frame is generally constructed of cold-rolled open-hearth steel, but sometimes of alloy steel to lighten the weight of the vehicle. The side members or rails are the heaviest parts of the frame. The cross members are fixed to the side members rigidly enough to prevent weaving and twisting of the frame. Angular pieces of metal called gusset plates are riveted or welded at the point where members are joined for added strength.

The number, size, and arrangement of cross members depend on the type of vehicle for which the frame is designed. Usually, a front cross member supports the radiator and front end of the engine as well as stiffens the frame. The rear cross members furnish support for the fuel tanks and rear trunk on passenger cars, and the two-bar connections for trucks. Additional cross members are added to the frame to support the rear of the engine and power train and to secure the rigidity required.

The cross members of most small vehicles are designed in either X or K form. The front cross members are wider and of heavier construction than the back members because they support the engine and the front wheels. The side members are shaped to accommodate the body and support its weight. They narrow toward the front of the vehicle to permit a shorter turning radius for the wheels and widen under the main part of the body where the body is secured to the frame. Trucks and trailers usually have frames with straight side members to accommodate several designs of bodies and to give the vehicle added strength to withstand heavier loads. Heavy duty trucks and trailers have I-beam frames.

Brackets and hangers which are bolted or riveted to the frame to support the shock absorbers, fenders, running boards, and springs are usually made of case or pressed steel.

GLOSSARY OF AUTOMOTIVE TERMS

CONTENTS

	Page
A-PILLAR..........ANTI-DIVE	1
ANTIFREEZE..........AXLE TRAMP	2
B-PILLAR..........BOND	3
BOOST PRESSURE..........C-PILLAR	4
CAB..........CHARGING RATE	5
CHASSIS..........COMPRESSION RATIO	6
COMPRESSION RINGS..........CRANKSHAFT	7
CRASH..........DEGASSER	8
DETONATION..........DUAL IGNITION	9
DUAL-RATIO AXLES..........EXHAUST PORT	10
EXHAUST STROKE..........FORCE	11
FOUR-STROKE-CYCLE ENGINE..........GASKET	12
GASOLINE..........HELICAL	13
HELICAL GEAR..........HYDROVAC BRAKES	14
IDLE..........INTAKE MANIFOLD	15
INTAKE PORT..........KNUCKLE	16
LAMINATED..........LUNETTE	17
MAGNET..........NEEDLE VALVE	18
NEGATIVE..........OVERHEAD CAM	19
OVERHEAD VALVE..........PITCH	20
PITMAN ARM..........PREIGNITION	21
PRIMER..........RELAY	22
RESIDUAL MAGNETISM..........RUBBER-ISOLATED CROSSMEMBER	23
SAE..........SHORT CIRCUIT	24
SHROUD..........STARTING SYSTEM	25
STATIC ELECTRICITY..........SYNCHROMESH	26
SYNCHRONIZE..........TOE-IN	27
TOE STEER..........TRAILING ARM	28
TRAILING LINK..........TWO-STROKE-CYCLE ENGINE	29
UNDERSTEER..........VALVE TAPPET	30
VALVE TIMING..........WHEEL BRAKE	31
WHEEL CYLINDER..........ZERO-OFFSET STEERING	32

GLOSSARY OF AUTOMOTIVE TERMS

A

A-PILLAR: The roof support on either side of a car's windshield.

AC: Alternating current, or current that reverses its direction at regular intervals.

ACCELERATING PUMP: A device in the carburetor that supplies an additional amount of fuel, temporarily enriching the fuel-air mixture when the throttle is suddenly opened.

ACCELERATION: The process of increasing velocity. Average rate of change of increasing velocity, usually in feet per second.

ACKERMAN STEERING: The steering system design that permits the front wheels to round a turn without sideslip by turning the inner wheel in more than the outer wheel.

ACTIVE SUSPENSION: An extremely sophisticated computer-controlled suspension system that uses powered actuators instead of conventional springs and shock absorbers. The actuators position a car's wheels in the best possible manner to deal with road disturbances and handling loads.

AERODYNAMIC DRAG: The drag produced by a moving object as it displaces the air in its path. Aerodynamic drag is a force usually measured in pounds; it increases in proportion to the object's frontal area, its drag coefficient, and the square of its speed.

AIR BLEED: A passage in the carburetor through which air can seep or bleed into fuel moving through a fuel passage.

AIR BRAKES: Vehicle brakes actuated by air pressure.

AIR CLEANER: A device, mounted on the carburetor or connected to the carburetor, through which air must pass before entering the carburetor air horn. A filtering device in the air cleaner removes dust and dirt particles from the air.

AIR-COOLED ENGINE: An engine cooled by air circulating between cylinders and around cylinder head as opposed to the liquid-cooled engine cooled by a liquid passing through jackets surrounding the cylinders.

AIR DAM: A front spoiler mounted beneath the bumper and shaped to reduce the airflow under the car. Air dams can increase the airflow to radiators, reduce aerodynamic drag, and/or reduce lift.

AIR FILTER: A filter through which air passes, and which removes dust and dirt particles from the air. Air filters are placed in passages through which air must pass, as in crankcase breather, air cleaner, etc.

AIR HORN: That part of the air passage in the carburetor which is on the atmospheric side of the venture. The choke valve is located in the air horn.

AIR-PAC BRAKES: A type of braking system using a vacuum.

AMMETER: An electric meter that measures current, in amperes, in an electric circuit.

AMPERE: Unit of electric-current-flow measurement. The current that will flow through a 1-ohm resistance when 1 volt is impressed across the resistance.

AMPHIBIOUS VEHICLE: A vehicle with a hull that permits it to float in water, and tracks or wheels that permit it to travel on land.

ANGLE OF APPROACH: The maximum angle of an incline onto which a vehicle can move from a horizontal plane without interference; as, for instance, from front bumpers.

ANGLE OF DEPARTURE: The maximum angle of an incline from which a vehicle can move onto a horizontal plane without interference; as, for instance, from rear bumpers.

ANTI-DIVE: A tuned-in front suspension characteristic that converts braking-induced forces in the suspension links into a vertical force that tends to lift the body, thereby reducing dive under braking.

ANTIFREEZE: A substance added to the coolant system in a liquid-cooled engine to prevent freezing.

ANTIFRICTION BEARING: A bearing of the type that supports the imposed load on rolling surfaces (balls, rollers, needles), minimizing friction.

ANTIKNOCK: Refers to substances that are added to automotive fuel to decrease the tendency to knock when fuel-air mixture is compressed and ignited in the engine cylinder.

ANTI-LOCK BRAKING SYSTEM: A braking system that senses when any of the wheels have locked up, or are about to, and automatically reduces the braking forces to keep the wheels rolling. Commonly called ABS, such a system can control all four wheels or only two.

ANTI-ROLL BAR: A suspension element (used at the front, the rear, or both ends of a car) that reduces body roll by resisting any unequal vertical motion between the pair of wheels to which it is connected. An anti-roller bar does not affect suspension stiffness when both wheels are deflected equally in the same direction. Often incorrectly called a sway bar.

ANTI-SQUAT: Similar to anti-dive, this suspension characteristic uses acceleration-induced forces in the rear suspension to reduce squat.

APEX: The point(s) or region on the line through a corner that touches the corner's inner radius.

ARMATURE: The rotating assembly in a direct current generator or motor. Also, the iron piece in certain electrical apparatus that completes a magnetic (and in many cases, an electric) circuit.

ASPECT RATIO: Generally the ratio between two dimensions of an object. In tire terminology, it applies to the unloaded sidewall height of the tire divided by its overall width. A lower aspect ratio implies a shorter, wider tire. When used to describe a wing, it is the span of the airfoil (the long dimension perpendicular to the airflow) divided by its chord (the dimension parallel to the airflow).

ATMOSPHERE: The mass of air that surrounds the earth.

ATMOSPHERIC PRESSURE: The weight of the atmosphere per unit area.

ATOM: The smallest particle, or part, of an element, composed of electrons and protons and also of neutrons (with exception of hydrogen).

ATOMIZATION: The spraying of a liquid through a nozzle so that the liquid is broken into tiny globules or particles.

AUTOMATIC CHOKE: A choke that operates automatically in accordance with certain engine conditions (usually temperature and intake manifold vacuum)(also electrically controlled.)

AUTOMATIC TRANSMISSION: A transmission that reduces or eliminates the necessity of hand-shifting of gears to secure different gear ratios in the transmission).

AXIAL: In a direction parallel to the axle. Axial movement is movement parallel to the axis.

AXIS: A center line. The line about which something rotates or about which something is evenly divided.

AXLE: A cross support on a vehicle on which supporting wheel, or wheels, turn. There are two general types: live axles that also transmit power to the wheels and dead axles that transmit no power.

AXLE TRAMP: It is a form of wheel hop that occurs on cars with live axles, caused by the axle repeatedly rotating slightly with the wheels and then springing back.

B

B-PILLAR: The roof support between a car's front door window and rear side window, if there is one.

BACKFIRING: Pre-explosion of fuel-air mixture so that explosion passes back around the opened intake valve and flashes back through the intake manifold.

BACKLASH: The backward rotation of driven gear that is permitted by clearance between meshing teeth of two gears.

BAFFLE: A plate or shield to divert the flow of liquid or gas.

BALANCE SHAFT: A shaft designed so that, as it rotates, it vibrates in a way that reduces or cancels some of the vibration produced by an engine. Not essential to an engine's operation, balance shafts are nonetheless becoming increasingly common as a means of engine refinement. Balanced-shafted four-cylinder engines use two shafts turning in opposite directions on either side of the engine's crankshaft. A single balance shaft is used when fitted to three-cylinder and V-6 engines.

BALL BEARING: A type of bearing which contains steel balls that roll between inner and outer races.

BALL JOINT: A flexible joint consisting of a ball in a socket, used primarily in front suspensions because it can accommodate a wide range of angular motion.

BATTERY: A device consisting of two or more cells for converting chemical energy into electrical energy.

BATTERY CHARGING: The process of supplying a battery with a flow of electric current to produce chemical actions in the battery; these actions reactivate the chemicals in the battery so they can again produce electrical energy.

BDC: Bottom dead center; the position of the piston when it reaches the lower limit of travel in the cylinder.

BEAM AXLE: A rigid axle supporting the non-driven wheels. Also called a dead axle.

BEARING: A part in which a journal pivot, or pia, turns or revolves. A part on or in which another part slides.

BELTLINE: The line running around a car's body formed by the bottom edges of its glass panels.

BENDIX DRIVE: A type of drive used in a starter which provides automatic coupling with the engine flywheel for cranking and automatic uncoupling when the engine starts.

BEVEL GEAR: One of a pair of meshing gears whose working surfaces are inclined to the center lines of the driving and driven shafts. Bevel gears are used to transmit motion through an angle.

BLACKOUT LIGHTS: A lamp installed on a vehicle for use during blackouts, which can be seen from the air only at very close range.

BLOCK: See Cylinder.

BLOCK BLOW-BY: Leakage of the compressed fuel-air mixture or burned gases from combustion, passing piston and rings and into the crankcase.

BLOWER: A mechanical device for compressing and delivering air to engine at higher than atmospheric pressure.

BODY: The assembly of sheet-metal sections, framework, doors, windows, etc., which provides an enclosure for passengers or carriage space for freight.

BOGIE: A suspension unit consisting of tandem axles jointed by a single cross support (trunnion axle) that also acts as a vertical pivot for the entire unit.

BOND: To bind together.

BOOST PRESSURE: The increase above atmospheric pressure produced inside the intake manifold by any supercharger. It is commonly measured in psi, inches of mercury, or bar.

BORE: The diameter of engine cylinder hole. Also diameter of any hole; as, for example, the hole into which a bushing is fitted.

BOSS: An extension or strengthened section, such as the projections within a piston which support the piston pin.

BRAKE BAND: A flexible band, usually of metal with an inner lining of brake fabric, which is tightened on a drum to slow or stop drum rotation.

BRAKE BIAS: The front/rear distribution of a car's braking power. For the shortest stopping distance, brake bias should match the car's traction at each end during hard braking.

BRAKE DRUM: Metal drum mounted on car wheel or other rotating members; brake shoes or brake band, mechanically forced against it, causes it to slow or stop.

BRAKE FLUID: A compounded fluid used in hydraulic braking system; it transmits hydraulic force from the brake master cylinder to the wheel cylinder and should be impervious to heat or freezing.

BRAKE HORSEPOWER: The power actually delivered by the engine which is available for driving the vehicle.

BRAKE LINING: A special woven fabric material with which brake shoes or brake bands are lined; it withstands high temperatures and pressures.

BRAKE MODULATION: The process of varying pedal pressure to hold a car's brakes on the verge of lockup. Ideally, the brakes will unlock with only a slight reduction in the pressure needed to lock them. Typically, however, a considerable pressure reduction is required.

BRAKE SHOES: The curved metal part, faced with brake lining, which is forced against the brake drum to produce braking or retarding action.

BRAKE SYSTEM: The system on a vehicle that slows or stops it as a pedal or lever is operated.

BRAKE TORQUING: A procedure generally used in performance tests to improve the off-the-line acceleration of a car equipped with an automatic transmission. It is executed by firmly depressing the brake with the left food, applying the throttle with the car in gear to increase engine rpm, then releasing the brakes. Brake torqueing is particularly effective with turbo-charged cars because it helps overcome turbo lag.

BRAKES: The mechanism that slows or stops a vehicle or mechanism when a pedal or other control is operated. Also called the brake system.

BREATHING (ENGINE): A term used to describe an engine's ability to fill its cylinders with air-fuel mixture and then discharge the burnt exhaust gases. In general, the more air-fuel mixture an engine burns, the more power it produces.

BRONZE: An alloy consisting essentially of copper and tin.

BRUSHES: The carbon or carbon and metal parts in a motor or generator that contact the rotating armature commutator or rings.

BUSHING: A sleeve placed in a bore to serve as a bearing surface. A simple suspension bearing that accommodates limited rotary motion, typically made of two coaxial steel tubes bonded to a sleeve of rubber between them. The compliance of the bushing in different directions has a great effect on ride harshness and handling.

BYPASS: A separate passage which permits a liquid, gas, or electric current to take a path other than that normally used.

C

C-PILLAR: The roof support between a car's rearmost side window and its rear window. On a vehicle with four side pillars, the rearmost roof support may be called a D-pillar.

CAB: Separate driver's compartment provided on trucks.

CAD/CAM: Computer-aided design and computer-aided manufacturing—the harnessing of computers to generate drawings, perform complex structural and design analyses, and directly program numerically controlled machines to produce automotive parts.

CAM: A moving part of an irregular form designed to move or alter the motion of another part.

CAMBER: To curve or bend; the amount in inches or degrees that the front wheels of an automotive vehicle are tilted from a true vertical at the top.

CAM PROFILE: The shape of each lobe on a camshaft. The profile determines the amount, or duration, of time the valve is open; it also largely determines the valve's maximum opening, or lift.

CAMSHAFT: A shaft fitted with several cams, whose lobes push on valve lifters to convert rotary motion into linear motion. The opening and closing of the valves in all piston engines is regulated by one or more camshafts.

CAPACITANCE: That property of a circuit which tends to increase the amount of current flowing in a circuit for a given voltage or to delete in its entirety.

CAPACITOR (CONDENSER): A device for inserting the property of capacitance into a circuit; two or more conductors separated by a dielectric.

CARBON FIBER: Threadlike strands of pure carbon that are extremely strong in tension (that is, when pulled) and are reasonably flexible. Carbon fiber can be bound in a matrix of plastic resin by heat, vacuum, or pressure to form a composite that is strong, light, and very expensive.

CARBON-PILE REGULATOR: A type of regulator for regulating or controlling voltage or amperage in a circuit, which makes use of a stack, or pile, of carbon disks.

CARBURETOR: The device in a fuel system which mixes fuel and air and delivers the combustible mixture to the intake manifold.

CASTER: The amount in degrees that the steering knuckle pivots are tilted forward or backward from a true vertical.

CATALYTIC CONVERTER: Often simply called a *catalyst*, a stainless steel canister fitted to a car's exhaust system that contains a thin layer of catalytic material spread over a large area of inert supports. The material used is some combination of platinum, rhodium, and palladium; it induces chemical reactions that convert an engine's exhaust emissions into less harmful products. So-called three-way catalysts are particularly efficient; their operation, however, demands very precise combustion control, which can be produced only by a feedback fuel-air ratio control system.

CELL: A combination of electrodes and electrolyte which converts chemical energy into electrical energy. Two or more cells connected together form a battery.

CENTER DIFFERENTIAL: A differential used in four-wheel-drive systems to distribute power to the front and rear differentials.

CENTER OF GRAVITY: The imaginary point in any object about which it is in perfect balance no matter how it is turned or rotated around that point.

CENTRIFUGAL ADVANCE: The mechanism in an ignition distributor by which the spark is advanced or retarded as the engine speed varies.

CENTRIFUGAL FORCE: The force acting on a rotating body, which tends to move its parts outward and away from the center of rotation.

CHARGE INDICATOR: The device on a vehicle that indicates, by a needle, whether or not the battery is receiving a charge from the generator.

CHARGING RATE: The rate of flow, in amperes, of electric current flowing through a battery while it is being charged.

CHASSIS: An assembly of mechanisms, attached to a frame, that make up the major operating part of an automotive vehicle (less body). In cars with unitized construction, the chassis comprises everything but the body of the car.

CHOKE: A device in the carburetor that chokes off, or reduces, the flow of air into the intake manifold; this produces a partial vacuum in the intake manifold and a consequent richer fuel-air mixture.

CIRCUIT: A closed path or combination of paths through which passage of the medium (electric current, air, liquid, etc.) is possible.

CIRCUIT BREAKER: In electric circuits, a mechanism designed to break or open the circuit when certain conditions exist; especially the device in automotive circuits that opens the circuit between the generator and battery to prevent overcharging the battery. (One of the three units comprising a generator regulator.)

CLOCKWISE: Direction of movement, usually rotary, which is the same as movement of hands on the face of a clock.

CLUTCH: The mechanism in an automotive vehicle, located in the power train, that connects the engine to, or disconnects the engine from, the remainder of the power train.

COIL: In electrical circuits, turns of wire, usually on a core and enclosed in a case, through which electric current passes.

COIL SPRING: A type of spring made of an elastic metal such as steel, formed into a wire or bar and wound into a coil. Coil springs have many automotive applications but are particularly important as suspension springs.

COMBAT VEHICLE: A type of vehicle, usually armored, for use in armed combat.

COMBUSTION: A chemical action, or burning; in an engine, the burning of a fuel-air mixture in the combustion chamber.

COMBUSTION CHAMBER: The space at the top of the cylinder and in the head in which combustion of the fuel-air mixture takes place. It is formed by the top of the piston and a cavity in the cylinder head. Since most of the air-fuel mixture's combustion takes place in this space, its design and shape can greatly affect the power, fuel, efficiency, and emissions of the engine.

COMMUTATION: The process of converting alternating current which flows in the armature windings of direct current generators into direct current.

COMMUTATOR: That part of rotating machinery which makes electrical contact with the brushes and connects the armature windings with the external circuit.

COMPLIANCE: A slight resiliency, or *give*, designed into suspension bushings to help absorb bumps. Good compliance allows the wheels to move rearward a bit as they hit bumps but doesn't allow them to move laterally during cornering.

COMPOSITE: Any material that consists of two or more components, typically one or more of high strength and one an adhesive binder. The most common composite is fiberglass, which consists of thin glass fibers bonded together in a plastic matrix. The structural properties of composites can be altered by controlling the orientation and configuration of the high-strength components.

COMPRESSION: Act of pressing into a smaller space or reducing in size or volume by pressure.

COMPRESSION RATIO: The ratio between the volume in the cylinder with the piston at bottom dead center and with the piston at top dead center. The ratio between the combined volume of a cylinder and a combustion chamber when the piston is at the bottom of its stroke, and the volume when the piston is at the top of its stroke. The higher the compression ratio, the more mechanical energy an engine can squeeze from its air-fuel mixture. Higher compression ratios, however, also make detonation more likely.

COMPRESSION RINGS: The upper rings on a piston; the rings designed to hold the compression in the cylinder and prevent blow-by.

COMPRESSION STROKE: The piston stroke from bottom dead center to top dead center during which both valves are closed and the gases in the cylinder are compressed.

CONCENTRIC: Having a common center, as circles or spheres, one within the other.

CONDENSER: See Capacitor.

CONDUCTOR: A material through which electricity will readily flow.

CONNECTING ROD: Linkage between the crankshaft and piston, usually attached to the piston by a piston pin and to the crankshaft by a split bearing and bearing cap.

CONSTANT-VELOCITY JOINT: A particular kind of universal joint designed so that there is no cyclic fluctuation between the speeds of its input and output shafts.

CONTACT PATCH: The portion of a tire tread that is in contact with the road. On modern tires, it varies from nearly a circle to a wide ellipse.

CONTROL ARM: A suspension element that has one joint at one end and two joints at the other end, typically the chassis side. Also known as a wishbone or an A-arm.

CONVERTIBLE: A car whose top can be completely lowered.

COOLANT: The liquid that circulates in an engine cooling system which reduces heat generated by the engine.

COOLING FAN: The fan in the engine cooling system that provides a forced circulation of air through the radiator or around the engine cylinders so that cooling is effected.

COOLING FINS: Thin metal projections on air-cooled-engine cylinder and head which greatly increases the heat-radiating surfaces and helps provide cooling of engine cylinder.

COOLING SYSTEM: A system which reduces heat generated by the engine and thereby prevents engine overheating; includes, in liquid-cooled engine, engine water jackets, radiator, and water pump.

CORE: An iron mass, generally the central portion of a coil or electromagnet or armature around which the wire is coiled.

CORNERING LIMIT: The maximum speed at which a car can negotiate a given curve.

COUNTERCLOCKWISE: Direction of movement, usually rotary, which is opposite in direction to movement of hands on the face of a clock.

COUPE: A closed car with two side doors and less than 33 cubic feet of rear interior volume, according to measurements based on SAE standard J1100. A two-door car is, therefore, not necessarily a coupe.

COWL: The front portion of the vehicle body or cab which partially encloses the dash panel and forms the windshield frame.

CRANK: A device for converting reciprocating motion into rotary motion, and vice versa.

CRANKCASE: The lower part of the engine in which the crankshaft rotates. In automotive practice, the upper part is lower section of cylinder block while lower section is the oil pan.

CRANKCASE BREATHER: The opening or tube that allows air to enter the crankcase and thus permit crankcase ventilation.

CRANKCASE DILUTION: Dilution of the lubricating oil in the oil pan by liquid gasoline seeping down the cylinder walls past the piston rings.

CRANKCASE VENTILATION: The circulation of air through the crankcase which removes water and other vapors, thereby preventing the formation of water sludge and other unwanted substances.

CRANKING MOTOR: See Starter.

CRANKSHAFT: The main rotating member or shaft of the engine, with cranks to which the connecting rods are attached. Together, the crankshaft and the con rods transform the pistons' reciprocating motion into rotary motion.

CRASH: Generally a high-speed parking maneuver. Often, the driver at fault will refer to it as a *shunt* or and *incident*.

CROSS-DRIVE TRANSMISSION: A special type of transmission used in tanks and other heavy vehicles which combines the actions of a transmission with torque converter, steering system, and differential.

CURRENT REGULATOR: A magnetic-controlled relay by which the field circuit of the generator is made and broken very rapidly to secure even current output from the generator and prevent generator overload from excessive output. (One of the three units comprising a generator regulator.)

CUTOUT RELAY: An automatic magnetic switch attached to the generator to cut out generator circuit and prevent overcharging of battery. See Circuit Breaker.

CYCLE: A series of events with a start and finish, during which a definite train of events takes place. In the engine, the four piston strokes (or two piston strokes on 2-stroke cycle engine) that complete the working process and produce power.

CYLINDER: A tubular-shaped structure. In the engine, the tubular opening in which the piston moves up and down. Typically made of cast iron and formed as a part of the block.

CYLINDER BLOCK: That part of an engine to which, and in which, other engine parts and accessories are attached or assembled.

CYLINDER HEAD: The part of the engine that encloses the cylinder bores. Contains water jackets (on liquid-cooled engine) and valves (on I-head engines). The aluminum or iron casting that houses the combustion chambers, the intake and exhaust ports, and much or all of the valve train. The head (or heads, if an engine has more than one bank of cylinders) is always directly above the cylinders.

CYLINDER LINER: The circular housing that the piston moves in when the cylinder is not an integral part of the block. Also known as a sleeve.

D

DBA: A unit of measure for decibels, the measure of sound intensity or pressure named after Alexander Graham Bell. It is a logarithmic measurement; every 3dB increase represents a doubling of the sound pressure. The A in dBA indicates that the measurement was taken with an A-weighted scale; sound pressure varies across the audible spectrum, and the A-weighted scale approximates the human ear's sensitivity to various frequencies.

DC: Direct current, or current that flows in one direction only.

DAMPER: A device for reducing the motion or oscillations of moving parts, air, or liquid.

DASH PANEL: The partition that separates the driver's compartment from the engine compartment. Sometimes called firewall.

DE DION SUSPENSION: A suspension system in which the rear, driven wheels are bolted to a transverse, lightweight, rigid member. Power is delivered to the wheels by universal-jointed half-shafts attached to a body-mounted differential.

DEAD AXLE: An axle that simply supports and does not turn or deliver power to the wheel or rotating member.

DEAD PEDAL: A footrest found to the left of the leftmost pedal. It provides a place for the driver to brace his left leg during hard cornering.

DECELERATION: The process of slowing down. Opposite to acceleration.

DEGASSER: A device used in connection with carburetors for shutting off the flow of fuel during deceleration so that gases from incomplete combustion during deceleration are prevented.

DETONATION: A condition in which, after the spark plug fires, some of the unburned air-fuel mixture in the combustion chamber explodes spontaneously, set off only by the heat and pressure of air-fuel mixture that has already been ignited. Detonation, or *knock*, greatly increases the mechanical and thermal stresses on the engine.

DIAPHRAGM: A flexible membrane, usually made of fabric and rubber in automotive components, clamped at the edges and usually spring-loaded; used in fuel pump, vacuum pump, distributor, etc.

DIESEL ENGINE: An engine using the diesel cycle of operation; air alone is compressed and diesel fuel is injected at the end of the compression stroke. Heat of compression produces ignition.

DIFFERENTIAL: A special gearbox designed so that the torque fed into it is split and delivered to two outputs that can turn at different speeds. Differentials within axles are designed to split torque evenly; however, when used between the front and rear axles in four-wheel-drive systems (a center differential), they can be designed to apportion torque unevenly.

DIFFERENTIAL WINDING: In electrical machinery, a winding that is wound in a reverse direction or different direction than the main operating windings. The differential winding acts to modify or change the action of the machine under certain conditions.

DISC BRAKES: Properly called caliper disc brakes—a type of brake that consists of a disc that rotates at wheel speed, straddled by a caliper that can squeeze the surfaces of the disc near it periphery. Disc brakes provide a more linear response and operate more efficiently at high temperatures and wet conditions than drum brakes.

DISTRIBUTOR: See Ignition Distributor.

DIVE: The dipping if a car's nose that occurs when the brakes are applied. Dive is caused by a load transfer from the rear to the front suspension; this transfer occurs because the car's center of gravity, through which all inertial forces pass, is higher than it contact patches, the points where the braking forces are exerted on the ground.

DOLLY: A two-wheel trailer coupled to a semitrailer to support and steer its front end when it is converted into a full trailer.

DOHC: Double overhead camshaft—a DOHC engine has two camshafts in each cylinder head; one camshaft operates the intake valve, the other actuates the exhaust valves.

DOWNFORCE: A vertical force directed downward, produced by airflow around an object—such as a car body.

DRAG COEFFICIENT: A dimensionless measure of the aerodynamic sleekness of an object. A sleek car has a drag coefficient, or Cd, of about .30; a square, flat plate's is 1.98. Also signified by Cx.

DRAG LINK: An intermediate link in the steering system between the Pitman arm and an intermediate arm or drag-link arm.

DRIVABILITY: The general qualitative evaluation of a power-train's operating qualities, including idle smoothness, cold and hot steering, throttle response, power delivery, and tolerance for altitude changes.

DRIVELINE: Everything in the drivetrain, less the engine and the transmission.

DRIVESHAFT: The shaft that transmits power from the transmission.

DRIVETRAIN: All of a car's components that create power and transmit it to the wheels; i.e., the engine, the transmission, the differential(s), the hubs, and any interconnecting shafts.

DRUM BRAKES: A type of brake that has an iron casting shaped like a shallow drum that rotates with the wheel. Curved brake shoes are forced into contact with the inner periphery of this drum to provide braking.

DUAL IGNITION: Ignition system using two spark plugs for each cylinder so that a dual spark effect takes place driving each power stroke.

DUAL-RATIO AXLES: Axle in truck with contains a mechanism for changing driving ratio of the wheels to either high or low ratio. Two-speed differential.
DYNAMOMETER: A device for measuring power output on an engine.

E

EGR: Exhaust-gas recirculation—a method of reducing NOx (oxides of nitrogen) exhaust emissions by recirculating some of the engine's exhaust gas into the intake manifold. The exhaust gas serves as inert filler that absorbs heat during the combustion process and reduces the peak temperature reached during combustion.
ECCENTRIC: Off center.
EDDY CURRENTS: Currents which are induced in an iron core and circulate in the core.
EFFICIENCY: Ratio between the effect produced and the power expended to produce the effect.
ELECTRIC BRAKES: A brake system which uses electric current for energization.
ELECTRICAL SYSTEM: In the automotive vehicle, the system that electrically cranks the engine for starting, furnishes high-voltage sparks to the engine cylinders to fire compressed fuel-air charges, lights the lights, operates heater motor, ratio, etc. Consists, in part, of starter, wiring, battery, generator, generator, ignition distributor, and ignition coil.
ELECTRICITY: A form of energy that involves the movement of electrons from one place to another, or the gathering of electrons in one area.
ELECTRODE: Either terminal of an electric source; either conductor by which the current enters and leaves an electrolyte.
ELECTROLYTE: The liquid in a battery or other electrochemical device, in which the conduction of electricity is accompanied by chemical decomposition.
ELECTROMAGNET: Temporary magnet constructed by winding a number of turns of insulated wire into a coil or around an iron core; it is energized by a flow of electric current through the coil.
ELECTRON: Negative charged particle that is a basic constituent of matter and electricity. Movement of electrons is an electric current.
ENERGY: The capacity for performing work.
ENGINE: An assembly that burns fuel to produce power sometimes referred to as the power plant.
ENGINE-CONTROL SYSTEM: A computerized brain that regulates an engine's operation by monitoring certain engine characteristics (rpm, coolant temperature, intake airflow, etc.) through a network of sensors and then controlling key variables (fuel metering, spark timing, EGR, etc.) according to pre-programmed schedules.
EPA FUEL ECONOMY: Laboratory fuel-economy tests administered by the Environmental Protection Agency using simulated weight and drag to re-create real driving conditions. The city fuel-economy test, also used to test emissions compliance, is based on a drive through typical Los Angeles urban traffic of about twenty years ago. The highway test uses a higher, steadier speed, averaging 49.4 mph.
EVAPORATION: The action that takes place when a liquid changes to a vapor or gas.
EXHAUST MANIFOLD: The network of passages that gathers the exhaust gases from the various exhaust ports and routes them toward the catalysts and mufflers of the exhaust system. A manifold with free-flowing passages of a carefully designed configuration, called a *header*, can improve breathing.
EXHAUST PORT: The passageway in the cylinder head leading from the exhaust valves to the exhaust manifold.

EXHAUST STROKE: The piston stroke from bottom dead center to top dead center during which the exhaust valve is opened so that burned gases are forced from the engine cylinder.

EXHAUST VALVE: The valve which opens to allow the burned gases to escape from the cylinder during the exhaust stroke.

F

FAN: See Cooling Fan.

FEEDBACK FUEL-AIR RATIO CONTROL: A feature of a computer-controlled fuel system. By using a sensor to measure the oxygen content of the engine's exhaust, the system keeps the fuel-air ratio very close to the proportion for chemically perfect combustion. Such tight control of the fuel-air ratio is mandatory for the proper operation of three-way catalysts.

F-HEAD: A type of engine with valves arranged to form an F; one valve is in the head, the other in the cylinder block.

FIBERGLASS: A composite material that relies on small glass fibers for its strength.

FIELD: In a generator or electric motor, the area in which a magnetic flow occurs.

FIELD COIL: A coil of wire, wound around an iron core, which produces the magnetic field in a generator or motor when current passes through it.

FIELD FRAME: The frame in a generator or motor into which the field coils are assembled.

FIELD WINDING: See Field Coil.

FIFTH WHEEL: The flat, round heavy steel plates (upper and lower) together with a kingpin for coupling semitrailer to truck-tractor. The lower plate is mounted on the truck-tractor, the upper on the semitrailer.

FILTER: A device through which gas or liquid is passed; dirt, dust, and other impurities are removed by the separating action.

FINAL DRIVE: That part of the power train on tractors, truck-tractors tanks, and tank-like vehicles that carries the driving power to the wheels or sprockets to produce the vehicle motion as they turn.

FINAL-DRIVE RATIO: The reduction ratio, found in the gearset of a drivetrain, that is furthest removed from the engine. Typically, the differential ratio.

FLOAT: In the carburetor, the metal shell that is suspended by the fuel in the float bowl and controls a needle valve that regulates the fuel level in the bowl.

FLOAT CIRCUIT: In the carburetor, the circuit that controls entry of fuel and fuel level in the float bowl.

FLOORPAN: The largest and most important stamped metal part in a car's body. Usually assembled from several smaller stampings, the floorpan forms the floor and fixes the dimensions for most of the car's external and structural panels. It is also the foundation for many of the car's mechanical parts.

FLUID COUPLING: Any device that transfers power through a fluid between its inputs and outputs. A fluid coupling basically consists of two fans in a sealed, oil-filled housing. The input fan churns the oil, and the churning oil in turn twirls the output fan. Such a coupling allows some speed difference between its input and output shafts.

FLYWHEEL: The rotating metal wheel, attached to the crankshaft, that helps level out the power surges from the power strokes and also serves as part of the clutch and engine-cranking system.

FOOT-POUND: A unit of work done in raising 1 pound avoirdupois against the force of gravity to the height of 1 foot.

FORCE: The action that one body may exert upon another to change its motion or shape.

FOUR-STROKE-CYCLE ENGINE: An engine that requires four piston strokes (intake, compression, power, exhaust) to make the complete cycle of events in the engine cylinder.

FOUR VALVES PER CYLINDER: A valvetrain with a total of four valves in the combustion chamber, typically two intakes and two exhausts. Compared to the more common two-valve-per-cylinder engine designs, a four-valve layout offers improved breathing and allows the spark plug to be located closer to center of the combustion chamber.

FOUR-WHEEL DRIFT: A somewhat imprecise term that describes a cornering situation in which all four tires are operating at large slip angles.

FOUR-WHEEL STEERING: A steering system that actively steers the rear wheels as well as the fronts to improve handling and maneuverability.

FOURTEEN-WHEEL STEERING: A stunning high-speed maneuver that occurs when a large semi-truck experiences four simultaneous blowouts while driving down a steep hill in the rain.

FRAME: An assembly of metal structural parts and channel sections that support the engine and body and that is supported by the vehicle wheels.

FREQUENCY: The number of vibrations, cycles, or changes in direction in a unit of time.

FRICTION: The resistance to motion between two bodies in contact with each other.

FUEL: The substance that is burned to produce heat and create motion of the piston on the power stroke in an engine.

FUEL FILTER: A device placed in the fuel line of the fuel system to remove dirt and other harmful solids.

FUEL GAGE: An indicating device in the fuel system that indicates the amount of fuel in the fuel tank.

FUEL INJECTION: Any system that meters fuel to an engine by measuring its needs and then regulating the fuel flow, by electronic or mechanical means, through a pump and injectors. Throttle-body injection locates the injector(s) centrally in the throttle-body housing, while port injection allocates at least one injector for each cylinder near its intake port.

FUEL LINE: The tube or tubes connecting the fuel tank and the carburetor and through which the fuel passes.

FUEL PASSAGE: Drilled holes in the carburetor body and tubes through which fuel passes from the float bowl to the fuel nozzles.

FUEL PUMP: The mechanism in the fuel system that transfers fuel from the fuel tank to the carburetor.

FUEL TANK: The storage tank for fuel on the vehicle.

FULCRUM: The support, as a wedge-shaped piece or a hinge, about which a lever turns.

FULL TRAILER: An independent and fully contained vehicle without motive power.

FUSE: A circuit-protecting device which makes use of a substance that has a low melting point. The substance melts if an overload occurs, thus protecting other devices in the system.

G

G: The unit of measure for lateral acceleration, or *roadholding*. One g is equivalent to 32.2 feet per second, the rate at which any object accelerates when dropped at sea level. If a car were cornering at 1.0g—a figure that very few production cars are able to approach—the driver's body would be pushing equally hard against the side of the seat as against the bottom of it.

GASKET: A flat strip, usually of cork or metal, or both, placed between two surfaces to provide a tight seal between them.

GASOLINE: A hydrocarbon, obtained from petroleum, is suitable as an internal combustion engine fuel.
GEAR RATIO: The relative speeds at which two gears turn; the proportional rate of rotation.
GEARS: Mechanical devices to transmit power or turning effort, from one shaft to another; more specifically, gears which contain teeth that engage or mesh upon turning.
GEARSET: A group of two or more gears used to transmit power.
GEARSHIFT: A mechanism by which the gears in a transmission system are engaged.
GENERATOR: In the electrical system, the device that changes mechanical energy to electrical energy for lighting lights, charging the battery, etc.
GENERATOR REGULATOR: In the electrical system, the unit which is composed of the current regulator voltage regulator, and circuit breaker relay.
GOVERNOR: A mechanism that controls speed or other variable. Specifically, speed governors used on automotive vehicles to prevent excessive engine speed by controlling actions in the carburetor.
GREENHOUSE: The portion of a car's body that rises above the belt-line of the car.
GROUND: Connection of an electrical unit to the engine or frame to return the current to its source.
GROUND EFFECT: The phenomenon that occurs when the airflow between a moving object and the ground creates downforce.
GUSSET PLATE: A plate at the joint of a frame structure of steel to strengthen the joint.

H

HALF-SHAFT: An articulating, rotating shaft used in independent-suspension systems to transmit power from a differential to a wheel.
HALF TRACK: A vehicle using tracks instead of wheels at the rear.
HANDBRAKE: A brake operated by hand. Also referred to as the parking brake.
HANDLING: A general term covering all the aspects of a car's behavior that are related to its directional control.
HARSHNESS: The aspect of a car's ride roughness that is characterized by small, sharp jolts.
HEADLIGHT: Lights at the front of the vehicle designed to illuminate the road ahead when the vehicle is traveling forward.
HEAT: A form of energy.
HEEL-AND-TOE: A performance-oriented technique of downshifting while braking that requires the driver to use all three pedals of a manual-transmission car simultaneously. To perform a heel-and-toe downshift, the driver brakes with the toe of his right foot and—while continuing to brake—uses the heel or the side of the same foot to blip the throttle and raise engine rpm as he downshifts. The left foot operates the clutch pedal in the normal fashion. The sequence is as follows: brake with the right toe; depress the clutch with the left foot; shift to neutral; while continuing to brake, blip the throttle with the side or the heel of the right foot to raise rpm; shift to a lower gear; let the clutch out; release the brakes. The technique is difficult to master, but after practice it can be performed in less than a second. This process is best for smooth power flow and long transmission life.
HEIM JOINT: An extremely rigid articulating joint, commonly known as a *spherical rod-end*, used in any precision linkage. Heim joints are often used in the suspension links of race cars because they locate wheels very precisely.
HELICAL: In the shape of a helix, which is the shape of a screw thread or coil spring.

HELICAL GEAR: A type of gear in which the teeth are cut at a slanting angle to the gear's circumference. A helical design produces an even, constant tooth loading in a gearset, thereby reducing noise.

HEMI: A term used to describe any engine that has hemispherical combustion chambers in its cylinder head. Although a four-valve design is more efficient, a hemi head provides room for a pair of large valves and offers good breathing characteristics.

HIGH-SPEED CIRCUIT: In the carburetor, the passages through which fuel flows when the throttle valve is fully opened.

HIGH TENSION: Another term for high voltage. In the electrical system, refers to the ignition secondary circuit since this circuit produces high-voltage surges to cause sparking at the spark plugs.

HILL HOLDER: A device in the transmission that automatically prevents the vehicle from rolling backward down a hill when the vehicle is brought to a stop.

HORN: An electrical signaling device on the vehicle.

HORNSEPOWER: The common unit of measurement of an engine's power. One horsepower equals 550 foot-pounds per second, the power needed to lift 550 pounds one foot off the ground in one second—or one pound 550 feet up in the same time.

HOTCHKISS DRIVE: Type of rear live axle suspension in which the springs serve as torque members.

HOTCHKISS SUSPENSION: A live-axle rear suspension in which leaf springs handle both the axle's springing and its location.

HULL: In a tank, the protective shell that encloses the vehicle components and occupants.

HYDRAMATIC: A type of automatic transmission containing a fluid coupling and automatic controls for shifting from one gear to another.

HYDRAULIC BRAKES: A braking system that uses a fluid to transmit hydraulic pressure from a master cylinder to wheel cylinders, which then cause brakeshoe movement and braking action.

HYDRAULIC LIFTER: A valve lifter that, using simple valving and the engine's oil pressure, can adjust its length slightly—thereby maintaining zero clearance in the valvetrain. Hydraulic lifters reduce valvetrain noise and are maintenance-free.

HYDRAULIC STEERING: A steering system that uses a fluid to produce an assisting hydraulic pressure on the steering linkage, thus reducing the steering effort on the part of the driver.

HYDRAULIC TRAVERSING MECHANISM: A turret traversing system that makes use of hydraulic pressure to furnish the motive power to traverse the turret.

HYDRAULIC VALVE TAPPET: A valve tappet that, by means of hydraulic pressure, maintains zero valve clearance so that valve noise is reduced.

HYDROMETER: A device to determine the specific gravity of a liquid. This indicates the freezing point of the coolant in a cooling system or, as another example, the state of charge of a battery.

HYDROVAC BRAKES: A type of braking system using vacuum to assist in brake operation. The vacuum action reduces the effort required from the driver to operate the vehicle brakes.

I

IDLE: Engine speed when accelerator pedal is fully released; generally assumed to mean when engine is doing no work.

IDLE CIRCUIT: The circuit in the carburetor through which fuel is fed when the engine is idling.

IDLER GEAR: A gear placed between a driving and a driven gear to make them rotate in the same direction. It does not affect the gear ratio.

IDLING ADJUSTMENT: Adjustment made on the carburetor to alter the fuel-air mixture ratio or engine speed on idle.

IGNITION: The action of setting fire to; in the engine, the initiating of the combustion process in the engine cylinders.

IGNITION ADVANCE: Refers to the spark advance produced by the distributor in accordance with engine speed and intake manifold vacuum.

IGNITION COIL: That component of the ignition system that acts as a transformer and steps up battery voltage to many thousand volts; the high voltage then produces a spark at the spark plug gap.

IGNITION DISTRIBUTOR: That component of the ignition system that closes and opens the circuit between the battery and ignition coil, and distributes the resultant high-voltage surges from the coil to the proper spark plugs.

IGNITION SWITCH: The switch in the ignition system that can be operated to open or close the ignition primary circuit.

IGNITION TIMING: Refers to the timing of the spark at the spark plug as related to the piston position in the engine cylinder.

I-HEAD: A type of engine with valves in the cylinder head.

IMPELLER: The rotor f a centrifugal pump which causes the fuel-air in an engine to be thrown into a diffuser chamber to effect thorough mixing and good distribution.

INDEPENDENT SUSPENSION: Any suspension in which the camber of a wheel is not directly affected by the vertical motion of the opposite wheel.

INDICATED HORSEPOWER: A measurement of engine power based on power actually developed in the engine cylinders.

INDUCTION: The action or process of producing voltage by the relative motion of a magnetic field and a conductor.

INJECTOR: The mechanism, including nozzle, which injects fuel into the engine combustion chamber on diesel engines.

IN-LINE ENGINE: An engine in which all engine cylinders are in a single row, or line.

INSERT: A form of screw thread insert to be placed in a tapped hole into which a screw or bolt will be screwed. The insert protects the part into which the hole was tapped, preventing enlargement due to repeated removal and replacement of the bolt.

INSTRUMENTS: The displays on the dashboard that communicate information about the mechanical operation of the car to the driver. Mechanically controlled instruments almost always feature analog displays (usually needles-and-numbers dials). Electronically controlled instruments use analog displays, digital readouts, or even graphics panels.

INSULATION: Substance that stops movement of electricity (electrical insulation) or heat (heat insulation).

INSULATOR: A substance (usually of glass or porcelain) that will not conduct electricity.

INTAKE CHARGE: The mixture of fuel and air that flows into the engine.

INTAKE MANIFOLD: The network of passages that directs air or air-fuel mixture from the throttle body to the intake ports in the cylinder head. The flow typically proceeds from the throttle body into a chamber called the plenum, which in turn feeds individual tubes, called runners, leading to each intake port. Engine breathing is enhanced if the intake manifold is configured to optimize the pressure pulses in the intake system.

INTAKE PORT: The passageway in a cylinder head leading from the intake manifold to the intake valve(s).

INTAKE STROKE: The piston stroke from top dead center to bottom dead center during which the intake valve is open and the cylinder receives a charge of fuel-mixture.

INTAKE VALVE: The valve in the engine which is opened during the intake stroke to permit the entrance of fuel-air mixture into the cylinder.

INTEGRAL: Whole; entire; lacking nothing of completeness.

INTERCOOLER: A heat exchanger that cools the air (or, in some installations, the intake charge) that has been heated by compression in any type of supercharger. An intercooler resembles a radiator; it houses large passages for the intake flow, and uses either outside air or water directed over it to lower the temperature of the intake flow inside.

INTERFERENCE: In radio, any signal received that overrides or prevents normal reception of the desired signal. In mechanical practice, anything that causes mismatching of parts so they cannot be normally assembled.

INTERNAL COMBUSTION ENGINE: An engine in which the fuel is burned inside the engine, as opposed to an external combustion engine where the fuel is burned outside the engine, such as a steam engine.

INTERNAL GEAR: A gear in which the teeth point inward rather than outward as with a standard spur gear.

J

JACKSHAFT: An intermediate driving shaft.

JET: A metered opening in an air or fuel passage to control the flow of fuel or air.

JOUNCE: The motion of a wheel that compresses its suspension.

JOUNCE BUMPER: An elastic cushion used to stiffen the suspension gradually as it approaches the end of its jounce travel.

JOURNAL: That part of a shaft that rotates in a bearing.

K

KEVLAR: A very flexible, strong, light, and abrasion-resistant artificial fiber, manufactured by DuPont, that can be combined with a plastic resin to produce an efficient composite material for chassis and body components.

KICKDOWN: A downshift in an automatic transmission caused by depressing the throttle.

KINGPIN: A pin by which a stud axle is articulated to an axle beam or steering head; also the enmeshing pin in a fifth wheel assembly.

KINGPIN INCLINATION: The number of degrees that the kingpin, which supports the front wheel, is tilted from the vertical.

KNOCK: In the engine, a rapping or hammering noise resulting from excessively rapid burning or detonation of the compressed fuel-air mixture.

KNOCK SENSOR: A sensor mounted on the engine that is designed to detect the high-frequency vibrations caused by detonation. By employing a knock sensor, a computerized engine-control system allows an engine to operate very near its detonation limit—thereby improving power and efficiency.

KNUCKLE: A joint or parts carrying a hinge pin which permit one part to swing about or move in relation to another.

L

LAMINATED: Made up of thin sheets, leaves, or plates.

LAMINATED LEAF SPRING: Spring made up of leaves of graduated size.

LANDING GEAR: Retractable support under the front end of a semitrailer to hold it up when it is uncoupled from the truck tractor.

LATERAL LINK: A suspension link that is aligned to resist sideways motions in a wheel.

LEADING LINK: A suspension link that is aligned to resist longitudinal motions in a wheel; it is mounted to the chassis behind the wheel.

LEAF SPRING: A long, flat, thin, flexible piece of spring steel or various composite materials that deflects by bending when forces act upon it. Leaf springs are used primarily in suspensions.

LEAN MIXTURE: A fuel-air mixture that has a high proportion of air and a low proportion of fuel.

LEVER: A rigid bar or beam of any shape capable of turning about one point, called the fulcrum; used for transmitting or changing force or motion.

LEVERAGE: The mechanical advantage obtained by use of lever; also an arrangement or combination of levers.

L-HEAD: A type of engine with valves in the cylinder block.

LIFT: A vertical force directed upward, produced by the airflow around a moving object—such as a car body.

LIFT-THROTTLE OVERSTEER: A handling characteristic that causes the rear tires to lose some of their cornering grip when the throttle is released during hard cornering.

LIGHT: In the electric circuit, an electrical device that includes a wire in a gas-filled bulb which glow brightly when current passes through it—often called a lamp.

LIGHTING SWITCH: In the electrical circuit, a switch that turns light on or off.

LIMITED-SLIP DIFFERENTIAL: A differential fitted with a mechanism that limits the speed and torque differences between its two outputs. Limited slip ensures that some torque is always distributed to both wheels, even when one is on very slippery pavement.

LINE: The path through a corner that best accommodates a late braking point, a high cornering speed, and the fastest-possible exit speed out of a corner.

LINK: A suspension member that has a single joint at each end.

LIVE AXLE: A rigid axle incorporating a differential and axle shafts to power the two wheels it is supporting.

LOCKUP: The juncture at which a tire starts to skid during braking. A tire's maximum braking force is developed when it is on the verge of lockup, so a car's shortest stopping distances are produced when its front and rear tires approach lockup simultaneously. This is very hard to achieve under varying conditions of load and traction, so one end typically locks up before the other. Front-wheel lockup is inherently more stable than rear-wheel lockup.

LOCKUP DIFFERENTIAL: A differential whose two outputs can be locked together, eliminating any differential action but maximizing traction under slippery conditions.

LOCKUP TORQUE CONVERTER: A torque converter fitted with a lockup clutch that can be engaged to eliminate the slip between the torque converter input and output, thereby improving fuel efficiency and performance.

LOOSE: A slang term for oversteer.

LUBRICATION: The process of supplying a coating of oil between moving surfaces to prevent actual contact between them. The oil film permits relative movement with little frictional resistance.

LUNETTE: An eye that hooks into a pintle assembly to tow vehicles.

M

MAGNET: Any body that has the ability to attract iron.
MAGNETIC FIELD: The space around a magnet which the magnetic lines of force permeate.
MAGNETIC FLUX: The total amount of magnetic induction across or through a given surface.
MAGNETIC POLE: Focus of magnetic lines of force entering or emanating from magnet.
MAGNETISM: The property exhibited by certain substances and produced by electron (or electric current) motion which results in the attraction of iron.
MAGNETO: A device that generates voltage surges, transforms them to high-voltage surges, and distributes them to the engine cylinder spark plugs.
MAIN BEARING: In the engine, the bearings that support the crankshaft.
MANIFOLD: See Intake Method or Exhaust Manifold.
MASTER CYLINDER: In the hydraulic braking system, the liquid-filled cylinder in which hydraulic pressure is developed by depression of the brake pedal.
MASTER ROD: In a radial engine, the rod to which all other connecting rods are attached, or articulated.
MATTER: Anything which has weight and occupies space.
MECHANICAL EFFICIENCY: In an engine, the ratio between brake horsepower and indicated horsepower.
MECHANISM: A system of parts or appliances which acts as a working agency to achieve a desired result.
MEMBER: Any essential part of a machine or structure.
MESHING: The mating or engaging of the teeth of two gears.
METERING ROD: A small rod, having a varied diameter, operated within a jet to vary the flow of fuel through the jet.
MID-ENGINE: A chassis layout that positions the engine behind the passenger compartment but ahead of the rear axle.
MOLECULE: The smallest particle into which a chemical compound can be divided.
MONOCOQUE: A type of body structure that derives its strength and rigidity from the use of thin, carefully shaped and joined panels, rather than from a framework of thick members. Also called *unit* or *unitized* construction.
MOTOR: A device for converting electrical energy into mechanical energy.
MOTORCYCLE: Two-wheeled vehicle similar to a bicycle but motor-driven.
MOTOR TRICYCLE: Similar to a motorcycle except the rear wheel has been replaced by two wheels.
MUFFLER: In the exhaust system, a device through which the exhaust gases must pass; in the muffler, the exhaust sounds are greatly reduced.
MULTILEAF SPRING: A leaf spring with several leaves bundled together by steel bands.
MULTILINK SUSPENSION: A rear suspension consisting of a least four links, or arms, and no struts. Because multilink suspensions assign specific wheel-locating duties to each element, they provide great flexibility for optimizing both ride and handling.
MUTUAL INDUCTION: Induction associated with more than one circuit, as two coils, one of which induces current in the other as the current in the first changes.

N

NEEDLE VALVE: Type of valve with rod-shaped, needle-pointed valve body which works into a valve seat so shaped that the needle point fits into it and closes the passage; the needle valve in the carburetor float circuit is an example.

NEGATIVE: A term designating the point of lower potential when the potential difference between two points is considered.

NEGATIVE TERMINAL: The terminal from which electrons depart when a circuit is completed from this terminal to the positive terminal of generator or battery.

NEUTRAL STEER: A cornering condition in which the front and rear slip angles are roughly the same. Although seemingly an ideal state of balance, perfect neutral steer is not as stable as slight understeer.

NORTH POLE: The pole of a magnet from which the lines of force are assumed to emanate.

NO-SPIN DIFFERENTIAL: A special type of differential which prevents the spinning of one of the driving wheels even if it is resting on smooth ice.

NOZZLE: An orifice or opening in a carburetor through which fuel feeds into the passing air stream on its way to the intake manifold.

O

OCTANE RATING: A measure of the anti-knock value of engine fuel.

ODOMETER: The part of the speedometer that measures, accumulatively, the number of vehicle miles traveled.

OHM: A measure of electrical resistance. A conductor of one ohm resistance will allow a flow of one ampere of current when one volt is imposed on it.

OHMMETER: A device for measuring ohms resistance of a circuit or electrical machine.

OIL: A liquid lubricant derived from petroleum and used in machinery to provide lubrication between moving parts. Also, fuel used in diesel engines.

OIL CONTROL RINGS: The lower rings on the piston which are designed to prevent excessive amounts of oil from working up into the combustion chamber.

OIL COOLER: A special cooling radiator through which hot oil passes. Air also passes through separate passages in the radiator, providing cooling of the oil.

OIL GAGE: Indicating device that indicates the pressure of the oil in the lubrication system. Also a bayonet-type rod to measure oil in the crankcase.

OIL PAN: The lower part of the crankcase in which a reservoir of oil is maintained.

OIL PUMP: The pump that transfers oil from the oil pan to the various moving parts in the engine that require lubrication.

OIL STRAINER: A strainer placed at the inlet end of the oil pump to strain out dirt and other particles, preventing these from getting into moving engine parts.

ON-CENTER FEEL: The responsiveness and feel of the steering when he wheel is approximately centered. In a car with good on-center feel, the steering wheel tends to return to center when slightly deflected, assisting straight-line stability.

OPPOSITE LOCK: A technique in which the steering wheel is turned in the direction away from where the car is turning. Opposite lock is used to control a car when it is oversteering and its tail is swinging wide.

OVERDRIVE: Any gearset in which the output shaft turns faster than the input shaft. Overdrive gears are used in most modern transmissions because they reduce engine rpm and improve fuel economy. Occasionally, a separate gearbox with an overdrive gearset is coupled to a conventional transmission.

OVERFLOW TANK: Special tank in cooling system (a surge tank) for hot or dry country to permit expansion and contraction of engine coolant without loss.

OVERHEAD CAM: The type of valvetrain arrangement in which the engine's camshaft(s) is in its cylinder head(s). When the camshaft(s) is(are) placed close to the valves, the valvetrain components can be stiffer and lighter, allowing the valves to open and close more rapidly and the engine to run at higher rpm. In a single-overhead-cam (SOHC) layout, one camshaft actuates all of the valves in a cylinder head. In a double-overhead-camshaft (DOHC) layout, one camshaft actuates the intake valves, and one camshaft operates the exhaust valves.

OVERHEAD VALVE: Valve mounted in head above combustion chamber. Valve in I-head engine.

OVERLOAD BREAKER: In an electrical circuit, a device that breaks or opens a circuit if it is overloaded by a short, ground, use of too much equipment, etc.

OVERRUNNING CLUTCH: A type of drive mechanism used in a starter which transmits cranking effort but overruns freely when engine tries to drive starter. Also, a special clutch used in several mechanism that permits a rotating member to turn freely under some conditions but not under other conditions.

OVERSQUARE: A description of an engine whose bore is larger than its stroke.

OVERSTEER: A handling condition in which the slip angles of the rear tires are greater than the slip angles of the front tires. An oversteering car is sometimes said to be *loose* because its tail tends to swing wide.

P

PANHARD ROD: A long lateral link that provides lateral location of a rigid axle. It usually sits roughly parallel to the axle, with one end attached to the body and the other attached to the axle.

PARABOLIC REFLECTOR: A reflector that sends all reflected light originating at the focal point outward in parallel rays.

PARALLEL CIRCUIT: The electrical circuit formed when two or more electrical devices have the terminals connected together (positive to positive and negative to negative) so that each may operate independently of the other.

PARKING BRAKE: See Handbrake.

PENT-ROOF: A combustion chamber whose upper surface resembles a shallow peaked roof. Usually used with four valves per cylinder.

PERIOD: The time required for the completion of one cycle.

PERMANENT MAGNET: Piece of steel or alloy in which molecules are so aligned that the piece continues to exhibit magnetism without application of external influence.

PHASE: That portion of a whole period which has elapsed since the activity in question passed through zero position in a positive direction.

PILOT: A short plug at the end of a shaft to align it with another shaft or rotating part.

PINION: The smaller of two mating or meshing gears.

PINTLE ASSEMBLY: A swivel-type assembly used to engage with a lunette for towing trailers.

PISTON: In an engine, the cylindrical part that moves up and down in the cylinder.

PISTON DISPLACEMENT: The volume displaced by the piston as it moves from the bottom to the top of the cylinder in one complete stroke.

PISTON PIN: The cylindrical or tubular metal pin that attaches the piston to the connecting rod (also called wrist pin).

PISTON RING: One of the rings fitted into grooves in the piston. There are two types: compression rings and oil-control rings.

PISTON ROD: See Connecting Rod.

PITCH: The rotation of a car about a horizontal axis, which causes its nose or tail to bob up and down. Dive and squat are pitching motions.

PITMAN ARM: The arm that is a part of the steering gear; it is connected by linkage to the wheel steering knuckle.

PIVOT INCLINATION: See Kingpin Inclination.

PLANETARY GEARS: A gearset in which all of the gears are in one plane, grouped around each other like the planets around the sun. The central gear is called the *sun gear*. In mesh with it is a circular grouping of gears, called *planet gears* mounted on a rotating carrier. The planet gears also engage teeth on the inner periphery of the *ring gear*. By holding any one of the three gear elements motionless, different ratios can be produced between the other two. Planetary gearsets are common in automatic transmissions.

PLENUM CHAMBER: A chamber, located between the throttle body and the runners of an intake manifold, used to describe the intake charge evenly and to enhance engine breathing.

POLAR MOMENT OF INERTIA: The resistance of an object to rotational acceleration. When the mass of an object is distributed far from its axis of rotation, the object is said to have a high polar moment of inertia. When the mass distribution is close to the axis of rotation, it has a low polar moment of inertia. A mid-engined car has most of its mass within its wheelbase, contributing to a low polar moment of inertia, which, in turn, improves cornering turn-in;

POPPET: A spring-loaded ball engaging a notch. A ball latch.

PORT FUEL INJECTION: A type of fuel injection with at least one injector mounted in the intake port(s) of each cylinder. Usually the injector is mounted on the air intake manifold close to the port. Port fuel injection improves fuel distribution and allows greater flexibility in intake-manifold design, which can contribute to improved engine breathing.

POSITIVE: A term designating the point of higher potential when the potential difference between two points is considered.

POTENTIAL: A characteristic of a point in an electric field or circuit indicated by the work necessary to bring a unit positive charge from infinity; the degree of electrification as compared to some standard (the earth, for example).

POTENTIAL DIFFERENCE: The arithmetical difference between two electrical potentials; same as electromotive force, electrical pressure, or voltage.

POUND-FEET: The unit of measurement for torque. One pound-foot is equal to the twisting force produced when a one-pound force is applied to the end of a one-foot-long lever.

POWER: The rate at which work is performed. Power is proportional to torque and rpm and is measured in horsepower.

POWER BAND: The subjectively defined rpm range over which an engine delivers a substantial fraction of its peak power. The power band usually extends from slightly below the engine's torque peak to slightly above its power peak.

POWER DIVIDER: A mechanism placed between dual rear axles to apportion driving effort between the two pairs of wheels to provide the maximum tractive effort.

POWER PLANT: The engine or power-producing mechanism on the vehicle.

POWER STEERING: Vehicle steering by use of hydraulic pressure to multiply the driver's steering effort so as to improve ease of steering.

POWER STROKE: The piston stroke from top dead center to bottom dead center during which the fuel-air mixture burns and forces the piston down so the engine produces power.

POWER TAKE-OFF: An attachment for connecting the engine to power driven auxiliary machinery when its use is required.

POWERTRAIN: An engine and transmission combination.

PREIGNITION: Premature ignition of the fuel-air mixture being compressed in the cylinder on the compression stroke.

PRIMER: An auxiliary fuel pump operated by hand to feed additional fuel into the engine to produce a richer mixture for starting.
PRISMATIC LENS: A lens with parallel grooves or flutes which deflect and distribute light rays.
PROFILE: The aspect ratio of a tire.
PROGRESSIVE-RATE SPRING: A spring with an increasing spring constant. For example, if the first inch of spring motion requires 100 pounds of force, the second inch would require more than an additional 100 pounds, and the third inch would require still more. Progressive-rate springs become stiffer as they are compressed, unlike single-rate springs, which have a fixed spring rate.
PROPELLER SHAFT: The driving shaft in the powertrain that carries engine power from the transmission to the differential; also, the shaft that turns the propeller in amphibian vehicles.
PROTON: Basic particle of matter having a positive electrical charge, normally associated with the nucleus of the atom.
PSI: Pounds per square inch, the common unit of measurement for pressure. Normal atmospheric pressure at sea level is 14.7 psi.
PUMP: A device that transfers gas or liquid from one place to another.
PUSH: A slang term for understeer.
PUSHROD: A general term for any rod that transfers force in compression. In a valvetrain, pushrods are used to transfer reciprocating motion from the cam followers to a more distant part of a valvetrain, typically the rocker arms.

R

RPM: Revolutions per minute, a measure of rotational speed.
RACK-AND-PINION: A steering mechanism that consists of a gear in mesh with a toothed bar, called a *rack*. The ends of the rack are linked to the steered wheels with tie rods. When the gear is rotated by the steering shaft, it moves the rack from side to side, turning the wheels.
RADIAL: Pertaining to the radius of a circle.
RADIAL ENGINE: An engine with each cylinder located on the radius of a circle and with all cylinders disposed around a common crankshaft.
RADIATOR: A device in the cooling system that removes heat from the coolant passing through it, permitting coolant to remove heat from the engine.
RADIUS: Distance from the center of a circle or from center of rotation.
REBOUND: The motion of a wheel that extends the suspension. The opposite of jounce.
RECIRCULATING BALL: A steering mechanism in which the steering shaft turns a worm gear that, in turn, causes a toothed metal block to move back and forth. Ball bearings in a recirculating track reduce friction between the worm gear and the block. As the block moves, its teeth rotate a gear connected to a steering arm, which then moves the steering linkage.
RECTIFIER: An electrical device that changes alternating current to direct current.
REDLINE: The maximum recommended revolutions per minute for an engine. In cars equipped with a tachometer—an instrument that measures engine rpm—the redline is usually indicated by, surprisingly enough, a red line. Some tachometers mark the redline with a colored sector. Others have two lines: the lower one marking the maximum allowable sustained engine rpm, the higher line indicating the absolute maximum rpm
RELAY: In the electrical system, a device that opens or closes a second circuit in response to voltage or amperage changes in a controlling circuit.

RESIDUAL MAGNETISM: The magnetism retained by a material after all magnetizing forces have been removed.
RESISTANCE: The opposition offered by a substance or body to the passage through it of an electric current.
RESISTOR: In an electrical system, a device made of resistance wire, carbon, or other resisting material, which has a definite value of resistance and serves a definite purpose in the system by virtue of that resistance.
RHEOSTAT: A resistor for regulating the current by means of variable resistance.
RICH MIXTURE: Fuel-air mixture with a high proportion of fuel.
RIDE HEIGHT: A measurement between the ground and some fixed reference point on a car's body (the reference point varies according to the whims of the particular automaker). This dimension can be used to measure the amount of suspension deflection or the height of the body from the ground.
RIDE STEER: A generally undesirable condition in which a wheel steers slightly as its suspension compresses or extends. Also called *bump steer*.
RIGID AXLE: A simple non-independent suspension, consisting of a rigid transverse member with wheel hubs solidly bolted to it. The axle can be attached to the body by leaf springs, or by a combination of suspension arms and links.
RIM: That part of a vehicle wheel on which the tire is mounted.
RING-AND-PINION GEAR: Any gearset consisting of a small gear (the pinion gear) which turns a large-diameter annular gear (the ring gear).
RING GEAR: A gear in the form of a ring such as the ring gear on a flywheel or differential.
ROADHOLDING: The ability of a car to grip the pavement. Technically described as *lateral acceleration*, because cornering is actually a continuous deviation from a straight path. Measured in gs.
ROAD-LOAD HORSEPOWER: The amount of power at the driving wheels needed to move a car down the road at a steady speed. This power varies according to the car's speed, aerodynamic drag, and mechanical friction, as well as the tires' rolling resistance. Road-load horsepower is distinct from engine power because the output of the engine is sapped by various mechanical losses between the engine's output at its flywheel and the driving wheels.
ROCK POSITION: The piston and connecting rod position (top or bottom dead center) at which the crank can rock or rotate a few degrees without appreciable movement of the piston.
ROD: See Connecting Rod.
ROD CAP: The lower detachable part of the connecting rod which can be taken off by removing bolts or nuts so the road can be detached from the crankshaft.
ROLL: The rotation of a car's body about a longitudinal axis. Also less accurately called *sway* or *lean*, it occurs in corners because the car's center of gravity is almost always higher than the axis about which it rotates.
ROLLER BEARING: A type of bearing with rollers positioned between two races
ROTOR: A part that revolves in a stationary part; especially the rotating member of an electrical mechanism.
RUBBER-ISOLATED CROSSMEMBER: A laterally aligned structural member that is attached to the body or the frame via vibration-absorbing rubber isolators. By bolting suspension or driveline components to such crossmembers, automotive engineers can reduce the transmission of noise and/or ride harshness to the body.

S

SAE: Society of Automotive Engineers—the professional association of transportation-industry engineers. The SAE sets most auto-industry standards for the testing, measuring, and designing of automobiles and their components.

SAE HORSEPOWER: A measurement based upon number of cylinders and cylinder diameter.

SCOOTER: A small version of a motorcycle.

SCRUB RADIUS: The distance from the point where the steering axis intersects the ground to the longitudinal line that runs through the center of the tire's contact patch. Also called *steering offset*.

SEALED-BEAM: A special type of headlight in which the reflector and lens are sealed together to enclose and protect the filaments.

SEDAN: As used by Car and Driver, the term *sedan* refers to a fixed-roof car with at least four doors or any fixed-roof two-door car with at least 33 cubic feet of rear interior volume, according to measurements based on SAE Standard J1100.

SELF-INDUCTION: A property of a circuit which causes it to magnetically affect voltage and current in the circuit.

SEMI-ELLIPTIC LEAF SPRING: A slightly curved leaf spring that is attached to a car's body at its ends and to a suspension component near its middle. One of the two body attachments is a shackle, which allows for changes in the spring's length as it flexes up and down.

SEMITRAILER: A type of trailer supported at the rear by attached wheels and at the front by the truck-tractor; the truck-tractor can be coupled and uncoupled by means of fifth wheel.

SEMI-TRAILING ARM SUSPENSION: An independent rear-suspension system in which each wheel hub is located only by a large, roughly triangular arm that pivots at two points. Viewed from the top, the line formed by the two pivots is somewhere between parallel and perpendicular to the car's longitudinal axis.

SEPARATOR: In the storage battery, the wood, rubber, or glass mat strip used as insulator to hold the battery plates apart.

SERIES CIRCUIT: The electrical circuit formed when two or more electrical devices have unlike terminals connected together (positive to negative) so that the same current must flow through all.

SERIES (TIRE): The numerical representation of a tire's aspect ratio. A 50-series tire has an aspect ratio of 0.50.

SHACKLE: A swinging support that permits a leaf spring to vary in length as it is deflected.

SHIFT GATE: The mechanism in a transmission linkage that controls the motion of the gearshift lever. The shift gate is usually an internal mechanism; however, in some transmissions—including Ferrari five-speeds and Mercedes-Benz automatics—the shift gate is an exposed guide around the shift lever.

SHIM: A strip of copper or similar material, used under a bearing cap for example, to adjust bearing clearance.

SHIMMY: Abnormal sidewise vibration, particularly of the front wheels.

SHOCK ABSORBER: A device that converts motion into heat, usually by forcing oil through small internal passages in a tubular housing. Used primarily to dampen suspension oscillations, shock absorbers respond to motion; their effects, therefore, are most obvious in transient maneuvers. Shock absorbers have no effect during steady-state conditions.

SHORT CIRCUIT: In electrical circuits, an abnormal connection that permits current to take a short path or circuit, thus bypassing important parts of the normal circuit.

SHROUD: Forward subassembly of a body or cab containing dash, cowl, and instrument panel. Also, a hood placed around a fan to improve fan action.

SHUNT: Parallel connections, in a portion of an electrical circuit.

SIDE CAR: A car attached to a motorcycle for carrying a passenger or cargo.

SINGLE-RATE SPRING: A spring with a constant spring rate. For example, if a 100-pound force deflects the spring by one inch, an additional 100 pounds will deflect it one more inch, and so on until the spring either bottoms or fails.

SKIDPAD: A large area of smooth, flat pavement used for various handling tests. Roadholding is measured by defining a large-diameter circle (Car and Driver uses 300 feet) on the skidpad and measuring the fastest speed at which the car can negotiate the circle without sliding off.

SLIP ANGLE: The angular distance between the direction in which a tire is rolling and the plane of its wheel. Slip angle is caused by deflections in the tire's sidewall and tread during cornering. A linear relationship between slip angles and cornering forces indicates an easily controllable tire.

SLIP JOINT: In the power train, a variable-length connection that permits the propeller shaft to change effective length.

SLUSHBOX: Slang for an automatic transmission.

SOHC: Single overhead camshaft—an SOHC engine uses one camshaft in each cylinder head to separate both the exhaust valves and the intake valves.

SOLENOID: A coil of wire that exhibits magnetic properties when electric current passes through it.

SOUTH POLE: The pole of the magnet into which it is assumed the magnetic lines of force pass.

SPACE FRAME: A particular kind of tube frame that consists exclusively of relatively short, small-diameter tubes. The tubes are welded together in a configuration that loads them primarily in tension and compression.

SPARK PLUG: The assembly that includes a pair of electrodes which has the purpose of providing a spark gap in the engine cylinder.

SPECIFIC GRAVITY: The ratio of the weight of a substance to weight of an equal volume of chemically pure water at 39.2°F.

SPEEDOMETER: An indicating device, usually connected to the transmission, that indicates the speed of motion of the vehicle.

SPIDER: In planetary gearsets, the frame, or part, on which the planetary gears are mounted.

SPIRAL BEVEL GEAR: A bevel bar having curved teeth.

SPLINE: Slot or groove cut in a shaft or bore; a splined shaft onto which a hub, wheel, etc., with matching splines in its bore is assembled so the two must engage and turn together.

SPOILER: An aerodynamic device that changes the direction of airflow in order to reduce lift or aerodynamic drag and/or improve engine cooling.

SPRAG UNIT: A form of overrunning clutch; power can be transmitted through it in one direction but not in the other.

SPRINGS: Flexible or elastic members that support the weight of a vehicle.

SPUR GEAR: A gear with radial teeth parallel to the axis.

SQUAT: The opposite of dive, squat is the dipping of a car's rear end that occurs during hard acceleration. Squat is caused by a load transfer from the front to the rear suspension.

STARTER: In the electrical system, the motor that cranks the engine to get it started.

STARTING SYSTEM: The electrical system, including the starter battery, cables, switch, and controls, that has the job of starting the engine.

STATIC ELECTRICITY: Accumulated electrical charges, usually considered to be those produced by friction.

STEERING AXIS: The line that intersects the upper and lower steering pivots on a steered wheel. On a car with a strut suspension, the steering axis is defined by the line through the strut mount on top and the ball joint on the bottom.

STEERING FEEL: The general relationship between forces at the steering wheel and handling. Ideally, the steering effort should increase smoothly as the wheel is rotated away from center. In addition, the steering effort should build as the cornering forces at the steered wheels increase. Finally, the friction built into the steering mechanism should be small in comparison with the handling-related steering forces.

STEERING GAIN: The relationship between yaw and the steering wheel's position and effort. All three should be proportional and should build up smoothly.

STEERING GEAR: That part of the steering system, located at the lower end of the steering shaft, which carries the rotary motion of the steering wheel to the vehicle wheels for steering.

STEERING GEOMETRY: Difference in angles between the two front wheels and the car frame during turns; the inside wheel turns more sharply than the other wheel turns since it must travel on an arc of a smaller radius. Also called *toe-out during turns*.

STEERING LINKAGE: Linkage between steering gear and vehicle wheels.

STEERING RESPONSE: A subjective term that combines steering feel and steering gain.

STEERING SYSTEM: The system of gears and linkage in the vehicle that permits the driver to turn the wheels for changing the direction of vehicle movement.

STORAGE BATTERY: A lead-acid electrochemical device that changes chemical energy into electric energy. The action is reversible; electric energy supplied to the battery stores chemical energy.

STRAIGHT-LINE TRACKING: The ability of a car to resist road irregularities and run in a straight line without steering corrections.

STROKE: The movement, or the distance of the movement, in either direction, of the piston travel in an engine.

STRUT: A suspension element in which a reinforced shock absorber is used as one of the wheel's locating members, typically by solidly bolting the wheel hub to the bottom end of the strut.

SULFATION: A crystalline formation of lead sulfate on storage battery plates.

SUMP: The space in the engine block under the crankshaft into which the oil drains from its various applications.

SUN GEAR: In a planetary gear system, the central gear.

SUPERCHARGER: A device used in connection with engine fuel-air systems to supply more air at greater pressure to the engine, thereby increasing volumetric efficiency. The term is frequently applied only to mechanically driven compressors, but it actually encompasses all varieties of compressors—including turbochargers.

SUPPRESSION: In the electrical system, the elimination of stray electromagnetic waves due to action of ignition, generator, etc., so that they cannot be detected by radio.

SUSPENSION: The system of springs, etc. supporting the upper part of a vehicle on its axles or wheels.

SWAY BAR: A connecting bar placed between wheel supports, parallel to the axles, which prevents excessive vehicle or sway on turns.

SWITCH: In the electrical system, a device used to open or complete an electrical circuit.

SYNCHROMESH: A name designating a certain type of transmission which has the virtue of permitting gear-ratio shifts without gear clashing.

SYNCHRONIZE: To make two or more events or operations occur at the same time.

T

TACHOMETER: A device for measuring revolutions per minute.

TACTICAL VEHICLE: Vehicle designated primarily to meet field requirements in direct connection with combat, tactical operations, and the training of troops for combat.

TANDEM AXLES: Two axles one placed directly in front of the other.

TAPER: To make gradually smaller toward one end; a gradual reduction in size in a given direction.

TARGA: A removable-roof body style popularized by Porsche that is similar to a convertible except that it incorporates a fixed, roll-bar-like structure running from side to side behind the front seats.

TDC: Top dead center; the position of the piston when it reaches the upper limit of travel in the cylinder.

TEMPERATURE GAGE: An indicating device in the cooling system that indicates the temperature of the coolant and gives warning if excessive engine temperatures develop.

TENSION: A stress caused by a pulling force.

THERMAL EFFICIENCY: Ratio between the power outlet and the energy in the fuel burned to produce the output.

THERMOSTAT: A device for automatic regulation of temperature.

THIRD-BRUSH GENERATOR: An auxiliary brush which regulates the current output of the generator by increasing or decreasing the field coil current.

THREE-QUARTER TRAILER: Trailers, usually 2-wheeled; used for light loads. The load is practically balanced on the trailer suspension, although some of the load is thrust on the truck-tractor connection.

THROTTLE: A mechanism in the fuel system that permits the driver to vary the amount of fuel-air mixture entering the engine and thus control the engine speed.

THROTTLE-BODY: A housing containing a valve to regulate the airflow through the intake manifold. The throttle-body is usually located between the air cleaner and the intake plenum.

THROTTLE-BODY FUEL INJECTION: A form of fuel injection in which the injectors are located at the engine's throttle-body, thereby feeding fuel to more than one cylinder. Such an arrangement saves money by using fewer injectors; but because it routes both fuel and air through the intake manifold, it eliminates some of the tuning possibilities offered by port fuel injection.

THROTTLE VALVE PLATE: The disk in the lower part of the carburetor air horn that can be tilted to pass more or less fuel-air mixture to the engine.

THRUST: A force tending to push a body out of alignment. A force exerted endwise through a member upon another member.

TIE ROD: A rod connection in the steering system between wheels.

TIMING: Refers to ignition or valve timing and pertains to the relation between the actions of the ignition or valve mechanism and piston position in the cylinder.

TIRE: The rubber and fabric part that is assembled on the wheel rim and filled with compressed air (pneumatic type).

TOE-CONTROL LINK: A lateral link in a multilink suspension designed to control a wheel's direction as the suspension moves up and down.

TOE-IN: The intentional nonparallel orientation of opposite wheels. Toe-in is measured by subtracting the distance between the front edges of a pair of tires from the distance between the rear edges of the same pair of tires. The toe-in dimension is positive when the fronts of the tires are turned toward the center of the car.

TOE-STEER: The changes in the direction of a wheel that occur without driver steering input. Toe steer can be caused by ride steer or by deflections in suspension components caused by the stresses of cornering, accelerating, and/or braking on smooth and bumpy roads.

TORQMATIC TRANSMISSION: A special type of transmission which includes a torque converter; it is designed for heavy-vehicle application.

TORQUE: A twisting or turning effort. Torque is the product, of force times the distance, from the center of rotation at which it is exerted. Measured in pound-feet.

TORQUE CONVERTER: A particular kind of fluid coupling with a third element added to the usual input and output turbines. Called the *stator*, this additional element redirects the churning liquid against the output turbine, increasing torque. This torque increase, however, is achieved at the expense of rpm and efficiency.

TORQUE ROD: Arm or rod used to insure accurate alignment of an axle with the frame and to relieve springs of driving and braking stresses.

TORQUE STEER: A tendency for a car to turn in a particular direction when power is applied. Torque steer is common in front-drive cars because reaction forces created in the half-shafts can generate uneven steering forces in the front tires.

TORQUE-TUBE DRIVE: The type of rear-end arrangement which includes a hollow tube that encloses the propeller shaft and also takes up stresses produced by braking and driving.

TORQUE WRENCH: A special wrench with a dial that indicates the amount of torque in pound-feet being applied to a bolt or nut.

TORSION BAR: A spring consisting of a long solid or tubular rod with one end fixed to the chassis and the other twisted by a lever connected to the suspension.

TORSIONAL VIBRATION: Vibration in a rotary direction; a portion of a rotating shaft that repeatedly moves ahead, or lags behind, the remainder of the shaft is exhibiting torsional vibration.

TORUS: Rotating member of fluid coupling.

TRACK: The endless tread on which a tank rides.

TRACKLAYING VEHICLE: A vehicle that uses tracks instead of wheels for mobility.

TRACTION: The force exerted in drawing a body along a plane as when a truck-trailer pulls a semitrailer.

TRACTION CONTROL: An electronic control system that prevents wheelspin by detecting when a driven wheel is about to break traction, and then reducing engine power and/or applying the appropriate brakes to prevent it.

TRACTIVE EFFORT: The pushing effort the driving wheels can make against the ground, which is the same as the forward thrust or push of the axles against the vehicle.

TRACTOR: A motor vehicle (wheeled or tracked) especially designed to tow trailers.

TRAIL-BRAKING: A driving technique in which the driver begins to brake before entering a turn and then continues to brake as he eases into the corner. As cornering forces build, the driver gradually feathers off the brakes—trading braking power for cornering grip. By increasing the vertical loading—and thus the traction, at the front tires, trail-braking can improve a car's turn-in.

TRAILER: A vehicle without motive power towed by a motor vehicle, designed primarily for cargo carrying.

TRAILING ARM: A suspension element consisting of a longitudinal member that pivots from the body at its forward end and has a wheel hub rigidly attached to its trailing end. A sufficiently rigid trailing arm can provide all of a wheel's location. In that case, it is similar to a semi-trailing arm, except that its pivot axis is exactly perpendicular to the car's longitudinal center line.

TRAILING LINK: A suspension link that is aligned to resist longitudinal motions in a wheel; it is mounted to the chassis ahead of the wheel.

TRANSAXLE: A transmission and a differential combined in one integrated assembly.

TRANSFER: The auxiliary assembly for applying power to both forward and rear propeller shafts, and to front wheels as well a rear wheels.

TRANSMISSION: The device in the power train that provides different gear ratios between the engine and driving wheels, as well as reverse.

TRANSMISSION BRAKE: A brake placed at the rear of the transmission, usually used for parking.

TREAD: The design on the road-contacting surface of a tire which provides improved frictional contact.

TREAD SQUIRM: The flexibility in the tire tread between the surface of the tread and the tire carcass. Snow tires, with their small, deep, unsupported tread blocks, have a large amount of tread squirm. Slick racing tires, which have no tread pattern, have very little squirm.

TRUCK-TRACTOR: A motor vehicle especially designed to tow semitrailers.

TRUNNION: Either of two opposite pivots or cylindrical projections from the sides of a part assembly, supported by bearings, to provide a means of swiveling or turning the part or assembly.

TRUNNION AXLE: A supporting axle which carries a load with other axles attached to it. It use as a part of a bogie permits independent wheel action in a vertical plane and within designed limits.

TUBE FRAME: A car frame made up of rigid tubing welded together. Tube frames are easier to manufacture in small quantities than unitized frames.

TUMBLEHOME: The term that describes the convex curvature on the side of a car body.

TUNED INTAKE AND EXHAUST SYSTEMS: Intake and exhaust systems that, by harnessing the pressure pulses and resonances inside the various passages and chambers of the intake and exhaust manifolds, increase the flow of intake charge into and out of the combustion chambers.

TURBINE: A mechanism containing a rotor with curved blades; the rotor is driven by the impact of a liquid or gas against the curved blades.

TURBOCHARGER: A supercharger powered by an exhaust-driven turbine. Turbochargers always use centrifugal-flow compressors, which operate at the high rotational speeds produced by the exhaust turbine.

TURBO LAG: Within a turbocharger's operating range, lag is the delay between the instant a car's accelerator is depressed and the time the turbocharged engine develops a large fraction of the power available at that point in the engine's power curve.

TURN-IN: The moment of transition between driving straight ahead and cornering.

TURRET TRAVERSING MECHANISM: A mechanism for rotating a tank turret on a horizontal plane.

TWO-STROKE-CYCLE ENGINE: An internal combustion engine requiring but two piston strokes to complete the cycle of events that produce power.

U

UNDERSTEER: A handling condition in which the slip angle of the front tires is greater than the slip angle of the rears. An understeering car is sometimes said to push, because it resists turning and tends to go straight.

UNITIZED CONSTRUCTION: A type of body construction that doesn't require a separate frame to provide structural strength or support for the car's mechanical components. A unitized body can employ monocoque construction, or it can utilize strong structural elements as an integral part of its construction.

UNIVERSAL JOINT: A joint that transmits rotary motion between two shafts that aren't in a straight line. Depending on its design, a universal joint can accommodate a large angular variation between its inputs and outputs. The simplest kind of universal joint, called a *Hooke joint*, causes the output shaft to speed up and slow down twice for every revolution of the input shaft. This speed fluctuation increases with the angular difference between the shafts.

UNSPRUNG WEIGHT: Weight of a vehicle that is not supported by springs.

V

VACUUM: A space entirely devoid of matter.

VACUUM ADVANCE: The mechanism on an ignition distributor that advances the spark in accordance with vacuum in the intake manifold.

VACUUM BRAKES: Vehicle brakes that are actuated by vacuum under the control of the driver.

VACUUM PUMP: A pump, used in a vacuum brake system (for example), that produces a vacuum in a designated chamber.

VACUUM SWITCH: In the starting system, an electric switch that is actuated by vacuum to open the starting system control circuit as the engine starts, producing a vacuum in the intake manifold.

VALVE: A mechanism that can be opened or closed too allow or stop the flow of a liquid, gas, or vapor from one to another place.

VALVE FLOAT: A high-rpm engine condition in which the valve lifters lose contact with the cam lobes because the valve springs are not strong enough to overcome the momentum of the various valvetrain components. The onset of valve load prevents higher-rpm operation. Extended periods of valve float will damage the valvetrain.

VALVE LIFTER: Also called a *valve follower*. The cylindrically shaped component that presses against the lobe of a camshaft and moves up and down as the cam lobe rotates. Most valve lifters have an oil-lubricated hardened face that slides on the cam lobe. So-called *roller lifter*, however, have a small roller in contact with the cam lobe, thereby reducing the friction between the cam lobe and the lifter.

VALVE SEAT: The surface, normally curved, against which the valve operating face comes to rest, to provide a seal against leakage of liquid, gas, or vapor.

VALVE SEAT INSERT: Metal ring inserted into valve seat; made of special metal that can withstand operating temperature satisfactorily.

VALVE SPRING: The compression-type spring that closes the valve when the valve-operating cam assumes a closed-valve position.

VALVE TAPPET: The part that rides on the valve-operating cam and transmits motion from the cam to the valve stem or push rod.

VALVE TIMING: Refers to the timing of valve closing and opening in relation to piston position in the cylinder.

VALVETRAIN: The collection of parts that make the valves operate. The valvetrain includes the camshaft(s) and all related drive components, the various parts that convert the camshaft's rotary motion into reciprocating motion at the valves, and the valves and their associated parts.

VAPOR LOCK: A condition in the fuel system in which gasoline has vaporized, as in the fuel line, so that fuel delivery to the carburetor is blocked or retarded.

VELOCITY: The rate of motion or speed at any instant, usually measured in miles-per-hour or feet-per-second or minute.

VENTURI: In the carburetor, the restriction in the air horn that produces the vacuum responsible for the movement of fuel into the passing air stream.

VIBRATION: An unceasing back and forth movement over the same path; often with reference to the rapid succession of motions of parts of an elastic body.

VISCOUS COUPLING: A particular kind of fluid coupling in which the input and output shafts mate with thin, alternately spaced discs in a cylindrical chamber. The chamber is filled with a viscous fluid that tends to cling to the discs, thereby resisting speed differences between the two shafts. Viscous couplings are used to limit the speed difference between the two outputs of a differential, or between the two axles of a car.

VOLATILITY: A measurement of the ease with which a liquid turns to vapor.

VOLT: Unit of potential, potential difference, or electrical pressure.

VOLTAGE REGULATOR: A device used in connection with generator to keep the voltage constant and to prevent it from exceeding a predetermined maximum. (One of the three units comprising a generator regulator.

VOLUMETRIC EFFICIENCY: Ratio between the amount of fuel-air mixture that actually enters an engine cylinder and the amount that could enter under ideal conditions.

VOLUTE SPRINGS: Helical coil springs made from flat steel tapered both in width and thickness.

V-TYPE ENGINE: Engine with two banks of cylinders set at an angle to each other in the shape of a 7.

W

WANDER: To ramble or move without control from a fixed course, as the front wheels of a vehicle.

WASTE GATE: A valve used to limit the boost developed in a turbocharger. A west gate operates by allowing some of the engine's exhaust flow to bypass the turbocharger's turbine section under certain conditions.

WATER JACKET: A jacket that surrounds cylinders and cylinder head, through which coolant flows.

WATER MANIFOLD: A manifold used to distribute coolant to several points in the cylinder block or cylinder head.

WATER PUMP: In the cooling system, the pump that circulates coolant between the engine water jackets and the radiator.

WHEEL ALIGNMENT: The mechanics of keeping all the parts of the steering system in correct relation with each other.

WHEEL BRAKE: A brake that operates at the wheel, usually on a brake drum attached to the wheel.

WHEEL CYLINDER: In hydraulic braking systems, the hydraulic cylinder that operates the brake shoes when hydraulic pressure is applied in the cylinder.

WHEEL HOP: An undesirable suspension characteristic in which a wheel (or several) moves up and down so violently that it actually leaves the ground. Wheel hop can be caused by many problems, including excessive unsprung weight, insufficient shock damping, or poor torsional axle control.

WINCH: A mechanism actuating a drum upon which a cable is cooled, so that when a rotating power is applied to the drum, a powerful pull is produced.

WOBBLE PLATE: That part of a special type of pump (wobble pump) which drives plungers back and forth as it rotates to produce pumping action. It is a disk or plate, set at an angle on a rotating shaft.

WORK: The result of a force acting against opposition to produce motion. It is measured in terms of the product of the force and the distance it acts.

WORM GEAR: A gear having concave, helical teeth that mesh with the threads of a worm. Also called a *worm wheel*.

Y

YAW: The rotation about a vertical axis that passes through the car's center of gravity.

Z

ZERO-OFFSET STEERING: A steering system whose geometry has a scrub radius of zero. This configuration minimizes the steering effects produced during acceleration (with front drive) or braking on varying traction surfaces.